Praise for *What Is Global Leadership?*

"This wonderful book addresses the hottest talent issue facing global organizations . . . a serious shortage of leaders who can work across the world. You'll have a deep grasp of the capabilities required to lead globally. Filled with concrete and insightful guidance, this is an invaluable resource."

—Jay A. Conger, Author of *Growing Your Company's Leaders* and
The Practice of Leadership

"Well Done! What I like about this book is the emphasis on the importance of the 'soft side' of global leadership."

—Fons Trompenaars, Managing Director of Trompenaars Hampden-
Turner Consulting, is Co-Author of *Riding the Waves of Culture* and a
world authority on cross-cultural management

"Understanding what a global leader is, and what they do, is becoming increasingly urgent. This book does a great job of answering these questions, combining hard science with organizational research and case studies. An excellent resource for anyone trying to select, develop, or work with global leaders in any way."

—David Rock, CEO, NeuroLeadership Group

"Recent financial, economic, and political turbulence has reconfirmed the importance of leadership in distinguishing global winners from global losers. Extreme diversity of outcomes among otherwise powerful players—banks, companies, investors, and even countries—is hard to explain any other way. This volume provides an authoritative, engaging, and readable primer on global leadership to help explain the past and gain a sharper perspective on the future."

—Ingo Walter, Vice Dean of Faculty and Seymour Milstein Professor of
Finance, Corporate Governance, and Ethics, Stern School of Business,
New York University

D1270203

"Engaging stories, interesting research findings, and worthwhile practical recommendations make this a valuable contribution for both scholars and practitioners. This book provides a comprehensive, insightful look at global leadership."

—Joyce Osland, Executive Director, Global Leadership Advancement Center and Lucas Endowed Professor of Global Leadership, College of Business, San Jose State University

"*What Is Global Leadership?* provides many, many fascinating vignettes and lessons learned from business leaders living and working in a cross-cultural milieu. Though the focus is business leadership, its insights and perspectives are equally valid to successful government, military, and non-profit leadership across cultural boundaries. *What Is Global Leadership?* is an essential read for *anyone* who leads cross-cultural teams or works in a cross-cultural environment."

—Bob Schoultz, Director, Master of Science in Global Leadership, University of San Diego, Captain USN (retired) and former career Navy SEAL

What Is Global Leadership?

10 KEY BEHAVIORS THAT DEFINE GREAT GLOBAL LEADERS

Ernest Gundling, Terry Hogan
and Karen Cvitkovich

NICHOLAS BREALEY
PUBLISHING

BOSTON • LONDON

This edition first published by Intercultural Press, an imprint of Nicholas Brealey Publishing, in 2011.

20 Park Plaza, Suite 1115A
Boston, MA 02116, USA
Tel: + 617-523-3801
Fax: + 617-523-3708

3-5 Spafield Street, Clerkenwell
London, EC1R 4QB, UK
Tel: +44-(0)-207-239-0360
Fax: +44-(0)-207-239-0370

www.nicholasbrealey.com

Printed in the United States of America

16 15   14   13   12   3   4   5   6

Library of Congress Cataloging-in-Publication Data

What is global leadership? : 10 key behaviors of great global leaders / Ernest Gundling . . . et al.].
       p. cm.
   ISBN-13: 978-1-904838-23-4 (pbk. : alk. paper)
   ISBN-10: 1-904838-23-5 (pbk. : alk. paper)
   1. Leadership—Cross-cultural studies. 2. International business enterprises—Management—Cross-cultural studies. 3. Management—Cross-cultural studies.
I. Gundling, Ernest. II. Title.

HD57.7.W45597 2011
658.4'092—dc22

                                                     2011004032

Ernest Gundling

To Christie Caldwell, for helping to make an idea real.

Terry Hogan

To Tom and Joan Hogan: lifelong learners, global explorers, and loving parents.

Karen Cvitkovich

To my father, Gary Baker, who inspires me with his deep love of learning and natural leadership ability and to my mother, Barbara Baker, whose focus and perseverance helps me strive to be a better leader and a better person every day.

Acknowledgments

This book represents a collective effort in many ways. We would first of all like to express our gratitude to colleagues at Aperian Global who supported our work on the project. In particular, Christie Caldwell participated in the project from start to finish over the last several years—conducting many interviews, doing research for text examples and graphics, and contributing a rich combination of intelligence, hard work, and humor undeterred by seemingly impossible tasks. Lexi Rifaat gathered a number of images and figures and carried out much of the correspondence for gaining permissions. Lyrae Myxter and Sarah Wiktorek cheerfully and efficiently carried forward with the next steps in working with the publisher and getting the book out to a general audience even while the authors were mired in the details of the writing process. Jeneva Patterson and Theresa Kneebone introduced valuable client contacts in Europe and Asia Pacific. Bryan Donnery provided timely help with the graphics. Other employees at Aperian offered their ideas, feedback, technical support, and willingness to experiment with new materials, including Simone-Eva Redrupp, Pamela Leri, David Everhart, Jorge Iriso, and Michael Van Vleet.

We are also sincerely grateful to the individuals who consented to have their stories portrayed in the text: Fernando Lopez-Bris of John Deere, Diawary Bouare of CARE, Gary Ashmore of AMD, Khalid al-Faddagh of Saudi Aramco, Gina Qiao of Lenovo, and Birgit Masjost of Roche. We appreciate as well the participation of the executive coaches from Citi in our training and research, along with all the other interviewees who are either not mentioned individually by name or who asked to be depicted with a pseudonym. The hard-won knowledge that each of you shared has been a real inspiration to us. We have done our very best to listen carefully and to faithfully represent your comments, and hope that the experiences we depict here are as inspirational and thought-provoking to readers as they have been to us. It has truly been a privilege to speak with each of you.

We would like to thank clients and friends who took an interest in our research during its early stages and were responsible for recruiting interviewees: Matthew Barney, Patrick Carmichael, Laura Lea Clinton, Yolanda Conyers, Greg Cripple, Tracy Ann Curtis, Frank Edwards, Ryan Larsen, and Yi Min. Thank you very much for believing in this project and for introducing us to so many terrific global leaders! Joann Coakley wrote initial drafts for two of the mini-cases at the end of Chapter Eight during our work together on a global leadership development project; we enjoyed very much our collaboration with her. And thanks to Kevin Engholm for his patience and perseverance under pressure.

Additional companies that contributed to our research include Fujitsu, Infosys, Kohler, L'Oreal, Novartis, Novo Nordisk, Philips, and Wal-Mart. Clients in a number of companies, conferences, and other venues provided candid feedback to us in response to early versions of the research results that shaped the ultimate outcome. Special thanks are due to MBA students at the Haas School of Business at the University of California, Berkeley, and participants in a seminar conducted by two of the authors during the Summer Institute of Intercultural Communication.

Academics and consultants who have stimulated our thinking over the years include Hal Gregersen, Rita Bennett, Joyce Osland, Allan Bird, Mark Mendenhall, Eamonn Kelly, Morgan McCall, George Hollenbeck, David Rock, Janet Bennett, and Fons Trompenaars. George Renwick has been unstintingly generous in sharing his wisdom and practical support, not only with us but with an entire field. In addition, we acknowledge our debt of gratitude to other researchers who have gone before us and those whose work is ongoing, whether or not they are mentioned by name here. We view this project as one contribution to a field of global leadership development that is increasingly broad and deep, and hope that the ideas presented in this book will provide fresh perspectives and open up new angles for discussion and debate.

Erika Heilman of Nicholas Brealey has patiently and capably supported this project since its inception, and Jill Schoenhaut has helped to shepherd it through the editing process.

Notwithstanding the efforts of so many capable people, there may be errors or omissions in the text that the authors have missed. For these we take full responsibility.

Contents

Contents

Contents

CHAPTER ONE

Why Global Leadership?

A compelling set of underlying trends drives the current focus on global leadership. Many companies have gone through enormous changes in recent times in response to dynamic—bordering on cataclysmic—economic events. They have shaken up their operations and increased, reallocated, or curtailed investments to cope with unprecedented market fluctuation. These megatrends have created a new landscape for the world at large and have made a significant impact on the ways companies conduct their daily business.

As strategic plans are shaped for the coming years, the task of determining global strategic priorities and deploying limited resources has never been more crucial. The challenge for most companies, which tend to react relatively quickly to the changing global landscape, is in getting their employees to change as rapidly. Stale mental models dictate outmoded leadership behaviors. The ability to deal with "multiplexity"—complexity in multiple forms—requires frequent retooling of previous skill sets and a new or expanded repertoire of leadership behaviors. There is an intense need for leaders who have both the vision and the skills to function effectively in a world that is simultaneously boundaryless *and* replete with boundaries that mark significant differences across a broad spectrum of business and culture: customer needs, supply chain issues, employee motivation, competition, ethical standards, legal frameworks, standard business practices, religious and political influences, educational systems, and so on.

Three Megatrends

Amidst the dynamic global landscape, full of uncertainty as well as clearer trend lines, what are the key underlying currents that we need to track, and what are their practical implications for global leadership strategy? Futurists have their own predilections and temperaments, and they paint different scenarios as well as more general pictures of where our planet is headed, both gloomy and optimistic.[1] Some focus on technological developments and their implications, others look at social trends, and still others analyze geopolitical forces. Futurism provides a unique license to speculate without immediate feedback on one's predictions, which can only be assessed years down the road (in contrast to investment advisors who must compete each year with monkeys throwing darts).

An important piece of futurist advice is that the years ahead will most probably bring discontinuous events that cannot be accurately predicted based strictly upon extrapolations from the present, as with unanticipated and trans-formative events of recent years such as armed conflicts, terrorism, financial crises, piracy, epidemics, and environmental disasters precipitated by either natural or human causes. Mixed in with these discontinuous events, the crystal ball of futurist projections also holds more easily predictable trends that are either already well-established or which are readily visible and can be expected to spread. Another piece of futurist wisdom maintains that the future is already present at certain locations in our midst (imagine those first clumsy prototype automobiles trundling down dirt roads in the early 1900s) if we have the eyes to perceive it and the imagination to anticipate where it could take us.

Three highly predictable megatrends have been steadily impacting the global business environment for decades; such trends are likely to continue to exert an increasing influence over the future and are shaping an arena in which global leadership skills will be a prerequisite for organizational survival and growth. These three trends are (1) population growth in the developing world, (2) changes in the balance of the gross domestic product (GDP) between developed and emerging markets, and (3) rapid urbanization in Asia and Africa. While they may sound familiar, each trend holds implications with which few, if any, corporations have fully come to terms.[2]

MEGATREND #1: POPULATION GROWTH IN THE DEVELOPING WORLD

Our planet is currently in the midst of the greatest boom in human population it has ever seen. Demographers project that in the short span of one hundred years, from 1950 to 2050, the world's population will have more than tripled from approximately 2.5 billion to over 9 billion. Such trend lines are slow to change, and even though population growth has moderated in some locations over the last decades, it is still probable that we will hit or exceed the 9 billion mark within our own lifetimes or those of our children.

What is less commonly recognized about this trend is that virtually one hundred percent of this population growth is occurring in the developing world. The number of people in the developed world was slightly under a billion in 1950, and the population of those same countries in 2050 will probably be little more than a billion. So almost the entire increase of six and a half billion people over this hundred-year span will be in countries that represented only one and a half billion people in 1950—a fourfold increase in the developing countries vis-à-vis the stagnant population size of the developed world (see Figure 1-1).[3] This trend has tremendous implications for future markets, consumer demand, workforce demographics, talent availability and readiness, and much more. Consider for a moment the implications of the related fact that nine out of ten of the world's children under the age of fifteen currently live in developing countries.[4]

As their markets and the people they lead continue to diverge from the demographic features that dominated the economy in the recent past, present and future leaders will be increasingly unable to cope using only the popular, culturally embedded ideals of leadership often seen on the domestic best-seller lists.

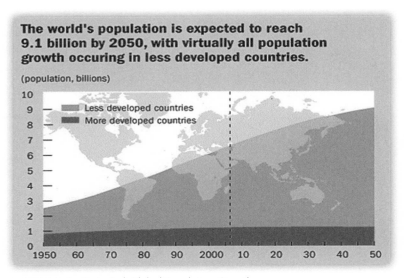

FIGURE 1-1 Projected Global Population Growth

MEGATREND #2: CHANGES IN THE BALANCE OF GDP

Companies accustomed to earning the bulk of their revenues in North America and Europe might argue that their biggest customers and business opportunities are still where they have always been in recent memory and therefore downplay the significance of developing countries' population growth. However, along with the shifting locus of the world's population has come a watershed change in the balance of global GDP. Estimates suggest that the combined GDP of the emerging economies has begun to exceed that of the developed world within the last few years, and that this trend will accelerate to the point where the size of the emerging economies will soon be as much as double that of developed economies (see Figure 1-2).[5]

These emerging economies are still in the process of adding another group of middle-class consumers, estimated variously at more than half a billion people, that will exceed the population of all of Europe. What makes this trend particularly hazardous to ignore is that patterns of both production and consumption in the emerging markets are no longer focused on basic commodities,

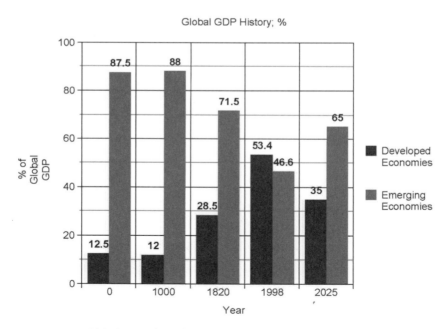

FIGURE 1-2   Global GDP of Developed and Emerging Economies

but now include products and services usually regarded as "high tech." Here are some examples:

- "SIA (Semiconductor Industry Association) expects . . . [that] developing countries will account for over half of world-wide PC sales and about two-thirds of mobile phone sales. . . . Demand for consumer electronic products in these new markets will continue to outpace growth in developed markets. . . ."[6]
- China has by far the largest number of Internet users. The country's online population of about 360 million already exceeds the entire population of the United States.[7]
- The largest automotive market in the world is now China, not the U.S., as vehicle sales in China are projected to surpass those in the U.S. by more than two million on an annual basis.[8]

In a sense, this shift represents a return to the old normal. Looking back, China was the world's largest economy for most of the last 2,000 years up until the last few centuries, and the Indian subcontinent had the world's second-largest economy for at least several hundred years—hence, the relatively greater size of the emerging economies prior to the mid-1800s(see Figure 1-2).[9]

These developing economies don't always want to act according to Western beliefs and values. Increasingly, they are asserting their own ideas of how the game should be played, notably at the inflection points between business, government, environmental resources, and social causes.

MEGATREND #3: RAPID URBANIZATION IN ASIA AND AFRICA

For the global economy, it makes a big difference where people live and what their occupations are. Rural populations that are engaged primarily in subsistence agriculture are less likely to purchase or provide goods and services delivered across geographic boundaries. When such people move to an urban center, however, their lifestyles tend to become far more enmeshed in the network of global commerce. For instance, they may go to work in factories that produce goods for customers on the other side of the world, and they gradually gain the purchasing power to buy clothes, foods, and consumer items produced elsewhere, while the natural resources of a local farming community are no longer immediately available to them.

North America and Europe already had a majority of their populations living in cities in 1950, and they have become progressively more urban since then, with well over seventy percent of their inhabitants now living in urban centers. In contrast, Asia and Africa were predominantly rural throughout the twentieth century, and are just now undergoing the transformation to a predominantly urban society that other parts of the world experienced many decades ago (see Figure 1-3 below).[10] Given the accompanying rapid population increase, we are witnessing the burgeoning growth of cities in the world's emerging markets of a size and scale never before seen on earth. Consumers in these new markets are already demanding different products and services, developed specifically for their needs and applications, and at price points unheard of in the past and recently regarded as unfeasible by most major corporations.

Implications for Strategy: The Need for a Global Mindset

Population growth, GDP shifts, and urbanization are driving an inexorable transformation in the blend of risks and opportunities faced by commercial enterprises worldwide. Global leadership is becoming an absolutely essential capability because such change can only be grasped and successfully met with a strategic global mindset. Companies will sooner or later need to respond to these trends through their impact on particular industries, and will eventually be rendered obsolete by them if their response is ineffective.

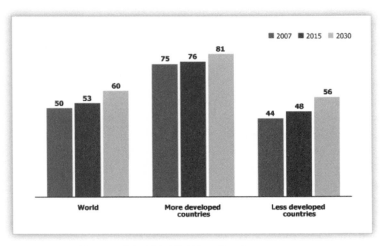

FIGURE 1-3 Percent of the World's Urban Population

Indeed, the three megatrends outlined previously have a pervasive combined impact that is affecting almost every aspect of life on earth. Climate change, energy supply issues, deforestation, water shortages, species extinction, fisheries depletion, and migration pressures can all be linked to changes in population, GDP, and urbanization. We are witnessing a rapid proliferation of so-called "tragedies of the commons" in which a person or even a country may derive short-term benefits from an activity that degrades the common natural heritage of humanity. While all people bear a shared responsibility for addressing these issues, commercial enterprises must learn how to manage their businesses through the changes that have occurred already and those—both predictable and unpredictable—yet to come.

For business leaders with an outlook shaped by the last century's events, it is essential to comprehend the full cumulative implications of such trends. Yet many executives still rely on an outmoded mental map without being fully aware of its strategic drawbacks. Although it is difficult to anticipate and prepare for discontinuous events, the trends that can be discerned already call for a reexamination of familiar topics using a fresh perspective. Executives and their organizations must learn to reevaluate and reshaped their responses to the following kinds of questions:

- Where are our key markets?
- What are the companies that matter to us?
- What are the major sources of innovation?
- Who are the model global leaders?

MINDSET CHANGE: WHERE ARE OUR KEY MARKETS?

The provocative futurist Eamonn Kelly asks us to compare the great cities of the not-so-distant past with those that are now rising to prominence. A list of the largest cities in the world in 1900 would include London, New York, Paris, Berlin, Chicago, and others, with the only non-Western city being Tokyo. By far the largest urban center on this list was London, with 6.5 million residents.[11] If we look at the roster projected for 2015, there are no U.S. or European cities among the top ten. The largest urban areas in the world are now or soon will be places such as Mumbai and Kolkata, India; São Paulo, Brazil; Chongqing and Shanghai, China; Jakarta, Indonesia; Lagos, Nigeria; Karachi, Pakistan; and Dhaka, Bangladesh. Each will have a population that easily exceeds 15 million.[12] Corporate managers who were raised in a world where the 1900 list was still the dominant reality may have trouble finding many of the cities in the more current roster on a map, let alone traveling or living in these locations and having a functional sense of their marketplace dynamics. And yet these are the markets of the future. Any effective global strategy will need to take them into account, considering which locations to target and how to achieve commercial success in a place that may have very different consumer tastes, supply chain resources, or pricing standards.

MINDSET CHANGE: WHAT ARE THE COMPANIES THAT MATTER TO US?

Knowing the competitive landscape is an important part of any strategy and an integral element of leadership skills. We tend to focus on "the usual suspects"— companies that have been rivals for many years and that are based in our own home market or another developed economy location. Yet strategy experts warn that the most dangerous competition can enter a market laterally from another industry or as a start-up with a disruptive product concept. There is a global version of this phenomenon, which is the emerging market company that was not previously on anyone's radar screen, but is growing rapidly and could soon become a potent force not only locally but around the world. Such companies are potential competitors, but also possible customers, suppliers, or partners.

A veteran of the electronics industry once described how his Western firm had been satisfied with its high rate of business growth in Japan, a promising market for the company at that time. Simultaneously, a small local competitor was growing at almost double that rate, although it was still too minor within the larger scheme of things to be regarded as a significant threat. That "small local competitor" continued to prosper and today is the global giant known as Sony; meanwhile, the competitive rival that the Western firm had been most focused on in that earlier growth era has since faded into obscurity, in part due to its lack of success in foreign markets. In the Chinese automotive market today, for example, there may be rapidly growing automobile makers or parts suppliers that could be the giants of the future.

If the world's growth markets with the most significant potential include the so-called BRIC countries—Brazil, Russia, India, and China—to what extent are the people who shape strategy in your organization aware of the competitive threats as well as the opportunities presented by firms that are growing quickly but less well-known outside their home countries? Figure 1-4 notes a few examples from various industries in BRIC countries.[13] Global team participants who are from these countries or nearby regions will immediately demonstrate

8

Company Name	Country	Industry
Cosan	Brazil	Ethanol and sugar
Gol Linhas Áereas Inteligentes	Brazil	Airline
Petrobras	Brazil	Energy
Vale (Companhia Vale do Rio Doce)	Brazil	Mining
Euroset	Russia	Mobile devices
JSC Mikron	Russia	Electronics
VimpelCom	Russia	Telecommunications
Wimm-Bill-Dann Foods	Russia	Juices, dairy products
Bharti Airtel	India	Mobile phone services
ICICI	India	Banking
Mahindra & Mahindra	India	Tractors, automobiles
Suzlon Energy	India	Wind turbines
BYD	China	Batteries; electric cars
Dangdang	China	E-commerce
Tencent	China	Instant messaging
Wanxiang	China	Auto parts

FIGURE 1-4 Sample List of BRIC Companies

their value when viewing such a list, as they will probably have a much more lively and well-informed sense of the competitive landscape.

MINDSET CHANGE: WHAT ARE THE MAJOR SOURCES OF INNOVATION?

There is a comforting myth believed by many in the developed world that emerging market firms are imitators rather than innovators, and that their products and services are nearly always derivative of those invented elsewhere. Historically, there is some truth to this claim, but it is increasingly the case that major innovations originate from developing rather than developed countries. A *disruptive innovation* is defined as a product that is introduced at a significantly lower price point with adequate although not stellar functionality, and which through continuous improvement comes to rival and possibly replace products

9

formerly regarded as higher-end offerings.[14] This turns out to be a rather good description of many products coming from the developing world.

The term *trickle up*—the opposite of the customary notion of technology that "trickles down" from advanced economies to the rest of the world—is even being used to describe the effects of these products. For example, General Electric's Healthcare India operation designed a portable electrocardiogram (ECG) device for the local market to be sold at one-tenth the price of larger, more sophisticated products used in North America and Europe. That same product has now been introduced into Germany, reversing of the previous trickle-down pattern.[15] Similarly, the Chinese company BYD has introduced a battery-powered car into the Chinese automotive market that is being offered at a far lower price than the advertised prices for competing Japanese and U.S. products—and BYD has made its product available to consumers sooner. Warren Buffett is a major stakeholder in BYD, and doubtless sees potential applications for its products that extend far beyond China.[16]

The value of continuous improvement should also not be underestimated. A series of incremental innovations introduced by energetic smaller players can have a highly disruptive impact over time, particularly in markets where large numbers of components are assembled to create the final product. Over the years, markets for major industries such as automobiles, shipbuilding, home appliances, and telecommunications have been turned upside down by former "imitators" who were initially looked down upon but gradually became quite skillful at continuous improvement. Companies such as Toyota, Hyundai Heavy Industries (shipbuilding), Haier (home appliances), and Huawei (telecommunications) are now formidable global competitors. Firms that seek to do business in emerging markets, and increasingly even in developed economies, must create compelling combinations of breakthrough pricing, adequate technology, and continuous improvement that is sustained over long periods of time in order to remain competitive.

MINDSET CHANGE: WHO ARE THE MODEL GLOBAL LEADERS?

The Western business press has celebrated a few current or former top executives in its pantheon of model global leaders over the past couple of decades, and it is often assumed that these models still have worldwide currency. Jack Welch of General Electric, Carlos Ghosn of Renault and Nissan, Akio Morita from Sony, and A. G. Lafley of Procter & Gamble have indeed led remarkable careers. But without continual revitalization, the companies their names are linked with may one day look like the list of the world's largest cities in 1900—in fact, most of the largest corporations from the first half of the twentieth century have already faded into obscurity. A host of other executives and firms in many different markets merit increasing recognition.

It is worth looking to developing markets to expand our view of model executives, both because there are individuals who deserve inclusion and because employees in other parts of the world may find such people and their careers easier to identify with and to emulate. In India, for example, Narayana Murthy of Infosys and Azim Premji of Wipro have started corporations and achieved unprecedented successes in the world's second-most populous nation. Each helped to build what are now two of Asia's most respected companies from very humble beginnings, and they are admired not only for their business acumen but for their ethics and substantial contributions to social causes.

Narayana Murthy, Infosys

Azim Premji, Wipro Technologies

In China, Zhang Ruimin, the CEO of Haier, is sometimes called the "Jack Welch of China," and he is probably much better known than Jack Welch to most businesspeople there. He led a destitute and dysfunctional state-owned enterprise from its former ruinous position into one of the world's most formidable home appliance companies; it has become a leading supplier even to Western enterprises such as Wal-Mart. Liu Chuanzhi, chairman of Lenovo, built the capabilities of a domestic Chinese computer-maker to the point where it executed the previously almost unimaginable purchase of IBM's personal computer division and is now among the world's top five industry players.

Zhang Ruimin, Haier

Liu Chuanzhi, Lenovo

Such names only begin to represent the rich variety of careers and characters that can be glimpsed within an expanded perspective. José Sergio Gabrielli de Azevedo of Petrobras (Brazil's massive state energy company, now the fourth largest in the world), Roger Agnelli of Companhia Vale do Rio Doce (a Brazilian mining enterprise), and even a colorful and controversial individual like Roman Abramovich (Russian oil tycoon, provincial governor, and football team owner in the United Kingdom) reflect unique features of their respective home markets, and offer insights about what may or may not work when doing business in the developing world.

Conclusion

Leadership was formerly a topic reserved for the corporate and political elite, and leading in a global context was simply not a reality even for many people in top-ranking jobs. Now, due at least in part to the megatrends described above, global leadership has become the target of much broader attention. Not only executives in line to step into top leadership roles, but also mid-level "high-potential" employees, MBA candidates, and even university undergraduates are receiving training and coaching in this area. There are a variety of factors related to this transformation.

- Organizations seeking to leverage emerging trends and to grow their business in key markets around the world have prioritized the need to build their global leadership pipeline and are willing to make significant investments for this purpose.
- The notion of "leadership at all levels," popularized by Noel Tichy and others, suggests that there are many roles—not just top executive positions—in which leadership capabilities can be meaningfully deployed.[17]
- Global leadership and its secrets are alluring to those who seek to move up the career ladder as quickly as possible. (Who wants to be a mere manager in a domestic operation when you could be a global leader instead?)
- A corporate and educational funding bandwagon sometimes makes it easier to receive funding for a prestigious and high-profile topic such as global leadership rather than more prosaic skills such as project or performance management.

Whatever their organizational role, present or future, only leaders with truly global vision and skills will be able to best position their enterprises to cope with the three megatrends portrayed here and their implications for global commerce and leadership. A keen sense of the strategic implications of population growth, GDP shifts, and urbanization will provide an important compass for navigation through stormy economic times. In addition to knowing the most critical markets, companies, sources of innovation, and examples of leadership, leaders will need to tap new sources of talent and ways to develop the global competencies of people on the other side of their world.

There is much that we don't know about where the world will go and how markets will evolve, but also much that is readily evident. Strategic plans must incorporate such insights without being "too early" or "too late." A global mindset and the global skill set that enable leaders to more readily discern and respond to key trends are part of the recipe for successful long-term growth.

CHAPTER TWO

What's Different About Global Leadership?

Most leaders have received formal or informal leadership training during the course of their careers. As their roles expand to include global responsibilities, the question naturally arises, "What's different about global leadership?" Proponents of various leadership development approaches are not necessarily aware of or in discussion with one another, and there is a great deal of confusion regarding the distinction between leadership in general and global leadership in particular, both in the corporate world and in academia. It is worth reviewing both generic and more specifically global approaches to arrive at a clearer picture. (Readers who are most interested in a practical description of global leadership behaviors based on our own research are advised to skip ahead to the summary of our findings beginning on p 29.)

Leadership: Common Approaches

Political rulers and military strategists of earlier eras drew upon numerous sources of advice, some of which still exert influence today. The topic of leadership is fascinating in part because there are many approaches and examples that have been held up as models over time. Confucius, Mencius, and Sun Tzu offered their versions of leadership consultation in past millennia in ancient China. Figures remembered from other countries in subsequent eras such as Plato, Cicero, Machiavelli, and von Clausewitz have also contributed their ideas and advice. Leaders engaged in commerce have received guidance in many forms as well, including instruction through the religious traditions of Judaism, Christianity, and Islam.

The focus in this section will be on leadership approaches in the post–World War II West, particularly in the United States, that have gained common currency in the business arena and have been applied in many countries around the world, albeit with mixed results. There has been a special fascination with these models, even in places such as Japan, the Middle East, and Northern Europe, due to the size and relative success of the U.S. economy, the reach of its business schools, and the ubiquity of its brand names. As the global balance of economic power shifts, this intellectual hegemony has already begun to slip, and those who once looked primarily to the U.S. for reference points have begun to cast a wider net for other leadership perspectives.

LEADERSHIP AND MANAGEMENT

John Kotter of the Harvard Business School articulates an approach that has probably gained the most widespread recognition over the last twenty years. In his seminal work *What Leaders Really Do*, he provides a definition of leadership that is also contrasted with management. Leadership, according to Kotter, involves *coping with change* by setting a direction, aligning people, and motivating and inspiring—often through leveraging informal networks within the organization.[1]

Others such as Jay Conger elaborate this picture of leadership by noting that it includes sensing an opportunity in the current situation, formulating a vision, communicating the vision, building trust and motivating followers, and ultimately achieving the vision through actions such as personal modeling and empowerment of coworkers.[2] Figure 2-1 provides a visual illustration that combines and embellishes the definitions of *leadership* from Kotter and Conger.

From a global leadership perspective, Kotter's definition of leadership is unquestionably helpful, but it is incomplete. It does not address issues such as how to read different futures for different markets, establish a vision with indigenous resonance in key locations, communicate effectively with people accustomed to a different communication style, create alignment across a complex matrix structure, motivate and engage emerging market employees, provide a personal example that inspires people in fifty countries, or identify high-potential future leaders who live ten thousand miles from headquarters.

Management, on the other hand, focuses on *coping with complexity* through planning and budgeting, organizing and staffing, and coordinating and problem solving; usually this means working through more formal organizational structures and systems. Figure 2-2 is a contrasting depiction of *management* based

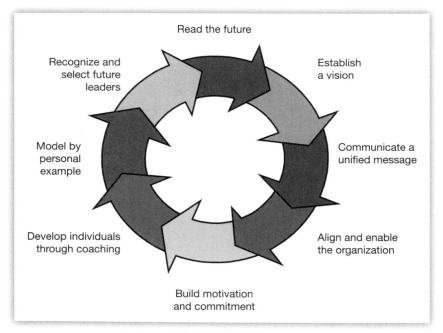

FIGURE 2-1 General Definitions of Leadership.

on Kotter's distinction. This definition, too, needs adaptation to a multicultural context, but that is a topic that has been addressed elsewhere.[3]

LEADERSHIP AT ALL LEVELS

Beyond the current general definition of leadership as setting and communicating a vision, aligning the organization, and motivating employees, there is also the question of to whom these activities apply. Leadership is sometimes seen as the sole purview of top executives—the culmination of a long path that begins with more ordinary management tasks. Noel Tichy's notion of "leadership at all levels" represents a different stance: he claims that the most effective companies are the ones that work assiduously to cultivate leadership capabilities at each level of the organization.

> "Organizations are winners because they have good leaders, not just at the top, but at all levels. Winning companies value leaders, they have cultures that expect and reward leadership, and they actively put time and resources into developing them. Winning companies win because they have

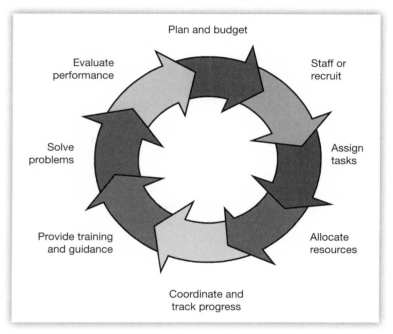

FIGURE 2-2 General Definition of Management

lots of leaders, and they have lots of leaders because they deliberately and systematically produce them."[4]

Tichy's emphasis on this open, multilevel approach to leadership development has been adopted by many corporations. They have invested considerable time and resources to enhance the capabilities of individuals designated as having "high-potential," and this has spawned an entire industry of leadership development professionals and approaches. At the same time, the increasingly fashionable focus on leadership at all levels has led to confusion about the nature of leadership and in some cases fostered a denigration of the vital workhorse skills of good management. Given the choice between attending a leadership development program or a more standard management course, ambitious younger employees are naturally attracted to leadership, even though they have not yet learned how to manage well or even had much management experience. And those who have risen to higher levels in an organization may now feel that they no longer need to manage, as ordinary management skills are beneath them—after all, leaders only need to worry about leadership, right?

A useful way to sort out the growing terminological confusion and to continue to recognize the substantial value of everyday management skills is to distinguish conceptually between "leaders" and "leadership," and between "managers" and "management," as illustrated in Figure 2-3. Regardless of whether one's official position in the organization (or self-concept, for that matter) is identified as that of leader or manager, both leadership and management skills are likely to be necessary. Even top executives are involved in budgeting, assigning tasks, and tracking and evaluating performance; meanwhile, a relatively new employee may take charge of a project or team for which it is necessary to establish a vision or direction, communicate that to others, and motivate team members to participate in its implementation. The balance of leadership and management skills that a person exercises over the course of a career may shift according to the nature of his or her changing roles, and some people are better at one set of skills than the other, but most jobs at any hierarchical level continue to call for a measure of both. In this book the term *leader* will be used as in common speech to refer broadly to anyone who must take on a leadership role, while *top executive* will be used to single out the highest-ranking leaders of an organization, keeping in mind that all leaders may need to carry out "management" roles as well.

Although Tichy's "leadership at all levels" has been popular and influential, it has also created head-scratching moments for global customers and counterparts in more hierarchically oriented countries when they meet a self-described leader who is twenty-eight years old and appears to be in his or her first basic management role. At its best, Tichy's concept fosters the rapid empowerment and development of young leaders with great promise. Defects stemming from its misapplication include a muddling of leadership and management as well

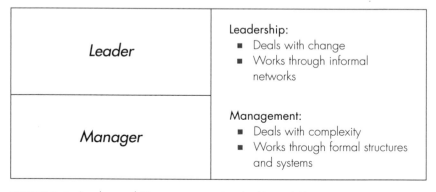

FIGURE 2-3 Leaders and Managers versus Leadership and Management

as culture clashes between those who consider themselves leaders already and others who regard them as just another junior employee.

Ram Charan and his coauthors of *The Leadership Pipeline* have helped to articulate the changing requirements of positions at various hierarchical levels in a large-scale organization. Their model highlights what a leader needs to value and be spending time on at a particular stage (e.g., helping others get work done versus doing it themselves). The authors describe a succession of leadership passages through which a person moves from being an individual contributor to a front-line management role, then takes on the responsibility of guiding other managers, and subsequently learns how to head up a function, business, group, or an entire enterprise. Their work reminds us that even in a primarily domestic organization the requirements of leadership evolve as a person moves to a new role with increased responsibilities. For instance, a person who was previously in charge of a function and who must now lead a business will have to deal with a new degree of complexity, set strategies for growth and profitability for the business as a whole, value other functions equally, and cope with intense visibility as well as scrutiny from above and below in the organization.[5] Limitations of this framework in a global context will be addressed in Chapter 7.

MULTIPLE INTELLIGENCES AND NEUROSCIENCE

Contemporary approaches to leadership have been further enriched by research on multiple forms of intelligence. In the 1980s, Howard Gardner introduced the concepts of intrapersonal and interpersonal intelligence to stress the importance of both self-understanding and the ability to understand the intentions and motivations of others.[6] The related notion of emotional intelligence, although criticized in scholarly circles for lack of supporting evidence, was later popularized by Daniel Goleman.[7] This thread of discussion has been taken up in recent years and recast under the rubric of "personal leadership," which emphasizes mindfulness, attending to emotions and even physical sensations, and crafting a life that is aligned with one's personal vision and yet creatively open to the unknown or the ambiguous.[8]

Another contribution to leadership research and practice has come through the rapid evolution in neuroscience. David Rock and Jeffrey Schwartz, for example, have explicitly sought to tie neuroscience to the challenges leaders face in achieving lasting organizational change. Rock's work highlights the importance of addressing "five domains of social experience that [the] brain treats the same as survival issues." These are basic human impulses associated with status, certainty, autonomy, relatedness, and fairness.[9] Triggering them in a negative way creates resistance and even trauma, while handling them smoothly improves concentration, focus, and performance along with receptivity to change. Rock and Schwartz also stress the value of a compelling vision that encourages employees to leave behind outmoded mental maps and to focus on solutions rather than problems. Effective leadership, they claim, creates opportunities for people to experience fresh insights related to a vision of the future that are then reinforced by a steady focus of attention on desirable changes; this combination of insight and attention reportedly enables the development of new neural connections that are linked with changes in behavior.[10]

Rock and Schwartz acknowledge the importance of both nature and nurture—that is, both brain physiology and cultural factors that shape neurological development. In this book we include a number of research vignettes that show how cultural factors may influence brain development and function. This line of thinking originates from the neuroscience of culture, a field of study that integrates neuroscience and cultural psychology. In recent years, scientists have come to believe that the brain has a seemingly endless capability to change its structure as a result of experience. Through functional magnetic resonance imaging (fMRI) studies, neuroscientists have proven that people from different cultures process information in different parts of the brain. Yet, over time, exposure to a new culture actually changes the way we use our brains, effectively giving us new mental maps that are not only metaphoric but physiological. Although our personal styles of perception and attention, for instance, may come hardwired at birth, through extended exposure to different social groups we can fundamentally alter the ways in which our brains process information.

Intercultural Perspectives on Leadership

Intercultural training and theory have approached leadership from another direction; they help to link generic approaches to leadership with the challenges of leading in a global context. Primary tenets of the intercultural approach include being aware of one's own culturally based values, beliefs, and assumptions; perceiving how others behave according to their own cultural lens; and leveraging differences and bridging gaps in thought and behavior to improve performance.

DIMENSIONS OF CULTURE

Interculturalists tend to focus on cultural contrasts, comparing countries and individuals along certain dimensions of culture. Geert Hofstede and

Fons Trompenaars, for example, have formulated or applied dimensions of behavior for which they have found strikingly divergent patterns in different countries.[11]

A number of survey tools are available for generating one's own cultural profile and comparing it with profiles for countries or other individuals; the *GlobeSmart*® self-assessment is one such tool, and a sample set of results for a multicultural team are displayed in Figure 2-4.[12]

While such broad cultural contrasts are useful to anyone who is working across borders, they can also be applied to the specific concerns of people who are in leadership roles. For example, a functional team leader who seeks to initiate a change process in a multicultural organization would be well-advised to consider attitudes toward risk-taking that are shaped by different cultural orientations and to formulate culturally appropriate strategies for handling them. If Steffi Hegel, for instance, were the leader of the team portrayed in Figure 2-4, she would probably find some team members who are eager to jump into the change effort immediately while others would want to engage in a detailed analysis of potential risks along with careful planning to address

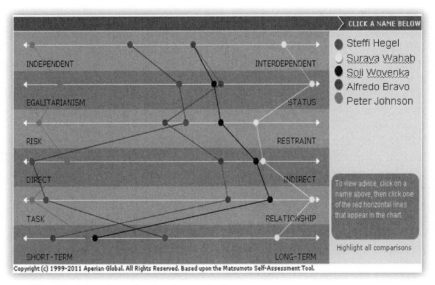

FIGURE 2-4 Sample Multicultural Team Profile

such risks, before proceeding. Similarly, she would likely discover that her direct communication style and task-focused orientation clash with the more indirect and relationship-oriented styles of other team members, and will need to model and promote "style-switching" among team members to ensure that everyone ultimately contributes to and owns the change process. Cultural knowledge can be similarly leveraged in other leadership tasks such as communicating a vision or strategy, motivating employees, creating organizational alignment and evaluating potential future leaders. Indeed, leaders working in diverse environments ignore such cultural variables at their peril.

The massive GLOBE (Global Leadership and Organizational Behavior Effectiveness) Study by Robert House and his associates attempts to identify leadership behaviors that have broad global application and those that are viewed in contrasting ways according to the cultural background of respondents. By comparing survey results from ten regional data clusters, the researchers identified universal factors of leadership effectiveness such as integrity, charismatic/value-based behaviors, and teamwork. On the other hand, they found there is

---

Neuroscience and Culture: Does "Self" Refer to "Me" or "We"?

Scientists studying the region of the brain called the prefrontal cortex, believed to represent the self, found that the area is active when U.S. volunteers think of their own identity and traits, while with Chinese volunteers this same region is activated by adjectives describing *both* themselves and their mothers. The Americans did not show a similar overlap between self and mother. The neural circuitry seems to function differently depending on whether the person hails from a culture that views the self as "autonomous and unique" or as "connected to and part of a larger whole." While the intercultural field has long since identified the cultural differences between "me" and "we" societies, this research attests to the strength of overlap between self and others in collectivist cultures.[13]

Defining oneself as an individual or part of a greater whole has obvious implications for one's everyday behavior and moral code. Global leaders who are able to see themselves (and even their very notion of the self!) as originating from a particular cultural context are much more likely to understand their leadership style as being one way among many possible approaches. They are also more likely to understand their employees' behavior and motivations as emanating from their own unique cultural backgrounds.

---

greater cultural variation when it comes to leadership that is described as self-protective (as in face-saving), participative, or humane-oriented.

For instance, the authors note that "a leadership exemplar for the Eastern Europe cluster would be one who is somewhat Charismatic/Value-Based, Team-Oriented, and Humane-Oriented, but is his or her own person, does not particularly believe in the effectiveness of Participative leadership, and is not reluctant to engage in Self-Protective behaviors if necessary." Nordic Europe, in contrast, rates high for participative and charismatic/value-based leadership but has lower scores for humane-oriented and self-protective leadership. It is interesting to consider how this study appears to support the general applicability of Kotter's model of visionary and inspirational leadership in a global as well as a domestic context, but not necessarily other approaches that assume the universal value of more egalitarian or nurturing leadership styles, even for two societal clusters on the same continent.[14]

CULTURES WITHIN CULTURES

Any national culture is full of complexity and internal contradictions. Beyond general contrasts between cultures, leaders need to be able to discern cultures within cultures along with a substantial degree of individual variation relative to cultural norms. As one global leader put it, "There is more diversity within India than is found in the whole of Europe. Here, there are followers of a religion you may have never heard of previously whose population is equal to that of many countries." These factors can affect consumer tastes, brand appeal, recruiting efforts, employee motivation, and so on. The social environment in China has gone through a series of upheavals, including the Great Leap Forward, the Cultural Revolution, and economic liberalization. Rather than distinguishing between Boomers, Gen X, and Gen Y, as in the U.S., in China it is more accurate to refer to four distinct generational groupings according to the decade of their birth: post-1950, post-1960, post-1970, post-1980 and post-1990.[15]

This internal diversity also calls for flexible approaches to leadership that take into account the behaviors of employees from the same country who identify with opposite ends of a given cultural spectrum. China's historical cultural patterns could reasonably be called highly interdependent, for example, and as recently as the 1970s, most Chinese lived within the collectivist *danwei* structure that simultaneously encompassed jobs, housing, health care, and community. However, an unintended side effect of the country's one-child policy, instituted in 1980, along with economic reforms begun in 1978, has been the creation of the "Little Emperor" generation of only children. Members of this generation, who have often been doted on throughout their lives by six adults—two sets of grandparents plus birth parents with rising incomes—frequently behave more independently in comparison with their Chinese elders, although perhaps not in comparison with people from cultures that have prized independence for generations. Such generational differences within China create challenges even for Chinese who are in leadership roles, let alone foreigners who are trying to work effectively with Chinese colleagues.

> "The collectivist post-'70 generation in China's workplace is often faced with the challenge of managing the individualistic post-'80 generation. In this context, post-'70 managers have found that, unlike themselves, their post-'80 subordinates typically have little respect for authority, actively seek to manage their own careers instead of having faith in the organization's system, and are far more likely to leave their job if the environment does not satisfy them. Furthermore, a recent survey shows that the '80s generation considers the '70s generation to be overly conservative, lacking in creativity, and reserved to the point of appearing fake."[16]

Chinese Schoolchildren

Contemporary Picture
of a Little Emperor

INTERCULTURAL DEVELOPMENT

One additional body of research in the intercultural field with significant implications for leadership focuses on the development of intercultural competence. This is defined by Mitch Hammer as "the capability to accurately understand and adapt behavior to cultural difference and commonality." Hammer and Milton Bennett have created and validated through extensive studies the Intercultural Development Inventory, or IDI, which uses a scale of five orientations—defense, polarization, minimization, acceptance, and adaptation—along a continuum from a monocultural mindset to an intercultural mindset. Corporate groups that use the inventory, including their leaders, most commonly fall in the stage known as *minimization*,[17] which Hammer defines as:

> "An orientation that highlights cultural commonality and universal values and principles that may also mask deeper recognition and appreciation of cultural differences."[18]

In other words, there is a tendency among such groups and their leaders to underscore similarities while underestimating differences. This kind of mindset is manifested in questions such as, "Aren't we all basically the same? Aren't others becoming more like us? Isn't the world converging toward common standards?" A challenge for many people in leadership roles as well as others working in multicultural environments is to be able to fully recognize and appreciate both commonality and difference (acceptance); then they need to transform their outlook and behaviors in a way that will make them most effective in handling the cultural differences that do exist (adaptation).

All of the cultural approaches described in this section help to explain differences that matter to leaders, but they must also be translated into practical action. Knowledge about cultural dimensions, cultures within cultures, or developmental stages is good to have, but only meaningful from a pragmatic standpoint when applied to specific relationships, events, or actions. It is essential to move from the "What"—the cultural differences that are identified—to the "So what," or why these matter from a leadership perspective, and then to the "Now what," as in what to do next. Some interculturalists falter because they are more comfortable with theory and general contrasts than they are in supporting leaders who need to determine how to proceed in a messy world that includes difficult personalities, organizational politics, thorny technical questions, and big investments. Add to this the fact that many cultural experts know a lot more about one country or region than about the rest of an increasingly interconnected planet, and the hurdles to surmount in successfully applying intercultural expertise to leadership become more formidable.

Global Leadership

Prior approaches to leadership, both generic and intercultural, do not provide an adequate set of answers for leaders facing the full hurricane force of globalization in which any or all of the following may occur.

- Disruptive technologies come from many different countries, including ones that have previously not been a competitive threat. Entire industries are threatened that have been mainstays of developed markets for decades.
- A wide array of robust and assertive global stakeholders—customers, employees, shareholders, governments, local communities—all seem to have a vested interest in the direction of the business.
- An effective vision must identify and capitalize on similarities and differences between customer and employee needs in both developed and emerging countries.
- Organizational structures mix matrix reporting across geography, product, and function, and individuals may have five or more direct line reporting relationships.
- Authority based on organizational structure is increasingly supplanted by the need to work horizontally and exert authority through a global network of relationships.
- Dispersed development projects may involve a dozen multicultural teams with people in various continents and time zones.
- Historical silos housing deep technical expertise must be linked to generate distinctive new products and services through cross-border systems thinking.
- Contradiction and ambiguity have become the norm, and besides making decisions with a finite set of "unknowns," leaders need to try to prepare for "unknown unknowns."

As the distinctive imperatives of leading in a *global* context have become both more obvious and more urgent, scholars and consultants have carried out a variety of studies to delineate the characteristics of effective global leaders. Joyce Osland provides a valuable overview of the global leadership literature, and we will not repeat her survey here.[19] However, it is worth summarizing the research approaches that have been used. Figure 2-5 notes the respective authors and titles of six of the best-known approaches to date and briefly describes their research methods.

Authors	Title	Primary Research Approach
Black, Morrison, and Gregersen	*Global Explorers: The Next Generation of Leaders*	Interviews with senior line and human resource managers, additional interviews with "archetypal" global leaders; interviewees asked to describe characteristics of effective global leaders and how these are developed
Goldsmith, Greenberg, Robertson, and Hu-Chan	*Global Leadership: The Next Generation*	Interviews with high-potential leaders from international companies (majority of interviewees under the age of forty) to elicit skills and characteristics of effective global leaders; survey of interviewees and others to compare perceptions of requirements for past, present, and future leaders
House, Hanges, Javidan, Dorfman, and Gupta	*Culture, Leadership, and Organizations: The GLOBE Study of 62 Societies*	Large-scale survey of managers in three industries that includes questions about effective leadership; assessment of results across ten societal clusters using six dimensions to compare leadership traits perceived to be universally endorsed or culturally based
Livermore	*Leading with Cultural Intelligence: The New Secret to Success*	Research on "cultural intelligence" (based on the multiple intelligences research) is applied to leadership tasks with a framework that addresses four aspects of intelligence: motivational, cognitive, metacognitive, and behavioral (drive, knowledge, strategy, action)
McCall and Hollenbeck	*Developing Global Executives*	Interviews with successful global executives focused on formative career events, derailers, experiences on international assignments, criteria for choosing people for international jobs, differences between international work and domestic assignments, and other factors
Mendenhall, Osland, Bird, Oddou, and Maznevski	*Global Leadership: Research, Practice, and Development*	Use of a panel of academic experts (modified Delphi technique) plus extensive literature review to identify key competencies of global managers; the model is expanded and adapted for global leaders in the form of a pyramid that portrays a cumulative acquisition of competencies, including global knowledge, threshold traits, attitudes and orientations, interpersonal skills, and system skills

FIGURE 2-5 Global Leadership Research Approaches

The research outlined in Figure 2-5 has done much to deepen our understanding of global leadership. Nonetheless, frameworks offered to date still have several key limitations:

- Global leadership competencies are often not clearly distinguished from more generic competencies that leaders need in any role, whether domestic or global.
- The leadership characteristics listed are often so broad or abstract (e.g., "flexibility," "integrity," or "business savvy") that they are difficult to cultivate and to utilize in a practical way.
- The requirements for leadership roles are often mixed with more general management skills or with intercultural skills needed by anyone who is working in a diverse environment.

Indeed, so-called global competencies are often haphazard extrapolations from domestic practices. Given the rising priority of global business opportunities in many industries, there is a tremendous temptation both inside and outside corporations to take whatever has been successful to date and slap onto it a "global" label. Headquarters executives sometimes assume, based on minimal evidence, that their own leadership styles can be readily exported. And leadership consultants are highly motivated to assert that their models have universal value, even when such models have not been derived from or systematically tested in multiple cultures and are greeted with puzzlement, resistance, misinterpretation, or even derision in foreign markets.

Joyce Osland and Allan Bird, among others, list a number of these flaws in the studies to date that have been focused on global leadership, and suggest that future research examine "whether and how global leaders differ from domestic leaders," and "what effective global leaders actually do."[20] Indeed, the topics they call attention to have shaped the research agenda for this book. It is important to keep in mind that people working in demanding global leadership roles quickly become impatient with competencies, survey tools, or forms of advice that look like what they have already learned in previous jobs as domestic leaders, and it is equally if not more essential to respond to their very practical priorities and concerns.

Research Background: What Is Distinctive About Global Leadership?

Based on the contributions and limitations of previous studies, we focused specifically on two questions:

- What is *global* leadership, and how is it different from leadership in general?
- How can effective global leadership behaviors be disseminated as rapidly and efficiently as possible throughout an organization?

PARTICIPANT DEMOGRAPHICS

To address these questions, we approached fourteen major organizations in a range of industries: energy, health care, information technology, manufacturing, pharmaceutical, retail, semiconductor, and telecommunications. One major nongovernmental organization (NGO) was included as well. The companies were located in various regions, with headquarters in North America, Europe, Asia, and the Middle East. We asked company representatives to select interviewees with the following characteristics:

- Service in a key leadership role as a current or former international assignee
- At least eighteen months or more of experience on assignment
- Evaluated by the organization as highly successful in their roles

We then interviewed approximately seventy international assignees selected by their companies according to these criteria. Eighty percent of interviewees had been on more than one international assignment, which makes this a group of very seasoned global leaders. Most were in positions as a country or regional director, or head of a major business or functional group. Because each had typically been in multiple prior leadership roles in his or her home country, they were well positioned to compare leadership in a global context with domestic leadership.

In all, the interviewees came from twenty-six different countries of origin and were on international assignments to thirty-two different country destinations. This rich mixture enabled us to identify themes that emerged across the board rather than characteristics of a particular nationality or destination. Figure 2-6 shows the national backgrounds of the interviewees, including the NGO leaders we interviewed, and Figure 2-7 calls out the countries to which they were assigned.

RESEARCH FINDINGS: A BRIEF OVERVIEW

The overriding consensus among our interviewees was that global leaders must carry out tasks similar to those of leaders in any location, yet they must be

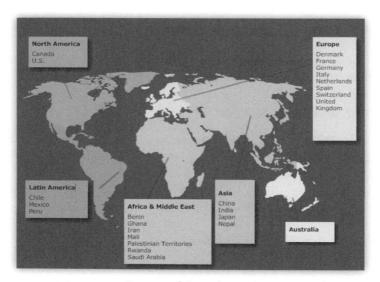

FIGURE 2-6 Countries of Origin for Leaders Interviewed

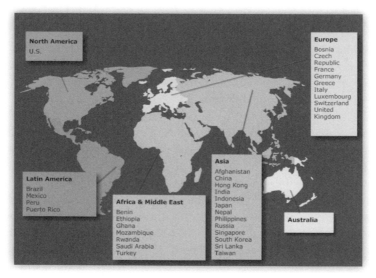

FIGURE 2-7 Assignment Locations of Leaders Interviewed

able to shift strategies, business processes, and personal styles to fit different cultural environments along with a broader range of employee backgrounds and motivations.[21]

Here are a few direct quotes from interviewees.

"Global leadership is very different, remarkably different. The business world has some global measures, but how to accomplish those things? We can all agree on growing ten percent, but what are the means to get there? The process? The people skills? All these are different to reach the same result."

"The core leadership skills prevail, such as getting results through people . . . but you have to adapt your style to the people, the environment, the way things are done, the things that help you get it done."

Many also noted that, in their experience, a different level of effort was required to perform effectively in their global leadership capacity compared with a purely domestic leadership role.

"I could do three out of five things in a domestic leadership role and still be successful, while in my global position I had to get all five right or the initiative would fail."

"If this is what I would normally do at home, here I have to ramp it up about fifty percent."

As these remarks suggest, global leadership behaviors are vital and yet easy to underestimate. The very people who most need to acquire them may minimize their significance by emphasizing similarities to generic leadership and repeating comforting but false mantras such as "leadership is the same everywhere." This is not what we heard from our interviewees. While there is indeed overlap between global leadership behaviors and more generic leadership and/or intercultural skills, as illustrated in Figure 2-8, it is also possible to delineate a distinctive combination of behaviors that are characteristic of effective global leadership in particular.

Figure 2-9 provides a distillation of our research findings. Detailed analysis of the interview data revealed that certain behaviors came up repeatedly when leaders described what they had learned while working in a global context. In total, there were ten behaviors interviewees consistently described as crucial to their success, and these behaviors can be categorized into five major stages. Later chapters in this book will cover each stage and the behaviors in detail.

For those who find acronyms useful, combining the first letter of each of these five stages produces the word SCOPE—many of our interviewees remarked on the significant expansion of job scope that occurred as they began

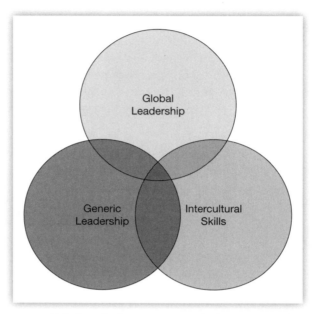

FIGURE 2-8 Global Leadership, Generic Leadership, and Intercultural Skills

to lead in a global context. One preliminary observation about these global leadership behaviors is that they begin with "seeing differences," a theme that is closely related to the more advanced developmental orientations of the Intercultural Development Inventory (IDI). In a sense, our research findings could be described as picking up where the IDI leaves off, exploring the specific implications of an intercultural mindset for people in leadership roles. In addition, the five stages illustrated in Figure 2-9 appear to be cumulative. Those

Seeing differences   **C**losing the gap   **O**pening the system   **P**reserving balance   **E**stablishing solutions

FIGURE 2-9 Global Leadership Behaviors: Five Stages

who acquire the capabilities associated with each stage are more likely to be successful at subsequent stages, although these steps don't always unfold in a sequential fashion and some may occur simultaneously.

The contents of each stage are described as behaviors because we exerted considerable effort to elicit concrete and specific descriptions from interviewees to avoid the drawbacks of more generalized models that refer to "traits" or "attitudes," although such models have merits as well. These behaviors deserve further research and testing for their potential to support and spell out the meaning of various competency frameworks, using the technical definition of a *competency* as a characteristic that is demonstrated to predict superior or effective performance on the job. Based on the distinction between "stable" competencies (enduring aspects of personality) and "dynamic" competencies (specific skills and abilities that can be taught), our behavioral focus places this work on the more dynamic end of the spectrum.[22]

POTENTIAL APPLICATIONS

The five stages and ten global leadership behaviors identified through this research have numerous potential applications. A common message we heard from interviewees is that the insights and experience they gained while serving in global leadership roles have been insufficiently leveraged by their employers. Indeed, many felt that others in their organizations were not even all that interested in what they had learned. However, these individuals were, without exception, eager to share their insights and were full of suggestions about how their experiences might be put to use.

Rapid and thorough dissemination of global leadership competencies throughout an organization requires a fundamental shift in mindset. Companies needing to expand their presence in global markets must learn to start every major effort with its global implications in mind instead of seeing global as an "add-on" to what already exists—not, for example, as an afterthought to a strategic initiative planned exclusively at headquarters, a single leadership competency called "Global Mindset," or a half-day module in a six-month leadership program. Possible areas for integrating global leadership behaviors into key organizational systems and processes include:

- Executive meetings
- Orientations for leaders of global teams and global projects
- Coaching/mentoring for global leaders and international assignees
- Competency definition and review

- Employee recruitment and retention policies
- Talent review and succession planning
- Stretch assignments for future leaders
- Candidate selection for top executives, international assignees, global "high potentials," positions with global responsibility, and global team leaders
- Nomination processes for executive education
- Executive/leadership development program design and delivery
- Predeparture training and on-site assimilation for international assignees
- Web-based resources

The various departments involved with developing global leaders—for example, Human Resources, Organizational Development, Mobility, Talent Management, Diversity, and Training and Development—seem at times to be attempting to guide the proverbial elephant in different and conflicting directions, each tugging on a separate body part of the larger animal known as leadership. Having a shared understanding of and commitment to a consistent set of global leadership behaviors could also serve to better align these efforts across different functions.[23]

GLOBAL LEADERSHIP: BENEFITS

Weaving a global perspective throughout an organization is increasingly a necessity rather than a "nice to have." Our interviewees spoke most eloquently about the benefits of the global leadership behaviors they learned as well as the tangible value they offer for companies that are competing in the world's fastest-growing markets.

Sample Benefits of Global Leadership

- **Global market awareness; better sensors:** "I've gained an acute awareness of global competition, demand, and global consumer trends. Awareness of the world is critical to survival."
- **Perspective on the organization:** "You have a better perspective on the company. We operate in a global market but are not necessarily global.... Markets are different all over the world."
- **Knowledge of global business drivers:** "A global company truly understands markets and their drivers and acts accordingly... When you understand the key drivers for the market, you can customize the product to those markets."
- **Senior executive candidates:** "It is impossible to explain China to senior management. Key leadership positions should be allocated to people with experience abroad for the company's sake."
- **Effectiveness in a diverse environment:** "We have a truly diverse workforce now, even domestically. It is a real challenge to be sensitive to all those styles, cultures, and approaches. To be a long-term effective leader in a diverse environment, you have to have a 'global mindset.' You need to have this if you want to be successful anywhere now—it is core."
- **Innovation:** "I'm now seen as someone who can come up with improvements and innovations and have been placed into a key role. Based on my global experience, I have an open mind to new solutions and the courage to make things happen."

CHAPTER **THREE**

Seeing Differences

Effective global leadership begins with the ability to see the differences that are most likely to make a difference. When companies do not notice or adequately address real differences in global markets, inappropriate solutions from headquarters tend to fill the knowledge gap. Leaders in a global environment must cultivate a range of vision that places their own previous leadership experience in context and enables them to sort through myriad factors, both familiar and unfamiliar, to identify and deal with the issues most crucial to success.

Global Leader: Fernando Lopez-Bris, John Deere

Fernando Lopez-Bris is the manager of Product Engineering for John Deere in its Coffeyville, Kansas, plant, which makes power transmission equipment. Fernando is originally from Madrid, and he speaks several languages, including Spanish, English, French, and German. In a previous job with a Japanese automotive company, he lived briefly in Japan.

Fernando's current role involves design control in his division of the company. His unit does the engineering for the product lines, and they work with a sister factory in Mexico that manufactures. His job is to oversee multiple projects and to provide support for all engineering teams, while handling budgeting, personnel, and other tasks. Before coming to the United States, Fernando performed a similar job in Spain, but with a different product range in Deere's agricultural division.

Fernando describes his previous leadership style in Europe as "pulling" rather than "pushing." He feels that by setting an example of hard work along with some basic principles, you can expect people to follow this example rather than needing to "crack the whip," as is common in more of a pushing style. He has learned through experience and through his MBA training in situational leadership that different people benefit from different approaches. "Not all people require the same type of management; some want close follow-up, looking over everything that they do. Others want to be turned loose and only report back when they have a problem."

Although Fernando had considerable leadership experience before coming to the United States, his current role has exposed him to a broader range of circumstances and stresses that have tested his skills in new ways. In addition to the quality and project issues he has encountered, Fernando has also had to cope with a natural disaster: the severe flooding that occurred in Coffeyville not long after his arrival. "The Friday before the flood, the general manager of the facility asked me if I could take care of operations while he was on vacation. The flooding was on Saturday, and I had to coordinate everything with City Hall. I had to spread the word around, make calls to ensure that people were okay, coordinate the team, stay in touch with the general manager, and make daily assessments. This was tough for all of us and a big experience for me."

FLOODING IN COFFEYVILLE, KANSAS

"All situations, if you are directly exposed to them, reveal your abilities. The more situations you are exposed to, the better skills you gain. I have gained from a broader range of experiences than I would have been exposed to in Spain [experiences like the flooding]. As a leader, you learn how you work under stress. In the U.S., the expectation is that you will stand up and work even harder in a crisis situation, that you will be proactive."

This exposure to a wide range of experiences has also provided Fernando with a broader perspective on global markets. As he notes, "In Europe, all of our operations are smaller than in the U.S., so you don't expect to sell a U.S. eight thousand to nine thousand model tractor frame there. But the six thousand model will sell in Europe. It was developed just for Europe, based on knowledge of the European market. You need to understand that small farms don't have the money for the big tractors. . . . Markets are different all over the world. A global company truly understands markets and acts accordingly. Something that is successful in the U.S. can be a disaster elsewhere. You can't drive the business the same in the U.S., Russia, China, or Africa. Even if it is a successful business model and team, it won't transfer to another country. When you understand the key drivers for a market, you can customize the product to those markets."

Along the way, Fernando has also encountered numerous other day-to-day challenges stemming from cultural contrasts in communication and leadership styles. For example, he has found that Spanish culture is more indirect: "You may need to go around." But the U.S. expectation is for clear and precise information, so long as it's not perceived as rude. "I can say to employees directly, 'I need you to work overtime.'" He misses business relationships that are developed around food. "In Spain, a meal is probably two to three hours at minimum. You talk and have food. You may cut a deal with a partner in the office and this is more formal. But sometimes you need to be less formal in order to capture the whole picture."

Fernando observes that his prior work experience in Japan made it easier for him to adjust to the United States. "I had a big breakthrough about this in my first international assignment. So in the U.S., I started by interacting with colleagues and neighbors to appreciate and understand the culture I am in. This helps you to understand your own culture, puts it into perspective, and you realize the differences. It helps you to look with more critical eyes. We take everything for granted when working domestically. But abroad, everything gets put into perspective, and you're checking for similarities and differences." Being flexible, he notes, means even being prepared to give up your customary style of living and to embrace a different style.

Cultural Self-Awareness

Cultural self-awareness is the first step toward seeing differences. It includes the realization that our leadership practices are shaped by the environment around us, and that there are different and perhaps equally or even more viable ways of getting things done in other locations. Many of our interviewees remarked that their global roles enabled them to see themselves and their own leadership style for the first time as the product of a particular cultural context, and this led them to question deeply their own actions and assumptions. Several described this experience as having a "helicopter view" of themselves, or the ability to view their own thoughts and ideas from an objective distance. As

Fernando Lopez-Bris indicates, being exposed to a wider set of circumstances requires leaders to constantly check for similarities and differences with what they already know, or think they know, and to recalibrate their expectations. They can no longer take things for granted, as is sometimes possible in a more familiar environment.

Cultural self-awareness may be stimulated through the questions that others ask. As another leader from a firm based in Asia said:

> "In my eight years abroad, I saw lots of new things that I hadn't seen at home. You learn to see your own country and yourself from an outsider's point of view. When you're at home, you don't think of it as 'just one country.' But when I talk to other Asians or to Europeans, people ask me about my country with questions like 'Why do you do things this way?' I get thousands of questions. When you are asked, it is difficult to answer. I wasn't ready."

Other leaders, perhaps because of their executive status, prior reputation, or global colleagues' deference to hierarchy, don't get such questions and must reach out in ways that are described in the next section of this chapter. The recipe for failure is to be "stuck inside yourself." A less polite way of referring to this is the person who has a box on his or her head, and who says once too often, "At headquarters we do it this way, so you have to do it this way as well." There is often a "new normal" to which one needs to become accustomed concerning the values of a different country, organization, or individual. As one

Insights from Global Followers[1]

I saw people who were prominent leaders at home who crumbled in global roles, while others who started at more mid-level positions rose to the top. Those who failed were inflexible, followed rules, and did what they were told to drive an existing process. They couldn't get the job done and couldn't understand why; they would raise their volume five times louder but the others still did not understand no matter how loudly these executives yelled or stamped their feet. This pattern of behavior turned into a downward spiral. My local counterparts would just look at me and shrug their shoulders. The people who failed tended to have little or no previous global experience, and had never spoken a second language. They had not been exposed to different cultures before; our executives thought we could plop them out in the world and they would be surrounded by the company bubble.

interviewee said, "You need to go back to zero and consider how to apply your expertise and values—you can't command or criticize others based on your own fixed ideas or assumptions. Yet at the same time, you may be able to find places where your own values and ways of doing things do apply."

WHAT ARE THE DIFFERENCES?

Academics who try to describe the different circumstances that global leaders face tend to invoke the term "complexity." While having to deal with complexity is not necessarily unique to a global role,[2] the nature of the challenges faced by people in global leadership roles is qualitatively different, and includes factors such as the following:

- Physical distance
- Time zones
- Language
- Historical influences
- Institutions: educational, legal, political, and religious
- Cultural values
- Common business practices

To better to understand what complexity actually means in a global setting, it is useful to look at two sample descriptions of global leadership roles and the challenges they entail. (See pages 41–42.)

The complexities Josefina and Bertrand face are certainly daunting. People working across boundaries in leadership roles are likely to encounter such difficulties sooner in their careers and with greater intensity than those working domestically. If they are not able to place their own prior leadership experience in perspective and adapt to these new environments, their chances for success are slim indeed. Each leader who takes on more complex responsibilities must reassess assumptions and patterns of behavior that are influenced by his or her own upbringing, prior work experience, and past successes. The patterns of success that people tend to cling to under pressure can become their greatest obstacles when exported to other environments.

For example, if Josefina were overly attached to product requirements from her home market, there is a good chance that her team would underperform or sink under the weight of ongoing conflicts, whether overt or hidden. This is true of her leadership style, too, as she is finding that she has to modify her approach to working with team members in different locations. Similarly, if

EXAMPLE 1: **GLOBAL TEAM LEADER**

Josefina Lopez is the leader of a global product development team. Although she is currently based in Mexico City, her team members are located on four continents spanning many time zones and speak eight different native languages. Scheduling virtual team meetings with colleagues in both Europe and Asia requires her to be on the phone with them either early in the morning or late at night her time. The team has had two face-to-face meetings to date—one at the project kick-off, and the other after the first year's milestones were completed. There were several team members with whom Josefina had worked in the past, but the others are all working together for the first time. Josefina's role is further complicated by the fact that two-thirds of the fifty people who are working on her team report in a direct line to other managers and have matrix reporting relationships to her. The larger team that she runs is also split into several subteams that need to coordinate with each other their roles in the product development effort.

More specific challenges that Josefina has encountered during the first year in her role include:

- Team meetings: Team members from certain countries tend to dominate the conversation, while others contribute little. It has been difficult to facilitate these meetings and create a common meeting format that allows everyone to contribute, especially since most participants are speaking in a second language. Josefina's attempts to build stronger personal ties between team members have been received warmly by some but more indifferently by others.
- Product requirements: Due to the influence on team members of local matrix managers who want to ensure a good fit between the new product and the needs of consumers in their markets, it has been difficult for the team to reconcile different and sometimes conflicting requests regarding the specifications of the new product. Josefina's attempts to establish shared goals for the team have been undermined by these competing country interests.
- Performance management: Josefina has found it challenging to clarify expectations and to assess the performance of individual team members reporting to her. Some seem to require constant supervision and consultation, while others—particularly team members from Northern Europe and the United States—reject the same kind of oversight as "micromanagement." Even though her employees have all logged their goals and are providing updates in electronic format, Josefina has the feeling that some are just going through the motions. She has started to contact each of them one-on-one on a monthly basis to share updates, but this has proved to be enormously time-consuming, and meetings are often hard to schedule due to various other commitments.

EXAMPLE 2: **GLOBAL BUSINESS LEADER**

Bertrand Favier is the head of a global business line for a large industrial firm based in France. Bertrand is in a key role, as his business has aggressive goals for future growth, most of it outside Europe. He is therefore under considerable pressure from the Executive Committee to meet these targets. The company has grown rapidly both organically and through acquisitions, and is currently attempting to integrate two medium-sized acquisitions into Bertrand's business line. There is some resistance on the part of the acquired entities to the corporate culture and processes of their new parent company, and they do not get along well with each other either. Almost every week Bertrand receives a message from one of his top managers in Hungary complaining about deadlines missed by a sister facility in India, and a similar message from India complaining about the lack of consistent policy and follow-up from Hungary.

Meanwhile, in China, an especially critical growth market in which the company has done well over the last ten years, Bertrand's business faces several new competitors. The rivals' low-cost structure, clever energy-saving features, and aggressive expansion have led three major customers to threaten to switch suppliers unless Bertrand's Chinese operation significantly lowers its prices. Yet another problem is that at least one of these competitors does not appear to follow standard international rules. During a recent visit to China, Bertrand found counterfeit products bearing his company's brand name installed in a client site that he visited. Besides the brand name violation and intellectual property theft, these products were dangerously substandard and could potentially create safety hazards for which his company might be blamed by consumers who are not able to distinguish fakes from the real thing. Upon further inquiry, it appears that the Chinese competitor making these products enjoys the support and investment of the provincial government where it is located and is regarded as a valued local employer. Counterfeit products from China have also begun to appear elsewhere in the global supply chain, turning up in markets in Taiwan, Thailand, and Vietnam.

Bertrand's division heads, mostly based in Europe, are focused on their largest current customers, which are major multinational companies. However, Bertrand is concerned that the best prospects for new growth and the greatest competitive threats are in emerging markets. Without a major shift in mindset and investment dollars on the part of his division heads, these growth prospects will probably not be realized and will instead be enjoyed by competitors.

And as if all of this weren't enough, Bertrand's cost analysis indicates that the fixed costs of his business are far too high in several countries, including the United States, Germany, and France. With different labor laws and employee contracts in each location, he must oversee the transfer of knowledge and operations that can be replicated elsewhere to lower cost locations, while handling the workplace engagement and morale issues that are likely to emerge along the way.

Bertrand remained focused on the major competitors he is accustomed to seeing in Europe without taking into account the threat posed by fast-growing new emerging market competitors, his business could be blindsided by disruptive innovations that arise from unanticipated directions. He faces a huge challenge in understanding the Chinese market and adapting not only his personal approach but that of his whole business. Only by distancing themselves from their own prior experiences—however successful they might have been—and assuming a broader perspective can both Josefina and Bertrand serve as effective global leaders.

TIPS FROM GLOBAL LEADERS

The global leaders we interviewed offered additional advice related to cultural self-awareness and why and how it should be cultivated. The following are the themes that we heard most frequently:

- You can't change a whole country, and your own country is not the center of the universe.

  "Culture never adapts to you; you have to adapt to country and organizational culture."

  "I was seeing so many different cultures, that the world is so different, while still trying to achieve results locally. I learned that I cannot change people, and have to accept them as they are and work within that for good solutions in other countries."

  "It is essential not to think 'headquarters-centric.' Most of world does not think in these terms, that the world revolves around my country. I didn't fully appreciate that. It gives you a much more global perspective, regardless of which country you are assigned to. I have to ask, 'How would they think? How will India receive this? What do they want?' My country is not the center of the universe. You express this in the way you talk to people or provide services—no one is better than anyone else."

- Previous patterns of success may be dysfunctional in a new environment, and rigid adherence to these is likely to be fatal.

  "We need to be cognizant of the things we take for granted."

  "You need to have self-awareness of your style, humility, and confidence to recognize that style can change and adapt if necessary."

"Knowing my own cultural style is critical; also, as a leader knowing about the group's style is critical."

"If you are rigid, you will be insane by the time it is over."

- There are different ways of looking at the same thing, and various ways to accomplish the same goal.

"I learned that the perception of reality is dependent on the cultural lens you are using. Other cultures are not programmed in the same way—you need to learn that."

"I came to the realization that different people will look at the same thing and understand it completely differently."

"We have to really understand that people in other countries don't always see our perspective—it is lost in translation."

"There is more than one right way to do things."

- It is good to experience differences early and often.

"It's important to accept that other cultures are different but have good reason to be different; they have other ways of doing things. The earlier you have this experience, the deeper it gets into your mindset."

"It becomes easier to adjust and change your style if you have done it before."

- Question your own approach without giving it up entirely; what matters the most is to get the job done.

"You may be trained to think that you know the right way to do something. But that may not work because you are in a different culture. You need to be able to question yourself without losing yourself. Some just say, 'This is the truth and I'm going to roll with it.'"

"Working globally heightens everything; you're more aware of what's at stake, and have to be very focused and clear. You need to have a broad perspective and an open mind, and freely challenge yourself."

"You need to be watchful, aware, proactive, always questioning your own approach—'Is it working?' You need to be focused on getting the job done; not getting it done your way."

Invite the Unexpected

Seeing differences also requires leaders to *invite the unexpected*. One of the many benefits of *cultural self-awareness* is that it contributes to a learning posture that is open to new information and experiences. When one's own way of doing things is seen as the product of a particular context, then it is natural to be curious about other styles of leadership and about business practices that are relevant to leading effectively elsewhere.

READINESS TO LEARN

If the standard recipe for global leadership failure is taking what worked in one environment and blindly applying it elsewhere, then the antidote is found through proactive inquiry about relevant aspects of another country's history and institutions.

> "Have an inquisitive mind; be prepared to learn. The fundamental thing is interest in learning, because this attitude comes across in your behavior. Show a real interest in the people and a willingness to learn."

A passion for learning is infectious, and leaders who demonstrate that they genuinely care about their global colleagues and the places they live in typically find that their counterparts respond with an increasing degree of openness. Many of the "getting to know you" questions that local colleagues or clients ask during informal conversations are intended to gauge the level of commitment that a global leader is consciously or unconsciously signaling toward a given market. Lack of interest in historical or cultural sites or an unwillingness to witness everyday lifestyles or to try local delicacies is often interpreted as a sign that the visitor does not take the country's market seriously. Business counterparts may construe such limited interest as an indicator of the level of effort and follow-through that the leader will apply to the business.

To some extent, curiosity is innate and can be traced to character traits that have been manifested starting much earlier in life.

> "A taste and desire for traveling and experiencing other things were already in my personality. It was already in my own spirit—this sense of adventure. These things undergird my flexibility and adaptability."

45

However, those who have previously had less exposure to working across borders can also learn how to learn, beginning even with simple choices related to travel schedules, lodging, meals, and transportation while in another country. It is one thing to arrive the day before a meeting, stay in a first-class hotel, and travel in a chauffeured limousine; it is quite another to arrive a day or two earlier or stay later in order to visit key cultural sites, select a place to stay that local businesspeople might use, and discover how to navigate the subway system. Do you try to replicate the comforts that you have at home or to immerse yourself as much possible in the social and business culture?

Knowledge regarding history, politics, and social networks contributes to informed business decisions while making local counterparts more forgiving of errors. One successful global leader advises, "Understand the culture and history. You can make a lot of mistakes that others will forgive if they believe you are really interested in them." More importantly, identifying existing strengths of the local organization and its members, as well as points of local pride, can tap into enormous sources of energy and enthusiasm that are not available when trying to standardize "global" practices on the basis of whatever is done at headquarters. Gradually, instead of learning *about* each other, global counterparts come to learn *from* each other.

Insights from Global Followers

It is easy to distinguish between the leaders who are going to do well and those who aren't. The ones who are most likely to succeed have a thirst for knowledge and are asking good questions. They have already learned about the country before they get here, and may arrive early or stay longer to learn more. They are prepared for the informal questions that customers are likely to ask early on in the conversation: "What's your favorite city here? Have you tried the food and what do you like best? Have you been to the national museum? How do you think the culture here is different from your country?" Such questions can be anticipated and should be considered before people land and look stupid with answers like, "I don't know; I have jet lag." No one is interested in your jet lag. The leaders who do well want to get out and talk to customers and see the business environment in person, and quickly become aware of the pulse of the people and the market. We're excited to have them because they're excited to be here. Instead of saying, "That's not how we do it at headquarters," which people don't want to hear, they say instead, "Here's what seems to be going well based on what I've learned, and here's a small thing that maybe we could change."

Ultimately, such learning influences a leader's own personal values, business practices, and lifestyle.

> "Even if you know about another culture and become an expert, you still need to be flexible enough to embrace some of the true values of the culture."

We will return to this topic in Chapter 6 in a discussion of how best to achieve balance between one's own values and those of the local environment.

SEEING WHAT WE DON'T EXPECT TO SEE

Beyond proactive inquiry, global leaders must also learn to consciously correct for the fact that human beings literally see what we expect to see, and that discipline and training are required to even notice the unexpected. There is even a psychological rationale for this. People leading busy lives, and especially those in leadership roles, process so much information and so many stimuli on a daily basis that they would be on complete overload without mental shortcuts. Our minds incorporate mental models—images of reality based upon past experience—that help us to quickly filter out superfluous information, hone in on the most important facts, and concentrate on responding to those matters. But what about vital messages from a previously unknown domain? Leaders risk missing critical data and framing problems in a way that leads to incomplete

---

Neuroscience and Culture: We Don't See What We Don't Expect

In an experiment entitled "Selective Attention Test," Professor Daniel J. Simons of the University of Illinois showed a video of people passing a basketball back and forth and told the experiment participants to count the number of passes. In the middle of the video, a person in a gorilla costume stepped into the middle of the screen, squarely faced the camera, and then walked out of view. After watching the video, the participants were asked if they saw anything unusual. Fifty percent of the participants did not report the gorilla.

This experiment demonstrates the concept of *inattentional blindness*, the idea that if we lack an internal frame of reference for something it is more than just confusing—our brain actually refuses to see it. In other words, if we are not expecting to see something, we will often not see what is right in front of us.[3]

---

solutions if they are not prepared to suspend or modify such autopilot filtering mechanisms in a global context.

To discover unfamiliar aspects of local cultural and market environments that will be crucial for solving business problems, it is essential to anticipate their occurrence and to position oneself by casting a wide net for contacts and other sources of information. Common examples of the unexpected in a global business context include:

- New competitors in expanding markets
- Potential new customers that are unknown or underestimated at head-quarters
- Consumer tastes that require substantial product modification
- Marketing concerns such as local perceptions of a word or symbol, or expectations regarding appropriate pricing
- Logistical challenges (e.g., same-day nationwide package delivery is not a reality in many markets)
- Supply chain issues with product quality or labor practices
- Employee relations issues, such as different labor laws or union protests
- Ethical issues that violate corporate policies or national laws
- Political changes that affect regulatory policies toward major projects
- Competition from government institutions as well as other companies
- Religious practices that are brought into the workplace

The Chinese market is especially rich with examples of the unexpected that Western firms have encountered. Amazon.com, which is rightfully proud of its efficient system of online payments and rapid shipping, found that the Chinese online merchant Dangdang became an effective competitor due in part to its use of bicycle couriers. Dangdang's vast fleet of relatively low-tech couriers responds effectively to consumer tastes by delivering merchandise in person and handling cash-on-delivery payments from consumers who like to see the physical product before they pay and prefer not to use credit cards.[4] Haier, now one of the world's top five appliance makers, has surprised its multinational competitors with innovations such as a washing machine that can be used to clean vegetables—perfect for rural Chinese consumers—and a small refrigerator that also features a fold-out table designed for U.S. college students in cramped dorm rooms.[5] Tencent QQ, the most popular instant messaging (IM) service in China (where IM is often preferred over email), has led the way in monetizing its social network of several hundred million users by selling memberships that allow users to create avatars for themselves, play online games, raise virtual pets, and listen to music.[6]

Sometimes the unexpected suddenly becomes very obvious, as happened to the country director of a multinational company in France who was locked into his own office and held hostage by the union for several days during negotiations (they did feed him well). He remarked that labor strife would never have led to such an outcome in his own country, while heated negotiations and strikes are relatively commonplace in France. In other cases, there may be unanticipated solutions that run counter to the views held regarding a particular market.

> "In Austria, we had bad financial returns because of a local competitor. We couldn't move the numbers. The organization believed we couldn't raise prices, but by listening and accepting more than my predecessors... by doing this I got better prices and market share."

The difficulty of perceiving the unexpected is compounded in many countries by the tendency to place people in global leadership roles on a pedestal and to follow their directions regardless of whether their decisions are seen as the best course of action. This happens in part based upon respect for hierarchy, and also because this can absolve those in subordinate roles from being accountable themselves.

> "We've tried to implement programs that worked at home, but they failed miserably here. In the first twelve months, if I wanted to do something wrong, they would go and do it. We face a lot of challenges in a tough economy. I don't know all the answers and we need to work things out together. But people look to you for answers. 'Why are you here if you don't know?' You have to get to the point where people will tell you you're wrong and explain why. That only happened to me after the first year on the job."

The bottom line for global leaders is that they need to be able to step aside from their status and accumulated expertise to experience what one leader called "the opening of your head" that makes you able to understand different perspectives and not work in such a linear way. "If you can sum up different perspectives, you end up with a better product."

LANGUAGE AND CULTURAL INSIGHT

Our interviewees emphasized language skills as a crucial vehicle for leaders to understand other cultures and to develop effective business relationships.

Although they acknowledged the effort required, they pointed out that culture is often embedded in language, and one cannot be readily understood without the other.

> "It is a huge mistake to think you don't need to learn the language or the culture. Things won't happen fast unless you are prepared to embrace the culture and learn the language. Thinking is reflected in language, and you can't understand things without that."

> "Languages are important. If someone is not interested in learning, that is a red flag. You need that openness, as it shows something to the people you are working with."

The persistent value of language may come as unwelcome news to those who do not have the time, ability, or inclination to study another one, or who may deal with so many countries that it is impossible to learn enough to achieve fluency. However, even relatively modest attempts at language learning are usually appreciated by global colleagues and can start to produce dividends quickly. "Learn a hundred words and use them; people will love you. Using common phrases is simple but important." More in-depth language study is not only a royal road to deeper insight, but also a demonstration of serious commitment to doing business in a country while building lasting ties with local colleagues—and not just on your own terms.

> "If you immerse yourself in the culture and language, you will automatically get into flexibility, adaptability; you will become more open-minded and teachable. If someone seeks to learn the language, it is very humbling, very difficult; they have to ask very simple things. Many don't have the willingness to be a child. But those who do are able to cross through barriers and gain humility and the open mindset that is a natural by-product of the process. It is embarrassing because you feel like a child, but you break down obstacles that will otherwise keep you from being successful."

> "It is very difficult to move forward with English in France. People really accept you and like you if you make an effort to speak French. It is very helpful in getting early acceptance as a person. Leadership is a lot about personality and being accepted."

Thankfully, there are multiple methods of language learning and new technologies that were previously unavailable. And as one learns more, the additional means of learning become accessible as well. One leader who went to Russia with no prior Russian language study or business experience in the country described his less traditional study methods along with how he began to apply what he had learned, including humor.

> "I was tenacious enough to study the language. If you watch the news, the sitcoms, you get a sense for the people and the humor and you come to understand. There is an interaction between language and the way of thinking. The more you know the language, the more capable you are to apply culturally relevant tactics to your leadership style."

TIPS FROM GLOBAL LEADERS

Here are some further comments and points of advice regarding the theme "invite the unexpected":

- Ask lots of questions and listen carefully while holding your own prior experience in check so that you can hear new messages.

  > "I ask a lot of questions, listen more than I speak, and start with the assumption that I am probably not right."

  > "It is challenging to hear different messages, to hear new messages that others are sending and cultural differences you need to be aware of; you need a more open filter."

  > "I learned to try to check cultural assumptions. Before you react to someone, make sure they meant what you think."

- Try to read nonverbal reactions, and don't fill the silence.

  > "The key thing is the ability to listen to other people, in the broadest sense: perspective, arguments, even in hidden speech, culture. Don't jump to conclusions before getting the rationale behind their behavior—investigate."

  > "Listen to subtleties and watch for cues. That skill translates to every culture, and you have to do that."

  > "I have to work harder to get feedback, because my colleagues here won't voluntarily give me the information on protocol, on what things are offensive culturally. I had to learn to ask. I have begun to read the body language and, if I notice something, I stop and ask, I slow down a bit. It's a listening

posture. I naturally like to get to the bottom line, so it's really important for me to stop."

"You can learn to listen. We try to fill silence vacuums; especially if in a leadership position, we fill silence by giving direction, but this is very dangerous. If we ask questions and give people time to answer, the period between when the question is asked and answered is where real learning can take place. You can learn to observe and read subtle signals during those periods."

"The answers are usually in the people themselves, so I must provide space for others' thoughts."

- Look for hidden issues and power dynamics.

  "I had to take it a little bit deeper in terms of observations. There were a lot of power dynamics that were not obvious, so it took a lot longer to figure things out."

  "When I came, I realized that there were some hidden issues that I was not prepared to deal with. Maybe I used to think that I could adapt to any situation, but it took me a while to understand the dynamics, the hidden agenda, and real culture of the people. Then I had to adapt my work and communication style."

- It is sometimes best to acknowledge what you don't know.

  "You have to be able to recognize that you don't know everything. Consumer shopping habits are very different. To come in and start giving directions right away is foolish."

  "What was helpful—I would call people and tell them that I did not know, but that I am open to learning. In this way I was trying to get people to raise issues and explain the culture, get them to tell me how they would deal with a situation."

  "Assume that you know nothing every day. Be ready to open yourself to learn and make mistakes; be open about it."

- Real listening is more likely to motivate than other methods.

  "If they don't believe you are listening, they won't work for you. You can threaten them only so much."

SUMMARY AND REVIEW: **QUESTIONS FOR LEADERS**

Here are questions related to *Seeing Differences* that are worth asking if you aspire to a global leadership role or are already in one. A larger set of questions similar to the ones in this book at the end of Chapters 3–7 are part of *Global Leadership Online* (*www.globalleadershiponline.com*), a web-based tool that enables leaders to both self-assess and to receive feedback from other raters on their performance.

1. What similarities and differences have you noticed between your own leadership style and the styles of counterparts from other cultures?
2. How does your own cultural background shape your leadership style?
3. Do you put yourself in the position of employees and customers from other parts of the world and ask, "What do they want?"
4. How do you check the effectiveness of your leadership style when working with people from different cultures?
5. Are you really interested in the history, institutions, and points of local pride in other country locations? If so, in what ways do you demonstrate this interest?
6. Do you recognize the existing strengths of people and practices in other locations before introducing your own ideas?
7. Have you made an effort to learn the language(s) of other country counterparts and customers? If you imagine an important customer from another country, how many words of that customer's language can you speak?
8. Have any of your assumptions about leadership been challenged when you have observed leadership practices in other locations? If so, which ones?

CHAPTER FOUR

Closing the Gap

Once leaders have discerned the real differences as well as the similarities between their global context and what they may have been accustomed to at home, they must learn how to constructively address the differences in order to achieve their organizational objectives. The first step is to find ways to close the gap between themselves and their counterparts from other cultures, both through building strong personal relationships and through "frame-shifting"—finding ways to shift their communication style, leadership style, and strategies. This is as true for many leaders sitting at their desks in their home country as it is for those who are living abroad.

Results Through Relationships

Although personal relationships are obviously important in any leadership role, our interviewees noted that global leaders must rely on others to a much greater extent because, in a foreign environment, they lack the local knowledge or skills that they would have in more familiar territory. The leadership behavior called *results through relationships* highlights the fact that strong, trusting relationships are nearly always the doorway to getting things done in a global context. Leaders who regard relationship-building as a no-brainer to be quickly checked off the list would do well to consider the nuances and the multiple facets of this behavior in other cultural environments: putting relationships before tasks, more interdependence or relying upon relationships to get the work done, leveraging relationship networks, and seeking out cultural guides who can help to trace a path through new territory by providing trustworthy advice. In certain cultures relationship-building is seen and cultivated in ways similar to a highly skilled art form or craft. What is true for crossing national boundaries is also valuable within complex organizations. Building relationships across organizational silos, stakeholder constituencies, and markets requires a similar focus and skill set.

Global Leader: Hannah de Zwaan, Northern European Manufacturer[1]

Hannah de Zwaan works for a Northern European manufacturer in their corporate headquarters. She is now a project manager responsible for new products from the design phase through their introduction to market. In addition to her native language, she speaks English, German, and French. She learned her French in part through nine months of living in Paris earlier in life.

Previous roles for Hannah included working in the logistics area as a manager of managers, controlling order flow, and taking responsibility for the warehouse, along with its blue-collar and white-collar staff. Several years ago, after having been at the company for ten years, Hannah was asked to join the leadership team that was moving an arm of its operations from headquarters to the Czech Republic. As the project manager for this transfer, she had a huge change management role that included both ramping up production in the Czech Republic and closing down the facility at headquarters. She then moved on to logistics management of the supply chain for a factory with over a thousand employees. Although she had been slated to return to headquarters, Hannah was asked to stay on longer to supervise the opening of a new European regional center for the company in the Czech Republic, and subsequently built up this center with an outsourcing partner and a large stakeholder group. She lived in the Czech Republic for a total of two and a half years.

Hannah describes her original leadership style as that of a typical Nordic egalitarian leader, which means "very much engaging in open, democratic discussion and involving staff in decisions." She allowed the people who worked for her a great deal of freedom, but she also asked them to take on a lot of responsibility.

After moving to the Czech Republic, Hannah felt quite alone in the beginning. She remarks, "First of all, you are leaving your personal network, but you are also leaving your boss and your own job networks." She also notes that she was not prepared for how her new Czech colleagues would react to her. "My husband and I actually skipped the cultural training because we were in a hurry. We just said, 'Let's get down there and see what things are like.' I would not recommend this, although it was helpful to me to have lived abroad before." At first Hannah kept a very low profile, telling employees what the task was and taking time to observe how they performed. "Once you have been there for one or two months, you see who the driver is, what games are played. Taking this time in the beginning to observe gives you good knowledge. You need to be able to step outside yourself and get into the other person's head. Your way of doing things is just one of many."

Although initially it was useful to observe, Hannah soon found that she had to significantly alter her leadership style in order to be effective. She discovered that her Czech employees were reluctant to take initiative, preferring instead to hold back and wait for direction. The quantity and quality of information expected from a leader was also very different from her headquarters experience. "This was new to me. Where I come from, people want to be informed about everything, but when I was in the Czech Republic, at first I really over-informed employees and they were bored, sleeping through meetings. I was used to democratic management, but this did not work at all in the Czech Republic. The most difficult task was being responsible for eighty blue-collar workers who spoke no English. At first I had a warehouse manager, but he left and then I had no one, so I needed to deal with employees myself. I had to go out on the warehouse floor, take a box, show exactly how to pack it, and tell them to finish by 3:00 P.M. It felt like being in the army to be giving such specific directions. They immediately respected me and did what they were told to do. Because of the cultural differences I had to change my leadership style and become stricter, more directive, and provide clearer deadlines." As time went on, Hannah discovered that she also had to differentiate between working with her production manager and with blue-collar workers, becoming more or less directive in her leadership approach. "You have to be able to switch as needed to get results."

Hannah eventually found herself sharing her hard-won understanding of both sides of the cross-cultural interaction. "I had a lot of colleagues from headquarters come down to deliver training in the Czech Republic. They kept saying that Czech people are so different, but I would respond, 'From their standpoint, you are very different. You are in their country so you are the one who is different.'" She also worked hard to manage others' expectations. "A lot of my time was used in setting the right expectations of people in other parts of the company, including headquarters. It is difficult for them to imagine what it is like, what is possible, what the price levels are, how the culture works. Being a bridge-builder and aligning expectations took a lot of time."

Many aspects of Hannah's leadership role were not easy, including her dealings with vendors outside the company. "You have to be pretty tough. I was the first woman general manager. I had to deal with the manager of a local company who was not cooperating. He saw me as a stupid female, and tried to slow things down and give me a lower budget. You have to be tough and not just accept people trying to fool or cheat you." She also struggled with the Czech language. "I ended up speaking a mixture of Czech and English to communicate. I tried to learn Czech, but it is a very difficult language. So I learned what I could and used it, and they respected me for this. Language should not be neglected."

On balance, however, Hannah says that she came to have great affection and respect for the culture and the qualities of the people. "My best experience was in the last nine months when I recruited a lot of people—they are now a high-performing team. The key to that success was that by then I had learned a few lessons about Czech culture and history. This helped me to understand the reasons for why they are the way they are. The lack of initiative, for example, is linked to the communist period in their history. This is how you had to act to survive." She also learned over time the critical importance of personal relationships for many aspects of leadership, including how to give effective feedback. "You need to be able to give positive but also corrective feedback. This is very difficult when you are sitting with a Czech employee whom you don't know. So I took time to get to know employees before I started giving feedback. I only started giving effective feedback when I really began to understand the culture, and became more direct, detailed, and concrete. I could be very honest and direct because I really knew the employees. But I didn't feel I could give feedback during the first six months I was there because I was not on my home turf and didn't know where the borders were."

Hannah observes that her experience in the Czech Republic has caused her to take a more holistic approach to leadership, and to enjoy having a job where she can see a task through from beginning to end and be responsible all the way. "The job in the Czech Republic involved a large role expansion with really open borders, many stakeholders, and work with different departments and competing interests. I had good training in being alone and making tough decisions, which gave me more confidence. Now I also have a much better general business understanding because I saw things from more than one side. I can say, 'Okay, this is what it looks like at headquarters,' but I can also look at the same issue from the perspective of different countries."

Among Hannah's current direct reports back at headquarters, there are six managers with six different nationalities. She says, "I felt that it was so easy to get to know them, to start a dialogue and engage in small talk because I can easily imagine how they feel being here, what kind of problems they have being new to this country and not knowing the language. I can put myself in their place. I have more empathy." Her frame of reference as a leader has broadened, and she has the ability to approach business problems from more than one perspective. "Sometimes I look at issues from the Czech point of view now and think that in my home country we discuss things too long! My experience in the Czech Republic moved my borders so that my own leadership style is different."

RELATIONSHIPS FIRST

A number of interviewees commented that they made the mistake of focusing immediately on the task at hand rather than starting with a foundation of strong personal relationships—a practice that is considered to be common sense for doing business in many parts of the world. One leader observed, "Relationships are first in Latin America; they're absolutely critical." Another interviewee said, "Working in Europe with the French, I was initially very task focused and people didn't respond. I needed to invest in the relationship before they would move." This appears to be true whether contacts are primarily virtual or take place in person; relationship and task are intertwined, and relationships often need to come first. "We take for granted the technology that we have, and need to remember the importance of face-to-face," another person remarked. "Take the time for that, to build those relationships. Relationship-building is a means to get things done."

While it is easy to accept in principle the notion that relationships are important, for global leaders the timing and the manner in which they are created are often quite different from their previous experiences. Fernando Lopez-Bris commented wistfully in the previous chapter that he misses the personal ties that are nourished through long meals and the art of conversation in his native Spain. Another interviewee who was more accustomed to a task-first style reported his experience. "I could sit down in the States for a meeting and get to know people by having a work-style dialogue. But in Brazil, those conversations can't start in the office. I had to earn trust over meals, away from work. It was a different way of getting to know people." Task-oriented leaders begin to feel trust toward others who complete tasks as promised within deadlines and who do each task well. Relationship-oriented leaders build trust by learning about their counterparts: their values, the way they think, their families, organizations, and extended networks. People who are relationship-oriented naturally also like to see work finished successfully and on time. Ultimately, it is difficult to say which method is more efficient. Relationship-building takes more time in the initial stages, but tends to save time later on through close collaboration and avoidance of rework that may be needed when business partners do not fully understand one another.

Following local relationship-building practices is crucial not just for getting to know people, but also for setting a tone that the leader is willing to join in and become a part of the group, to get to know the employees on their own terms. Acceptance of others through sincere cultivation of personal relationships tends to be reciprocated in acceptance of a new leader.

Insights from Global Followers

When new leaders are appointed to global roles, we watch very carefully to see what is most important to them. Are they in a hurry to build their own resumé with a "success story" and then move on to a higher position? Sometimes we have to clean up afterward because the effects of their actions only appear later. Or are they truly interested in us, in our market, and in our customers? We don't want to take people to see our most important clients who are going to push too hard and not show any personal interest. If they are willing to really get to know the employees and customers here and to work closely with us, then we can help them with many contacts that they don't even know about yet. On the other hand, if they are in a big hurry and not really interested in us, we can help them to feel comfortable and respected while they are living on an island, with the main business happening elsewhere. We know what we are doing in this market, and don't want them to be involved too closely if they are going to get in the way. Leaders come and go, and we have to live with the results of their actions for a long time.

"You are always being tested abroad, not intentionally, but it is part of trust building. If you go in with the perception that they are beneath you, you will have a huge problem. First submerge yourself in the culture. Talk with them one-on-one, eat with them without an aloof attitude."

As relationships are in fact built across linguistic and cultural barriers, vital tasks soon become more feasible. Hannah de Zwaan noted that it became far easier to provide direct critical feedback to her Czech colleagues—in spite of their generally more indirect communication style—as she got to know them better and learned the local practices for what could be said when. Sometimes the proper place for exchanging feedback is not at work, but in a more casual social setting.

"Be more open to people, not only at work. My colleagues need to talk to me, and not just on the job; it took me a long time to learn this. In this position, people want to learn from you or give advice—you need to be open to this."

INTERDEPENDENCE

Beyond the value of relationships for a global leader in establishing his or her credibility, they take on still greater significance because of the leader's increased reliance on others in unfamiliar organizational and market settings for information, guidance, leverage, and implementation.

> "Back home it is easier to influence the necessary players. Abroad, you don't have as much leverage, and you can't tell what people really mean in a second language, so you automatically have to be more reliant on people around you. You are dependent on them to help you. I need to make sure they know more about me as a person, my goals, and why we want to get to the goals."

Indeed, a sign of a failed global leader is the person who works long hours to compensate for the perceived shortcomings of colleagues from other countries because "they don't get it." An interesting paradox that emerged from many of our conversations with effective leaders was that they were less sure than in previous roles that they could get things done themselves, but more confident that they could accomplish their objectives through working with others. One leader stated, "You have to have confidence that you can be successful while knowing that you can't do it alone—that you do rely on others for success and are not a one-man show."

Thus global leadership is a profoundly interdependent job. To fully recognize and cultivate this interdependence is the indispensable groundwork for further progress.

> "If you are truly good with people and respect your local colleagues, this will spill over into respect for the culture and the new environment. This is really the foundation for leading abroad. It means that you can work well under pressure. Fundamentally, you need to be able to get things done while connected with the group—get things done with the help of other people; get things done in a state of interdependence. These are inseparable."

LEVERAGING RELATIONSHIP NETWORKS

Good relationships accelerate the forging of new connections across regional and functional lines. Having a familiar third party who can make an introduction or provide a shared bond reassures relationship-oriented colleagues. "Things go so much faster when the person you've just met says, 'Oh, I'm so glad you know Mr. Wong in Singapore; he's an old friend.'"

Accessing strong local networks through relationship ties can have an exponential impact on business results. Many enterprises in countries around the world have been painstakingly built up over generations through relationships based upon common family connections, places of origin, educational backgrounds, and long-term friendships. It makes a huge difference whether you are seen as an insider or as an outsider from the perspective of people who are linked together within these networks. If your relationships with counterparts are such that they feel comfortable sharing key contacts from within their own networks, this can become an invaluable personal and professional asset. And a personal touch or even flair in such situations thus becomes not just nice to have but essential to accomplish everyday tasks such as building a viable supply chain or to receive input on how you are doing.

> "The problem was not the numbers but in building relationships with key suppliers at the beginning to create a better supply chain. I had to look at it from their perspective, culturally how they built their business, establishing friendships and networks to move things along—this is just being practical. You work through friendships to get feedback and opinions and do not do things unilaterally."

FINDING A CULTURAL GUIDE

A number of interviewees also mentioned the value of establishing a relationship with another person who can serve as an objective sounding board and answer questions about standard practices in an unfamiliar environment. One leader said, "I was observing that I didn't feel connected, so I got to know a confidante there who told me when I was out of line culturally." This person might be a well-connected local counterpart who is a seasoned business veteran, or a fellow executive or sponsor from one's own country who is sufficiently open and experienced in working globally to have a balanced view. When facing major decisions related to strategic direction, personnel issues, responding to client requests, or internal conflicts, the advice and consultation provided by such cultural guides can be a lifesaver.

> "It's good to have a sounding board—someone with whom you can speak regularly and get reactions and a second opinion from, or someone who can even tell you that you are wrong. Otherwise, the pressure of general

business can affect your judgment and decision making. There are some things that may feel right at the time, but which then take a lot of undoing to fix. It's better to talk to a third party and say, 'Here's where I'm at, here's what I'm facing,' and get a neutral, objective point of view. Find someone whom you can completely trust with all aspects of the business, not just within one department or functional area—someone whom you can ask, 'What is your experience? Does this sound right to you?'"

"You have to not worry about going to others and saying, 'I don't know and I need some help.'"

The best cultural guides are able to balance outsider and insider perspectives: they know the local culture intimately, yet can also see it from a visitor's point of view and understand what others might find puzzling or difficult. If you are very comfortable with your guide, yet he or she seems unclear about local practices, it could be that this guide is better at relating to you than to the local culture. On the other hand, some would-be guides, however well informed and well intentioned, are so enmeshed in their own commonsense worldview that they are not able to articulate how things work to outsiders, and may find the explanation process exasperating. Depending on the dominant communication style in a particular culture, leaders who sincerely seek advice from qualified individuals still may not get it without adjusting their own styles. "One of my best cultural guides in China (bless her) was always 'telling' me what I was doing wrong in China, but due to her indirect style, it took me over a year to figure out that she was, indeed, giving me feedback." So, even when the cultural guide is trying to deliver a message, you still need to be able to "hear" it.

Frame-Shifting

Another way to close the gaps across national and cultural borders when major differences are identified is to start *frame-shifting*. Once leaders have come to view themselves as the product of a particular cultural context, are positioned to listen for the unexpected, and have built strong relationships with their global counterparts, they must learn to shift their perspectives and leadership methods to better fit different circumstances. Frame-shifting requires the cognitive and behavioral agility to alter both one's leadership style and strategic approach. Successful global leaders are nimble enough to take on new frames of reference and to modify their approach to various environments without losing sight of their primary business objectives.

COMMUNICATION STYLE

The first stylistic challenge that emerges for many global leaders is how they communicate. This area overlaps with general intercultural communication issues that affect anyone working across borders. However, leaders have an urgent need to get certain kinds of communication right, including asking others to take on tasks, giving and receiving critical feedback, getting to the bottom of key issues through their questions, and knowing when others have truly committed to a course of action.

Direct versus Indirect Communication

Fernando Lopez-Bris described how he learned to ask U.S. employees more directly to take on overtime tasks, whereas in Spain he was accustomed to taking a more roundabout approach (see Chapter 3).

> "In some countries you expect information to be clear and precise. You can say directly, 'I need you to work overtime.' In Spanish culture, you may need to go around and not be so direct. If you are not aware of these differences it may compromise your effectiveness."

Other leaders face the opposite challenge: if they are used to a direct approach, they need to learn how to understand and work with employees who are indirect. Subtle communication style differences have greater consequences than is often recognized. Some interviewees commented that leaders in Northern Europe tend to be more direct than those in the United States, but that leadership styles in the United Kingdom are relatively indirect and reserved in comparison with Northern Europe and the U.S. They also pointed to distinctions within South and Central America.

> "In the export business, you are communicating with 14 nations under one roof and dealing externally with 103 countries, and the styles are totally different. Scandinavians are completely direct. Many others—after one hour they have not told you the point. You need to have respect and know about these styles and how to work with them. Communication style training is essential for those working with other units around globe, even virtually."

63

"In the U.K., we had weekly meetings, and some people were not carrying their load, and I lit into them heavily. Human Resources said to back down, but those guys had to be fired eventually. It was the right thing to do but the wrong method of doing it. I learned that."

"Argentina and Brazil are more confrontational. In Central America, there is more of a passive-aggressive stance; in my experience, the partners I worked with there would sometimes say yes, but just not do it."

Even within the same country there are different levels of directness depending upon the situation, and each country has its own version of commonsense communication standards taken for granted by insiders but not easily discernable to others. Situational factors may include whether you are in the workplace or in a social setting, your hierarchical status in relation to others, and the degree of closeness of a relationship. In some countries it is customary for a leader to be directly critical of a subordinate, whereas the reverse is unacceptable except in certain social settings. The accepted practice with very critical messages may be to convey them through a third party or in private. And causing embarrassment or loss of face, even when unintended, can lead an entire team or organization to turn on its leader.

"In South Korea they will not give you their ideas because it is impolite to give your superior an idea. . . . You need to take them out and drink with them so they can open up and give you their views—if they do this when they are drinking, this is acceptable. If you start going out and eating from the same plate, then they feel that the boss is like us and eats Korean food, so they open up. If you ask for a fork and a knife, this will turn them off."

"In the Philippines people don't like to confront; they will tell someone off to a third party or do it in private. This is so critical. You will have the whole organization against you if you embarrass someone in public."

"Here in Central America people may get offended for life if you have an argument with them in public."

Use of Questions

Leaders with global experience frequently describe how they have learned to use questions differently. They may ask more questions, pose questions in more than one form, or employ questions to challenge or to provide feedback.

"You need to ask questions and follow-up questions; working globally you need to do that three times as much to get a true answer. People won't necessarily volunteer the information if it isn't exactly what you asked. I have taken up smoking with others for better communication—after ten minutes together, you get a completely different story."

"In some countries you have to ask more questions, challenge in a positive way: 'How do you think we can do it?' 'Do you think there are better ways?'"

"Questions, if asked properly, are not intimidating in any way; they can be used to convey directions. This is a way to give indirect feedback in China, to get information, and to know what is going on."

What is the best course of action in countries where it is considered proper to agree with your boss regardless of your true feelings, and where subordinates are reluctant to bring bad news of any kind? Here a refined questioning approach that probes persistently without interrogating can make the difference for a leader between knowing what is actually going on and having no idea. One highly successful leader in South Asia noted that she had learned to "ask fifteen questions"—that is, to pose variations of the same question in order to determine the true state of affairs.

Leader: "Have all the preparations been made for the event next month?"
Employee: "Oh yes."
Leader: "How about the location?"
Employee: "Yes, we have a very nice location."
Leader: "And the speakers?"
Employee: "Yes, very good speakers."
Leader: "Have all the speakers agreed to participate and made time in their schedules?"
Employee: "Almost."
Leader: "Who is still a question mark? Can I help?"
Employee: "The first day's schedule is complete."
Leader: "What about the second day?"
Employee: "Well, the keynote speaker on the second day may have a conflict. . . ."

Gaining Commitment

Most global businesspeople have heard about the "yes" that means "no," and the "maybe" that means "forget about it." Less well-known but equally puzzling for some is the dramatic display of passion or emotion that ultimately means very little. Leaders seeking commitments from customers or employees are likely to hear these kinds of messages and must alter their interpretations and responses based upon an understanding of the local communication style.

> "Commitment may mean something different. For the Italians I worked with, if I said I needed something, they would say 'yes.' To me, this meant yes, but to them it meant, 'Yes, your lips are moving.'"

> "I thought that I had a dispute, but then a colleague explained to me that the guy was agreeing with me in a Greek way. He said, 'I disagree with you!' but then said exactly what I had said."

> "In gaining commitment, certain cultures don't like to disappoint and won't bring bad news. Once I figured that out, I began to ask different questions and get different commitments. I learned by getting disappointed. I have become much more explicit, with a lot of follow-up and reminding. They are learning to adjust to me and my meanings as well. We are both seeing things from different vantage points. You can live with these different perspectives, and they make it interesting if you know what is going on."

Leaders struggling to work across diverse communication styles are often up against more than just direct or indirect manners of speaking. A subordinate providing what seems like vague answers or information may be relying on other, nonverbal contextual cues to convey his or her meaning while assuming that the leader has a shared understanding of the unspoken context. If the leader is coming from a more low-context and verbal culture, he or she may not be equipped with the mental tools to even look for the unspoken sources of meaning, so misunderstandings can, and often do, occur. Global leaders must hone new ways to search out and hear messages coming to them in unfamiliar packages.

LEADERSHIP STYLE

The need to "frame-shift" in terms of communication practices is linked with more comprehensive shifts in leadership style. Leaders such as Hannah de Zwaan who are trained in a consultative approach that constantly informs and draws upon the expertise of other team members might find that colleagues

Neuroscience and Culture: Attention to Objects or Context

Recent behavioral studies show distinct attentional bias along cultural lines. In a study involving both Western and East Asian participants, Westerners, whose cultures place a high value on independence and individuality, tended to focus their attention on individual objects, with less regard for context and relationships among items. In contrast, East Asian participants, whose cultures emphasize interdependent relationships and awareness of context, showed attentional bias toward contextual, relational processing of information.

These information-processing differences manifest themselves in cognitive behaviors. In a separate change blindness test, East Asians noticed more changes in background contexts, whereas U.S. Americans detected more changes in foreground objects. In addition, Americans recognized previously seen objects in changed contexts better than their East Asian counterparts, due to their increased focus on object information without regard to context.

Taking this one step further, in a study involving Asian-Americans and non-Asian-Americans, both groups were shown photos of complex, busy scenes while connected to devices measuring brain activity. The neurological study found that the Asian-Americans and non-Asian-Americans actually used different regions of the brain to process the scenes they were shown. The Asian-Americans showed activity in the area of the brain used to process figure-ground relationships, or holistic context. The non-Asian-Americans showed brain activity in the area used to recognize objects.

All of these results suggest that cultural influences subtly direct neural activity throughout the brain's development.[2]

in another country expect them to take a more directive stance—indeed, failing to do so may be seen as a sign of weakness or lack of capability. Similarly, a person who is used to being positioned as an expert technical resource may need to shift to a broader team leadership perspective or vice versa, and the emotionally expressive style that worked in one country must be toned down in another. Here are some more representative comments about these kinds of leadership style shifts from our interviewees.

- **Consultative/directive:** "I learned to modify my leadership style in order to be effective in other cultures. For example, when I was working in Mexico, they expected a more authoritarian style of leadership. This is the opposite of my U.S. MBA training. My style did not work in Mexico—the U.S. participatory style was viewed as ineffective."

- **Specialist knowledge/general team leadership:** "In Mali, leadership was based on technical skills and leading by example; in Benin, it required more of a team approach, so I learned more about team leadership."
- **Emotional expression:** "If you contrast Mexico with Indonesia, in Mexico it is about emotion; I could use a highly emotional devil's advocate approach to challenge people. This style completely flopped in Indonesia. They use small teams, give homework, and are nonconfrontational. You have to understand the culture you are working with and adapt your style."

Frame-Shifting and Generic Leadership

Frame-shifting for global leaders at times seems to contradict standard practices associated with generic leadership (see Chapter 2). For example, a key element of a leader's role in the generic sense is that he or she should provide a vision that gives the organization a clear and compelling sense of direction. Yet some of the leaders we interviewed, especially those with experience in communist or formerly communist countries, commented that the notion of "vision" reminded employees of propaganda. Vision also seemed to matter less in places where strong personal relationships and the mutual obligations that come with them are the first priority. Leaders had to start instead by focusing on other factors such as building personal loyalty, and then articulate their vision at a later date or perhaps not at all.

- **Vision/personal loyalty:**

  "Once you build up a loyal group of people around you, when they are lined up behind you and they feel like you are a good chief to have, then you just set the expectation and it gets done, with no questioning; they just execute and go through every road block. At home I spent a lot of time building consensus. In Russia, they just line up if they trust you."

  "In most of Latin America, our U.S.-centric model didn't work. There, it was more the patron relationship of employer to employee, the loyalty factor. The leader is there to take care of them, and they take care of you. If you threaten them, they will hang you from a tree. Other leaders didn't adapt and failed hugely. You have to adapt to the local leadership style. Once you develop the patron relationship, loyalty kicks in and you get exceptional results."

Leadership in the generic sense means driving change, and this includes changing organizational systems to create better alignment. However, in a global context, leaders who set out to drive an organizational transformation may find that they have to cope with larger bureaucratic and political systems that are not going to change, and which predetermine many of the processes that their own organizations must follow.

- **Changing the system/beating the system:**

  "You have to understand the culture you are working with and adapt your style. Russians have always lived in a situation where the system of life is very rigid, so they had to get their needs met while the system stayed the same. In my country we change the system because we have that option. . . . Russians are more clever about getting through an awful system, figuring out circuitous ways to get from point A to point B. The system is the way it is. You ask yourself, 'How do I shift my perspective and work with it?'"

Pace and Timing

Another frame-shifting topic often raised by global leaders pertained to pace and timing. Their own pace of work did not match that of their colleagues in another country, and their sense of timing was off. Work habits vary considerably, and there are locations around the world where the norm is to start work at mid-morning, catch up socially, do some light work, and then break for lunch, with a nap after lunch—but then the employees will work until late in the evening to get things done. So global leaders must learn to accelerate or decelerate their daily schedules, and to make decisions sooner or later than was their habit. The penalties for getting the timing wrong are very serious; a number of people mentioned that this could become a costly if not fatal error.

"I have received feedback about my fast pace: I work, speak, and even type quickly. The feedback is that I need to slow down and work at other people's pace. It took me a while to get that."

"When you come into a foreign culture, you need to make an initial investment of time and cannot play the leadership role all up front. If you go too fast too far in too strong a way, you get rejected and have to rework."

"Issues related to style and culture matter a lot. If you are too execution focused, and want everything done in your own time, you will get stonewalled, nothing will happen, and you will become the joke of the company. I have seen very accomplished people come and offend everyone and nothing gets done."

Such shifts in leadership style may be required on a permanent basis in order to work smoothly with colleagues in other parts of the world. On the other hand, in cases where leaders had been working with the same group of people over many months or years, some reported that as relationships deepened they were able to gradually revert to a style that was more natural for them.

> "I had to adapt my style a lot initially and then recovered my normal self gradually. My leadership role to get started required almost a 180-degree initial adaptation, a compromise of my entire personality and work style. Within a year to fifteen months, I was able to revert to the style I am most comfortable with."

Insights from Global Followers

It was such a relief to meet a leader who was willing to shift her approach to doing business in this market. So many people who come here seem to be proud to say, "This is the way I am, and I'm sure you'll get used to it. This is our corporate culture. This is the way we do business." They are so tied to the approach that has made them successful in other places that they are unable to see what is in front of them, and end up lowering the motivation of their own employees because they have no idea what is really going on here.

But our new leader was well-informed about the market, had learned a bit of the language, spoke English in a way that was very easy for us to understand, and even pronounced people's names correctly, which is not easy for visitors. She was also willing to hold back and take her time to learn more and make the right decisions. We had several meals together with her and the whole team while she was in our city, and I could see that she was asking good questions and listening carefully, not just about the business but also about people's personal lives. She seemed really interested in where they lived, what their children were doing, what the educational system was like, what was in the newspapers, and so on. She asked to see an average home, so I invited her to my small house to meet my wife and family. We traveled on a crowded train, and she said that this trip and being in our home helped her to better understand some of the consumer preference data we have been providing. She also brought a nice gift that my wife was very pleased to receive, and found ways to include her in the conversation.

Our managers in this country are relatively young and inexperienced, and they need more guidance than the managers in other places; we talked about how to ensure that on future visits and through virtual communication she could arrange more formal and informal training opportunities for them. We also began to discuss strategies for shrinking our product footprint and setting prices differently in order to respond to customer requests that we are getting. I'm optimistic that we are going to be very successful under her leadership.

LEADERSHIP STRATEGY

In addition to communication and leadership styles, frame-shifting extends to the strategic approach that a leader takes to working in different markets. If a sign of intelligence is being able to hold two contradictory ideas in the mind at the same time, global leaders who recognize major differences between country and regional markets must be able to shape strategies for other markets that sometimes run contrary to the basic value proposition or intent of strategies born at home. There are many possible reasons that strategic shifts could be required:

- Distinctive products or services have various levels of appeal in global markets.
- New environments present different customer requirements for product features, quality, cost, and delivery.
- Local innovations offer fresh opportunities.
- Unanticipated sources of local competition call for a response that is not required elsewhere.
- The local organizational support system or supply chain may be inadequate to implement strategies conceived in other locations.
- High economic growth in one region in contrast to a stagnant or slow-growing domestic market can create the need for disparate people strategies for recruitment, retention, and development.
- The rate and pace of project implementation is affected by how local cultures perceive and adapt to change.

Given this kind of volatility, leaders have a constant need to weigh the potential costs of adaptation against the size and potential of each market, and strategic flexibility is essential. As one interviewee commented, "The problem is when you get married to one strategy or the other. You need to apply the best one for the situation to get results." This happens not only with individual leaders but with whole teams who are assigned to new markets, especially when they feel the pressure to get things done quickly. Their style of action and sense of timing can undermine their ability to conceive of a viable strategy.

> "The initial team fails in most countries where we are trying to start up operations. The expectations are so high for immediate action that they fall all over themselves trying to do things and fail because they are not accustomed to doing nonstandard things."

Frame-shifting on the strategic level is easier to grasp by considering some examples.

EXAMPLE 1: **SOFTWARE ROLLOUT IN JAPAN**

A major software firm found that its Japanese customers had extremely high quality expectations for initial product releases and would not tolerate software bugs that were less critical for customers in other regions, including the company's home market. There were several painful and expensive experiences in which customers found bugs that they demanded to be rectified immediately, and the company had to fly software engineers to Tokyo to work with its local engineers to fix the bugs. The software company later modified its strategy for approaching the Japanese market in several ways. Among other things, they (1) paced product release schedules differently in Japan to ensure that any problems that emerged could be immediately addressed; (2) arranged for their Tokyo-based software engineers to participate at an earlier stage in product development efforts in order for them to increase their own knowledge and contribute to the development team's awareness of Japanese customer needs; and (3) used the high sensitivity in Japan toward product defects to drive their global quality assurance process by ensuring that local fixes were rapidly disseminated elsewhere whenever relevant.

EXAMPLE 2: **SELLING IN CHINA**

A Western consumer products company in China that distributed its products door-to-door found that its business model was adopted with alacrity by Chinese associates and consumers. The networking skills of its Chinese salespeople, mostly women, made it natural for them to sell products through their personal ties, and to recruit others to sell in a similar fashion. For several years the company expanded rapidly in the Chinese market and did quite well. Indeed, the model was so successful that many local imitators sprung up selling all kinds of products door-to-door, often escalating the business model to create multilayer Ponzi schemes that victimized participants. The Chinese government soon banned door-to-door sales completely, permitting only brick-and-mortar retail operations. So in order to stay in China, the Western company that had helped to create the market was forced to abandon the approach that had made it famous worldwide and sell through more traditional and less lucrative retail outlets, while repositioning the employees and associates that it could afford to keep. In short, it had to completely transform its business model and strategy in order to stay in the Chinese market. Eventually, after many years of lobbying and working to reassure ministry officials that the industry could conduct itself responsibly, the government allowed door-to-door operations to resume on a limited basis by licensed entities only. So the company once again had to reverse its strategy, this time going at least part way back toward its original business model of selling door-to-door.

In both of these cases, the leaders in charge of these businesses had to make fundamental shifts in their operating strategies to accommodate different and even changing market circumstances. In the absence of such strategic frame-shifting, they would have lost market share or have become unable to do business altogether.

Working with a new country or market environment typically requires a new frame of reference and action. In a different setting, leaders may have to distance themselves from deep-rooted patterns of action—including those associated with past successes—on multiple levels: communication style, leadership style, and strategy. And this is not just a one-time shift but something that needs to become a regular pattern of action in order for a person to alternate effectively between established markets and emerging markets, between the familiar and the new. These shifts are symbolized in Figure 4-1.

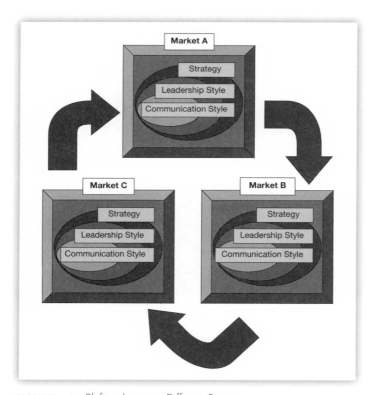

FIGURE 4-1 Shifting between Different Frames

SUMMARY AND REVIEW: **QUESTIONS FOR LEADERS**

1. Do you prioritize relationship-building with colleagues from other countries ahead of your own task agenda?

2. Are the relationships that you have with your global counterparts strong enough to have a positive impact on business results?

3. Have global colleagues shared their employee, industry, and governmental relationship networks with you to help you accomplish your business goals?

4. Are you authentically committed to relationships with counterparts from different cultures?

5. Can you distinguish between real agreement and polite responses that do not necessarily signify agreement or commitment?

6. Do you work well with global colleagues and/or customers who have a different sense of pace or timing regarding the completion of key tasks?

7. Do you maintain the same leadership style wherever you go, or modify your style in different environments?

8. Have you developed new strategies to fit different global business environments, even when those strategies diverge from those in your home country?

CHAPTER FIVE

Opening the System

Once significant differences between markets and business practices have been identified, it is often necessary to address systemic issues in order for a global business to expand. Leaders can close the gap between themselves and their global counterparts through more personal steps such as cultivating strong relationships and frame-shifting. However, they must also look for ways to expand the circle of ownership and accountability for solutions across various kinds of boundaries, and in so doing support the development of future leaders who may have very different backgrounds and styles. Employees who are potential sources of new leadership talent in locations far away from headquarters can be particularly sensitive to the suggestion that they are carrying out a strategy that has been decided elsewhere, or that they are lacking vital information that is considered too sensitive for them to know.

Global Leader: Diawary Bouare, CARE

Diawary Bouare, originally from Mali in West Africa, is a veteran of a number of global assignments within CARE. Having previously worked in Benin for five years, Burundi for two and a half years, and Nepal for three and a half years, he recently moved to Sierra Leone, where he is now the country director for an operation involving 200 employees. In addition to his native language of Bambara, he also speaks French (Mali's official language), Spanish, and English. In 2000, Diawary was the first national staff member from CARE Mali to be assigned to another country as a Global staff member since the beginning of its operations in 1975. Diawary's example inspired other colleagues who decided to follow his path. To date, six other people from CARE Mali have been promoted to become CARE Global staff members. He was also one of the first CARE employees from

Africa to hold a senior leadership position in a country operation in Asia. Diawary has come a long way from his underprivileged upbringing, which included a sixteen-kilometer daily round-trip walk to school and back.

While working for CARE in Mali, one of Diawary's jobs was to lead partnership and institutional capacity building. This was a very challenging task, as he had to both manage changes inside CARE and create a viable process for assessing potential partners. "We were introducing a new working approach at CARE, and this was a threat to CARE job security because we were now working with NGO partners. Change cannot always happen with the same staff, so we brought in people with new perspectives to help bring change. And as one of the few local nationals on the leadership team at that time, I was also facing a lot of pressure to subcontract, recruit friends, and so on. But I dealt very fairly and critically with this. Friends came to me to get a position, but I told them to go through the process based on their own accomplishments, saying to them, 'If as a manager, I hire you and you are not competent, then I will have to fire you so it will become more of a problem.' Local NGOs were using personal contacts to try to convince me to have them partner with CARE. But I had to refuse and say that our decisions are based on process, not on preference. When I was reviewing a partner's progress, there was always political pressure to give good reviews. It is routine for me now to do the right thing, and to demonstrate the rationale behind this. I can develop social relationships but don't compromise principles. This has been successful—people respect you in every difficult situation, and you gain respect in every culture. It has been critical to my success as a leader."

Based upon his performance in Mali, Diawary moved to a project manager position in nearby Benin, working with local NGOs on good internal governance, transparency, and quality of service delivery. He became country coordinator for CARE operations in Benin, channeling CARE funds through a meticulous process to ensure that they were properly used. He changed his approach to fit this new environment and role. "In Mali my leadership style was based on technical skills, leading by example. In Benin, I had to take more of a team approach and so learned about leading a team and how to adjust myself to be a team player." Again his efforts met with success, and he began to take on wider responsibilities as civil society sector coordinator for CARE Gulf of Guinea, covering Ghana, Togo, and Benin.

Diawary's next career role was to become assistant country director in Burundi, in a post-conflict context in Central Africa that is still rife with ethnic tensions (Burundi shares a border with Rwanda). In this new leadership role, he says, "I had to change again. From my time in Mali and Benin, I had a very direct approach, and I am most comfortable with this. I was trying to be very fair with everyone, and very clear about how I work. I was seen as fair and transparent.

Some other leaders treated people differently based on personal relationships. I used to be very critical of this. I am fair and rigorous, analytical in decisions, and work according to policies and procedures. Coming to Burundi, I kept some of this style because this is me, but tried to be softer instead of using a strong style of delivery for this approach. The security situation is not good, but if you are fair, you become respected. People tended to use the ethnic divisions and conflict to try to stop what we were doing, claiming that we were favoring one ethnic group or another. They were using the security threat to avoid changing our approach. So everything had to be very transparent, and I had to be more self-aware. The biggest change we made was the food distribution program restructuring—we succeeded where other leadership failed in aligning this project and reducing staff. I was leading the process, but sometimes I pushed them to make the decision. I had to lead by example and through my experience, by convincing, not by pushing too hard. I tried to make sure that others developed their own leadership, working in a team. I learned from colleagues and coached colleagues. I had to give others the chance to prove themselves successful in ways that no one had been successful before, and to utilize their own values and styles to be successful. Timing is critical; it's important not to push too quickly."

In Diawary's recent role in Nepal he faced a new kind of conflict, not ethnic but more social and political. In addition, he had to work in a large operation with experienced staff members, many of whom had probably never met or worked directly with an African in person before. "The shift from Africa to Asia was difficult. Because of the long history of CARE in Nepal, it was quite difficult for staff members who had been working there for fifteen or twenty years to accept an African in a leadership position. But I did come to feel accepted, based on CARE global values and my own leadership approach: critical analysis, generating debate, helping them to understand issues. This has gone well. People in Nepal already have a lot of technical knowledge, so I needed to focus on the strategic level and stay out of the details, as that would create frustration. If I maintained a strategic approach and challenged the status quo, then they felt I was adding value. Also, I recognized the contributions of staff members; I gave them space and a voice because they had been there for so long. My role as a leader is to provide room for them to use their skills and make critical decisions, and to have CARE demonstrate internally the values of diversity, respect, excellence, and transparency. This creates ownership and commitment among all staff—these things are critical here."

As in the move to Burundi, Diawary's leadership style in Nepal was again very different from the one he had used in West Africa. "If I had pushed in Nepal, I would have been rejected, so my style had to change. I had to make a clear distinction between cultures. In Nepal, you have to show your perspective through coaching and mentoring, not pushing. Because of the deeply rooted social, cultural, gender, and caste issues, the existing structures are very strong and resistant to change. We are trying to change the power dynamic, to get at the causes of poverty, discrimination, and conflict. We do this by building awareness among marginalized groups such as women or the Dalit (untouchable) caste, helping them to analyze the causes of their own poverty and empowering them to act. We also do our best to show by example. We try to empower those who feel marginalized within CARE and give them a voice. We try to manage within the social context and adapt but also question the status quo at the same time, keeping a balance. If you want to create ownership, you need to demonstrate your values and your commitment to a vision. It is critical to be an example. You need to coach the staff to give them confidence. You have to be approachable so that your staff will feel free to come to you for support, but coach in way that they are not just trying to please you but to be real leaders themselves. If you want real change, you need to build the capacity of your core team to become more strategic, and gradually widen the scope of those who are facilitating change."

The grass-roots development approach that Diawary and his colleagues took at CARE in Nepal has borne considerable results. Rather than bringing in large sums of aid money from outside the country, only to have that be distributed in ways that reinforce the existing power structures, they have helped numerous communities address the unjust distribution of existing resources as well as better leverage the use of funds from elsewhere. For example, it is common in Nepal for landholders to pay women half the wages they pay to men, even though the women perform the same or greater amounts of work. When the women themselves became ready to demand that this discrepancy be addressed because of its dire consequences for them, the result in some communities has been a one hundred percent increase in women's wages just through bringing them into parity with men's. Likewise, very poor communities that had previously received no government support because they were not favored by government officials have begun to receive money that was supposed to be allocated to them in the first place, thanks to their newfound willingness to challenge the status quo.

Diawary has now returned to West Africa, where he is the country director for Sierra Leone. "I am happy and proud to get the opportunity to serve at the most senior leadership position for CARE operations in Sierra Leone. I am also aware this represents the biggest challenge for me—to become the first ever African national in the country director position for CARE in this country since the start of its operations in 1961. My success in fulfilling the overall responsibility associated with the country director position will certainly require a mixed balance of several leadership styles, including adaptive, bureaucratic, and democratic."

Expand Ownership

Diawary Bouare has made an impressive journey with many firsts. He is working in the context of a nongovernmental organization, which of course differs from the corporate world. However, along the way he has learned to practice a number of the successful leadership behaviors described in earlier chapters: seeing the influence of his home environment upon his own approach to leadership; dealing with unexpected circumstances in new work settings; frame-shifting in terms of his communication and leadership styles from more to less direct, technical to strategic, and so on. Moreover, he speaks eloquently about widening the scope of those involved with leadership and decision making to include people who are usually excluded due to social and organizational barriers.

The global leadership behavior *expand ownership* means to create a sense of engagement in a shared process and accountability for setting and achieving targets with both global and local significance. Expanding ownership is a commonsense part of any change effort, whether domestic or global. But working in a global context brings new and sometimes hidden obstacles to involving those who are best informed and able to contribute to decision making, and who will also be critical to effective implementation. These obstacles may include leadership habits so deeply ingrained that they are not easily recognized, particularly by leaders whose previous successes are rooted in tried-and-true patterns of problem formation and resolution.

OBSTACLES TO OWNERSHIP: OUTDATED SYSTEMS

In the corporate arena as well as within the history of many nongovernmental organizations, there is a typical pattern of evolution experienced by organizations: they start with a focus on their national market and then evolve with their business toward a global presence. A firm is typically born as a "domestic" enterprise preoccupied with its home market. Later it may become an "international" company, run from a centralized headquarters that tries to replicate its operations in subsidiary locations around the world. The most complex stage of evolution is the "global" company, which consists of a matrixed, interlinked network of operations that are constantly exchanging information and expertise. This type of organization strives to balance the simultaneous need for global consistency and efficiency with the equally pressing imperative to respond to local market conditions.[1] More simply put, along the road to full-scale globalization, it is commonly necessary to move from a "mother ship/baby ship" type of structure (international, illustrated in Figure 5-1) to a model that consists of a more interdependent horizontal network, in which subsidiaries have greater autonomy while being closely linked with each other as well as with headquarters (global, depicted in Figure 5-2).

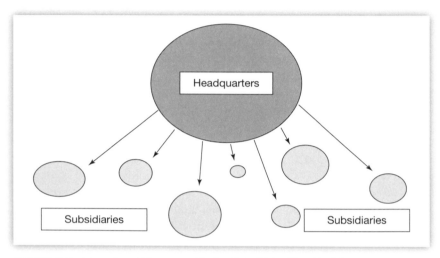

FIGURE 5-1 International Company: Mother Ship/Baby Ship Model

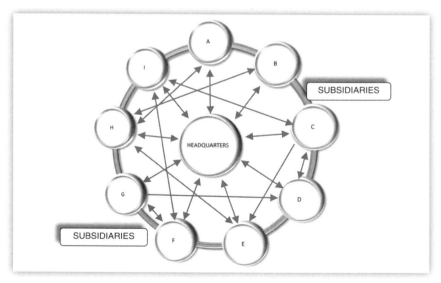

FIGURE 5-2 Global Company: The Horizontal Network

There is a great deal of confusion about the term "global." It is used in several overlapping ways, at times even by people within the same enterprise, to refer to:

1. An organization that has cultivated its structures, systems, and employee mindset to work effectively on a worldwide basis in a structure where the emphasis is on horizontal collaboration rather than vertical hierarchy, as in the global company type depicted in Figure 5-2.
2. Central control and authority that are exerted in contrast to local control—there is always a need to balance "global" in this sense with local, even when some aspects of an organization are relatively decentralized.
3. Functions or business units that are designed to achieve their objectives across national boundaries, as in "global business unit," "global IT," or "global" as a term for "headquarters" (such labels may represent more wishful thinking than reality).

Regarding the first meaning of the term "global" as a horizontal network, companies globalize in different forms and at different rates based upon their business environment and strategic choices. There is no single formula for success, but the higher the percentage of a firm's revenues that come from outside its home country, the more likely its leaders will perceive an increasing need to evolve in the direction of the global network model. Firms experiencing explosive revenue increases in markets abroad, whether through organic growth or as the result of mergers and acquisitions, may suddenly find themselves with an outdated organizational structure that is closer to the international type; other companies may evolve more gradually.

Whatever path a firm takes, there are common requirements for handling the complications that arise from doing business on a global scale. A new level of global understanding and day-to-day collaboration across business units and staff functions becomes essential to handle the distinctive cultural requirements and tastes of various customers, fresh competitive threats, supply chain logistics that span many countries, intellectual property violations, and/or labor laws and employment conditions that vary dramatically from one location to the next.

Predictable problems tend to occur as an organization moves toward a more globalized business while retaining the systems, mindsets, and behaviors that served it well in a previous stage of evolution but which have now become obstacles. The mentality of an international firm regarding a new product or project is, "We'll develop it here at headquarters and then roll it out to the rest of the world; we can tweak whatever we need to for local markets later on."

Employees who have been accustomed to designing products or initiatives for their home market and who now need to develop global solutions must fundamentally change their approach. Instead of seeing global solutions as an "add-on," they have to learn to think globally from the start, engaging their global counterparts to expand ownership. The following is an example of how this problem surfaced in the context of a marketing strategy.

EXAMPLE: **CREATING A GLOBAL MARKETING STRATEGY**

A highly successful retail firm with a proud history and a very strong brand in its home market was seeking to expand into new markets where it was less well-known, including China. The headquarters marketing staff members found themselves and their attempts to enforce company guidelines in direct conflict with their China-based counterparts, who sought to promote the brand in ways that ran completely counter to the brand strategy at home. Rather than the traditional low-key emphasis on quality and durability, which had long appealed to the firm's domestic customers, marketing staff in China sought to promote the brand in a more eye-catching way through association with glamorous celebrities, special events, and flashy store presentations. As one Chinese marketing employee put it, "Here we're just one brand among many, and local consumers don't have any idea who we are. So, we have to reach out and appeal to them by showing them how we are special. The marketing strategy and campaigns created at headquarters are just not relevant to this market."

Addressing this kind of marketing challenge will clearly require frame-shifting, with a mindset flexible enough to support both the traditional, soft-pedaled marketing approach at home and a more flashy and aggressive strategy in China. But systemic changes are needed as well that involve the task of achieving the optimum global/local balance. Headquarters must not only revamp the marketing guidelines, but also address an outmoded decision-making process that places the locus of control and authority for marketing decisions firmly at headquarters, while subsidiary employees who are on the front lines with customers have to petition for support.

Such a shift in power and control is particularly difficult to achieve, because employees in subsidiary locations need to overcome numerous disadvantages for their voices to be taken seriously: physical distance, language barriers, a virtual communication context, shorter tenure in the company and less experience at their jobs, a smaller scale of business that tends to draw less attention and resources, customer demands that seem eccentric or unreasonable to counter-parts at headquarters, and so on. Meanwhile, people at headquarters typically worry about becoming less important or less employable if they cede responsi-bility to others. And yet, as nearly all of our interviewees emphasized, persist-ing with an overly centralized approach can be self-defeating. It is necessary for leaders, regardless of their location, to use an approach that takes broader cross-border considerations into account from the beginning, bringing others into the process to expand ownership as they proceed.

"It's the kiss of death to say, 'This is the way we do it back at head-quarters.'"

"If they see that you are there to do your job and they are just pawns, you are done and there will be no buy in."

OBSTACLES TO OWNERSHIP: LOCAL CUSTOMS

Diawary Bouare has striven to expand ownership in each of the locations where he has worked. The greatest systemic obstacles he faced to further enfranchising employees while in Nepal appear to have been local barriers of caste and class; he tried to impact these gradually through demonstrating a commitment to organizational values of respect, excellence, and transparency. Ironically, in light of the problems often associated with central control, in this case the values that came from headquarters were a primary source of leverage in expanding local ownership in the face of entrenched barriers. On the spectrum of central to local control, CARE is a highly decentralized organization relative to most corporations. Its services such as emergency relief, economic development, education, and health care are customized and delivered on the ground to approximately sixty million people in seventy-two countries. The small CARE USA headquarters in Atlanta is dwarfed in size by its large country operations and the many thousands of local employees as well as the staff of its NGO partners. CARE USA and CARE International together have about 10,000 employees, and only 350 of these are in the United States. In spite of its high degree of decentralization and a mission statement that emphasizes self-help, even CARE must still struggle with a variety of issues related to headquarters versus local dynamics, and headquarters continues to serve a vital role.

For example, Diawary notes that he has had to combat pressures to show favoritism toward individuals or ethnic groups, and at least part of his success with the organization can be traced to the fact that he has successfully imple-mented organization-wide CARE principles in his leadership roles in the face of these pressures. Likewise, CARE must focus on achieving headquarters-driven standards of efficiency and financial reporting in raising and spending donor money, while also complying with the regulations of donor governments. And there are continuous forms of knowledge transfer that take place between CARE's centers of expertise in developed countries and its local operations around the world.

So complete decentralization should not be the ultimate goal of a globalized organization; instead, every organization must constantly work to achieve the optimum balance of centralization with decentralized authority. Sometimes outmoded forms of central control can be the primary obstacle to expanding local ownership; on the other hand, global values and processes that come from the center may turn out to be the primary vehicle for enabling greater enfranchisement.

OWNERSHIP AND PARAMETERS

The dynamic between centralization and decentralization is by no means unique to CARE. Although it is possible to paint a picture of successive globalization stages on the enterprise-wide level, it is actually necessary for leaders to scrutinize every segment of their operations on a micro level to determine the best form of headquarters/subsidiary balance for each business, function, and task.[2] In CARE's case, the proper balance in most locations will probably require strict compliance with standardized ethical and accounting principles driven by headquarters, with greater latitude in the mix of services and the way that they are delivered to people in different places like Mali, Burundi, and Nepal. Similarly, companies generally need to have more uniform solutions for their IT platforms or financial accounting systems, while functions such as sales, marketing, and human resources must be more flexible to accommodate local consumer tastes and labor laws. Figure 5-3 depicts this contrast between varying degrees of global standards and local flexibility for a number of common functions; a comparable range of solutions is required for different types of businesses as well as for specific tasks.

The proper balance between centrally and locally driven systems is often a moving target that shifts over time with the skill level of employees and the growing sophistication of particular markets. For example, many companies are currently altering the roles of their research and development functions in China and India from the adaptation of products designed elsewhere to more autonomous and demanding roles such as designing new products and finding cutting-edge technologies that originate in those rapid growth markets. At the

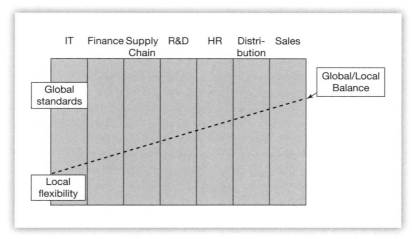

FIGURE 5-3 Global Standards and Local Flexibility by Function

same time, the critical nature of these countries for the success of the whole company calls for extensive ongoing communication and coordination between headquarters and subsidiary operations that are still not necessarily coequal but exist within a changing balance of power.

The global leaders who we interviewed sought to balance global standards with local flexibility by providing their employees freedom within structure—that is, parameters for their contributions that invited real creativity and ownership while also acknowledging the constraints as well as the opportunities inherent in a global business.

"It's about setting the parameters and then letting them do what they need to do to get things done. As an ancient Asian proverb goes, 'If I want to control an ox, I give it the whole paddock.' If they have boundaries and objectives, then I just need to be trusting and give them space to get there . . . let people do it their own way, not yours."

"Successful leaders are the ones who have been the most flexible—not about achieving the goal, but in how wide the path is, how far you can go from one side of the road to the other on the way there."

"Instead of telling people what to do, it is best to introduce a set of ideas and then let them work those ideas through and engage in some translation as well as trial and error until they own them. This is ultimately much faster."

Insights from Global Followers

Our executives use the word *empowerment* a lot. But the reality is that we don't have much input regarding our goals. These are set at headquarters by people who are looking at spreadsheets but don't fully understand our market or haven't been here for more than a week at a time. Then we are *empowered* to meet targets that have been forced on us and asked to commit to achieving these goals. They also use the word *global* for headquarters, but have no idea what *global* really means.

When we hear about this kind of "ownership" and "commitment," it is meaningless. If the leader of our business unit asked us, we could provide her with very detailed information about what is possible and what is impossible, but maybe she does not want to hear what we have to say because she is listening more carefully to her own bosses at headquarters, or thinks that we do not have sufficient experience or capability. It feels like she does not trust us even though she talks about trust-building.

Setting the right parameters may require a very active process of instruction along with clarity about the degree of freedom that others do have. What does not work well in promoting genuine ownership is either premature pushing of an approach formulated elsewhere or rhetoric about empowerment that does not match the actual opportunities available.

"You have to put it out there, teach it, show why and how, help them to understand, give them a choice; let them know that a different answer is okay too. Tell them you're painting a picture of an elephant rather than jumping in and pushing it on them."

OWNERSHIP AND PROCESS

Our interviewees also suggested crafting processes for gathering and sharing information, exchanging ideas, and making decisions that are systematically inclusive rather than exclusive. Based on his experiences in leadership roles in several countries, Diawary Bouare highlighted the importance of giving local employees a voice, ensuring broad understanding of issues, and creating a format for joint critical analysis and debate. Others noted the importance of seeking opinions at multiple levels of the organization to avoid being boxed into a narrow perspective due to barriers of hierarchy or language.

"Listen and do not make quick judgments, but rather take time to get all sides and perspectives, and verify these on different levels. Hold open discussions, not only one-on-one, but with different levels of staff. Some countries are more hierarchical so they have a fear of this; as a leader, don't let the conversation be dominated by a single voice, including yours. Meet with groups at their level. Don't take what you hear at face value; go into every level, get every perspective. Create a venue and space to share freely without fear of recrimination. Establish a process for this, and allow for anonymous feedback. Language is also key to this process of gaining input at every level; you will be limited to the senior perspective only if you don't learn the local language and are insulated from employees by a leadership team that speaks your language while other people do not."

Notwithstanding the frame-shifting experience of interviewees such as Hannah de Zwaan (described in Chapter 4), who had to adjust their leadership style to a more hierarchical environment, the majority of our interviewees expressed a preference for processes that expand involvement in decision making. They accomplish this through means such as increasing access to information, providing process instructions, and shaping options or offering a set of new practices from which management team members can choose.

"If local managers are not part of the decision-making process, then I have to take on an authoritarian attitude and this goes against my deepest values. People are adequately empowered through access to information. They need to have a venue to discuss, argue, and create, with the organizational space to talk about issues. Without this, there is no real decision-making process. I give them all the information necessary so they are not fearful about participating in the process. The dissemination of information creates a correlation between knowledge and power."

"We are normally in such a hurry to do everything; it's better to let people make decisions. Say, 'Here are some options you can choose from.' Then let them discuss and think for a few days and come back with their own version. Allow that to happen naturally."

"It's best to say, 'Here's something we're working on. I have some things I'd like to share. Do you think this would work for you?' So they can figure out the best way to accomplish the goal."

Yet these leaders were also not shy about stepping up to push for a timely decision or to make decisions themselves when necessary, meanwhile communicating as clearly as possible the reasons for selecting a particular direction.

> "I was leading the process, but sometimes I pushed them to make the decision. It is really a balance—you need to take decisions but also be participatory."

> "If the group can't agree, I give it another try, and if it still doesn't move, I get more active as a leader. I encourage the team to proceed on their own, but give guidance at a certain point."

> "Even when I have to make the decision, I have an obligation to understand the local perspective, and to have them understand why I am doing what I am doing. I do this by communicating verbally one-on-one and through meetings. I work through the people I know to reiterate the ideas to their colleagues."

There are many aspects of "diversity"—at least as this term is defined in the United States—that do not translate well to other countries due to different historical backgrounds and social priorities.[3] However, the diversity principle of inclusiveness seems to have considerable global appeal when embedded into decision-making processes, even if there are perverse advantages for employees in avoiding accountability for decisions that are made without their input. Inclusiveness can take many shapes as described above; there is probably an applicable form in most locations. Figure 5-4 lists components that a successful intercultural collaboration is likely to include.

■ Project initiated jointly between regions	■ Jointly agreed upon deadlines
■ Senior level support and access	■ Stakeholders agree on plan and resource commitments
■ Shared vision and values	■ Milestones set together and revisited
■ Mutual sense of urgency and priority	■ Multilevel communication
■ Common goals and objectives	■ Conflict resolution procedures in place
■ Shared process and criteria for decision making	■ Escalation process set
■ Information-sharing protocols: who, when, mode, and frequency	■ Access to and facility with the same technology

FIGURE 5-4 Expanding Ownership: Sample Process Elements

ACCOUNTABILITY

It is possible to err on the side of being too culturally sensitive and not holding others accountable for their performance, or failing to act decisively to reprimand or remove poor performers, even in places where this is challenging based on local laws and customs. Once global leaders have established parameters that provide some degree of autonomy and processes that incorporate information-sharing, joint discussion, and involvement in decision making, they can then demand greater accountability. Interviewees noted that inclusivity and accountability go together, and that empathy, cultural understanding, and a system that is open to participation do not preclude an emphasis on performance.

> "You need to have the same emphasis on accountability as inclusivity. People must be accountable for the results of inclusive decisions—there has to be balance."

> "Don't be afraid to hold people accountable. Our senior manager in Japan did a great job of adapting to the culture. He would go out with the team after hours to bars, and he understood the team well. But he didn't hold team members accountable, and nothing was accomplished. As a leader, you need vision, and must have confidence in that vision. You can't go in with your vision already decided. You need to assess and listen first, understand what they are doing, utilize their feedback, and engage in roundtable-type inquiry in a culturally appropriate way. Then three to four months down the road, come out with a vision, objectives, high standards, and expectations. You get buy-in, give people the support they need, and then you can hold them accountable. If people don't respond, you have to do something about it: get further buy-in, improve the process, or move people out—how to do that varies. But people need to know you are there to accomplish something and expect to get it done."

> "In some cultures, people find it very difficult to reprimand or fire someone. There is a risk involved with this, but if there is a poor performer in the office, other staff members know about it. You are seen as a weak leader if you don't do anything about it, and this may undermine your position."

> "You can have a strong sense of empathy for others and understand people but still insist on performance and results."

Leaders working in hierarchical and group-oriented cultures sometimes found value in empowering the local management team as a whole and holding them accountable for results on a collective as well as an individual basis.

"I have been really trying to empower the management team, getting them on board and using that group as an influential body. This group was previously seen as a rubber stamp, just doing what the country director wanted them to do; I am trying to change that. The power structure in this country is rigid, a real hierarchy. There is a tendency to let the senior person make the decision. I am getting the management team to take on a collective leadership role so that I don't have to make all the decisions. I am pretty happy with this team, and we have expanded so that there is participation from every department. I am trying to get this kind of decision-making structure out to all of the staff by sharing minutes, trying to make this process more transparent."

"My approach is a team approach: empower teams to have individual responsibility and balance that with team responsibility. Help them to understand their roles and commit to success. We have agreed upon standards and expectations in teams, and then we let people go on with their tasks. And we measure the results at the other end—this is very important."

Develop Future Leaders

Many of the interview comments regarding expanding ownership referred to leadership development. Beyond widening employees' sense of ownership for particular projects or initiatives, "opening the system" also means enabling capable people from anywhere in a global organization to step into leadership roles over time. Indeed, for an organization to achieve ambitious targets in key growth markets around the world, it is essential to develop local talent. Such development must include the capability to weigh global and local perspectives with the best interests of the company as a whole in mind. Some companies need to complete a massive transfer of knowledge from home-country employees with vital technical and project leadership skills to high-potential individuals in different world regions. In other cases, local employees need an infusion of more generic leadership experience as well as the skills to deal effectively with headquarters.

To develop future leaders, those who are currently in global leadership roles must identify and cultivate high-potential individuals, regardless of their country of origin, who can provide the future impetus to growth in key global markets. Although this sounds relatively straightforward, errors in judgment frequently occur when working across cultural and linguistic boundaries.

"It is so easy to arrive in a country with preconceived ideas about the country and individuals. I did stereotype and was one hundred percent wrong. I judged a person based on a couple of meetings as not right for the role. He turned out to be one of the very best people for the job. The problem was my lack of understanding of specific issues. You have to ask open-ended questions. I jumped to conclusions based on the wrong questions—people will answer the specific question. I judged that a proposal this person presented was not well thought through, but my preconceived idea of what he was trying to present was wrong. You have to take the time to explore and ask the right questions. Everything takes two or three times as long. I have only one direct report who speaks English."

Neuroscience and Culture: Valuing "Modesty" or "Assertiveness"

A study of Japanese and U.S. volunteers at Tufts University in 2009 found that the area of the brain that produces dopamine, the "feel-good hormone," in response to reward stimulation functions in alignment with the participants' cultural values. Researchers showed both groups of volunteers drawings of people standing in a submissive pose with their head down and shoulders hunched, and drawings of people standing in a dominant pose with arms crossed and face forward. The brain's positive reward circuit in the Japanese group was activated by the submissive stance, which may have been interpreted as a modest or respectful posture in Japan and thus aligned with core Japanese values. Meanwhile, the U.S. group showed brain activity in this same region for the dominant stance, which may have been interpreted as confident or appropriately assertive, both behaviors that are rewarded in American society.

This study demonstrates yet another way in which culture shapes human neurological functions. Hardwiring that is often assumed to be universal is actually shaped by our cultural values. In this case, the brain is wired to reward opposite behaviors and attitudes in Japan and the United States. This study gives us a valuable insight into the difficulties global leaders face in evaluating subordinates and selecting talent within a different cultural environment. A Japanese boss may seek to hire and promote a North American employee who is respectful according to Japanese norms, but who lacks the assertiveness to succeed in the U.S. business environment. Similarly, a U.S. leader in Japan may pass over the most talented candidate due to a perceived lack of confidence. Leaders are likely to find that they need cultural knowledge to properly interpret their employees' behavior.[4]

There are a number of typical reasons why leaders tend to misjudge others who come from a different background. These include:

- A tendency to evaluate most highly those who are most like us
- Incorrect assessment of a candidate's general capabilities based upon language skill level
- Evaluation of performance based on activities, not results—there may be different and more effective ways to get the job done in other settings than with the leader's customary style
- Misinterpretation of leadership conduct based on different cultural values, such as direct versus indirect communication or the acceptable degree of emotional expression

Another factor adding to the complexity of leadership development in a global context is that not only do leaders often misjudge others, but future leadership candidates may be looking at their own leaders inaccurately through the lens of cultural stereotypes or the performance of a predecessor.

"Just as I stereotype others, I am also stereotyped based upon the effectiveness or lack thereof of the previous people in my role. Knowing who was

Insights from Global Followers

It is very discouraging to see "apple polishers" get promoted into leadership roles. By this I mean the person whose primary skill is making friends with executives from headquarters. They have the language skills to communicate well, but lack technical skills or knowledge of our customers, and other employees don't respect them. I think even these apple polishers are surprised when they are promoted, but they like the power and the nice salary, and sometimes in order to protect their own position they will say negative things to foreign executives about the people who are really doing the work.

Recently a new global leader who is very good at judging people took over our line of business. It was so exciting to see him listen carefully to each person on the executive team, speak to other employees, and go on customer visits even when he had to communicate mostly through an interpreter. We gradually began to open up and tell him who is really capable, and he has begun to promote these people, including one local sales guy who doesn't speak other languages well but has won a lot of business with customers and is very much respected by employees.

in the country before has a bearing on how you're accepted when you first arrive."

Diawary Bouare noted that real change means building the capacity of your core team to be more strategic, while gradually widening the scope of those who are driving the change. What is especially challenging is that team members may go about accomplishing their tasks using unfamiliar methods. As one interviewee observed, "I had to give others the chance to prove themselves successful in ways that no one had been successful before, and to utilize their own values and styles to be successful." In other words, a leader may need to become a champion for others even when they take an approach that is very different from what executives at headquarters or the leader him- or herself would do.

Developmental practices and objectives will probably also require adjust-ment—for example, a leader who is accustomed to a consultative style or to an extreme task focus might have to help more junior staff cultivate a different leadership style more suitable to the local context. One common denomina-tor recommended by our interviewees for successful leadership development is accessibility.

"You need to coach the staff, to empower and give them confidence. You have to be approachable so that your staff will come to you for support."

"It is important to spend time with employees and their work, recognizing what they do. I have an open-door policy. If staff members have issues, they can come in at any time. This often means that I end up reading documents at home because I have been interrupted all day, but this works for me."

A commitment to being approachable and to employee development can produce other kinds of dividends, including feedback that global leaders find difficult to obtain through other means along with genuine employee motiva-tion and commitment.

"A tool that I used to keep myself engaged was to work on my direct reports' personal development. I would sit down with them on a monthly basis, develop an action plan, and look at their gaps and strengths. I received a lot of 360-degree feedback that way as well. This was great for me in this context—an excellent tool for building relationships, honesty, and a network. They trust me because they see that I am applying what they say and incorporating it. If you are honest with people and show them you are trying to help their career, they will give you everything they've got."

The ultimate goal for global leaders is to work themselves out of a job, with new people stepping in who may do things in a different but nonetheless effective way.

"I facilitated other people doing things through empowering, giving skills, instruction, and space and time to carry out a task rather than to do it myself. It is really helpful and important to have leaders draw on their global experiences and then try to work themselves out of a job. I have given responsibilities to a local national in all the countries I have been in previously. I work with national staff to train and coach them to leadership."

"You are allowing people to decide about their own futures, develop self-esteem and capabilities, and shape their own lives. My role is to make myself irrelevant—the more that people are doing things on their own, the more successful I have been. How should we promote local people's interests and abilities and inspire initiative? We need to break the dependency cycle to have them stand on their own feet."

SUMMARY AND REVIEW: **QUESTIONS FOR LEADERS**

1. Do you set guidelines that give employees a degree of freedom in shaping projects while also defining limits based upon their ability to contribute effectively?
2. Is your decision-making process structured in a way that increases the participation and involvement of global talent?
3. Once inclusive decisions have been made, do you hold employees accountable for achieving results?
4. Are you able to guide new ideas or proposals from start to implementation in a way that builds shared pride of authorship on the part of global employees?
5. Do you develop future global leaders from various cultural backgrounds based on their performance and potential?
6. Are you available to provide coaching and support to help develop future global leaders?
7. Have you created opportunities for high-potential local leaders to serve in more strategic regional and/or global roles?
8. Are you a passionate advocate for talented leaders from other countries even when their styles depart from corporate culture norms?

CHAPTER SIX

Preserving Balance

Thus far we have focused on how global leaders can recognize differences and adjust to them, either through changes in their own behaviors or through making organizational systems more inclusive. For decades, in fact, the research on working across borders has emphasized the importance of flexibility and adaptation. While adaptation is essential in a foreign environment—as one interviewee put it, "the local culture is not going to adapt to you"—the leaders we spoke with were also quite clear that they had to preserve a balance that entailed knowing when to adapt and when *not* to adapt. They found it necessary both to accommodate local circumstances and to select the right moments to contribute their own expertise, exert authority, or take a stand based upon certain values. The behaviors we have labeled *adapt and add value* and *core values and flexibility* reflect the kinds of balance that these leaders deemed to be most vital.

Global Leader: Gary Ashmore, AMD

Gary Ashmore is the director of AMD's Shanghai Research and Development Center. Originally from the United States, he has been in China for two years. His background includes a seven-year stint in the U.S. Air Force, during which he spent time in Germany, Italy, and the Middle East. He also lived previously in Mexico and Panama while doing work for a development firm. Gary has been with AMD for fifteen years, has an MBA from Rutgers University, and he served in a previous assignment for the company in Taiwan before moving to China. In addition to speaking Spanish and German, Gary speaks some Mandarin, and his wife is a native Mandarin speaker.

Gary notes that his time in the military made him more organized, confident, and better at taking risks, and after starting in a technical support role at AMD, he worked his way up into team leadership roles. However, he discovered, "It was a whole new world to start managing engineering groups in Asia. In Taiwan I had to adapt my style a lot initially and then recovered my normal self gradually." He brought in a coach to do communication style profiling with his staff and to build awareness of different communication styles and how to work together when mixing cultures.

Gary describes himself as a very outgoing person in comparison to most of his engineering colleagues in the United States. In Taiwan and then in China the differences he encountered were even greater. "I always had to watch my style, as engineering folks are quieter and analytical. When I came to Asia, I was dealing with engineers who were also culturally shy and reserved, and not very good at giving feedback, criticizing, or challenging management. I had to completely quiet down so as not to come off as a pushy American, and cut out the jokes—culturally my humor was not always understood. I had to take time to understand the local culture better, and if I wanted to be humorous, I had to learn what was relaxing and made sense in context for them. And there was a whole new level of organizational politics to learn. I had to go deeper in terms of observations. There is a lot of not-so-obvious power, and it takes a lot longer to understand this and to exert influence in the right ways."

There were many standard local practices that were unfamiliar to Gary, and he found it necessary to adapt. "I became more open-minded to the HR side of things. For example, everyone comes to work around 10 A.M., catches up socially, checks email, and then breaks for lunch. Then after lunch they may take a nap break, but they stay and work until 10 P.M. at night to get things done. Things are simply not done like in the U.S., and you can't expect the same productivity in the same time frame. But the work gets done; it's not that they are unproductive. You have to choose your battles. I also had to be more open about special seating arrangements in meetings, whom to give business cards to, the protocol—I had to be open even if it made no sense to me. I had to push to get more feedback, because people won't always voluntarily give you the information on protocol or what is offensive, so you have to learn to ask. I started to read and learn the body language and stop and ask more, while slowing down a bit and taking more of a listening posture."

Other adjustments that Gary has made include exercising more patience. "Sometimes we are talking about methodologies or Western references that people don't have experience with here, and they're also using a second language to listen. I try to watch my speed and pronunciation and be aware of using idioms or other words they don't understand. Folks from the U.S. come over with presentations geared toward a U.S. audience, and the employees here can't always absorb the information or the main message as easily. I usually try to review visitors' presentations in advance and help them to condense the content."

It took time for him to establish his own credibility with his Chinese colleagues. "I had to earn respect through work, coming out with ideas and then relaxing and letting them come up with specific details and questions in their own time—then listening to them and explaining things to them. If this is what I would normally do in the U.S., I had to ramp it up by about fifty percent. It's a question of degree. Once the team gets used to you, they start to understand what needs to happen."

A major step forward for Gary was "getting a local person to be my business manager, to explain local nuances to me. I had to find a confidante, build trust, and ask that person to fill me in on the dynamics. It was good to have someone who had worked for a multinational corporation before, who understood how the local people see things. I used that person as a sounding board to seek out advice. Over time I didn't need to rely on this advisor as much. Local managers can be trained to fill that role as well. It is important to have someone whom you can completely trust with all aspects of the business, not just within their department. Having a second opinion really helped me to navigate through obstacles."

Gary describes himself as a kind of cheerleader in his current leadership role. "Everyone at work has a job to do, and when they are here, I want them not to be suffering but excited, with lots of teambuilding activities including things like a tug of war, barbecue on the roof, and pictures on the wall from every fun activity we do so that they can call us a 'family.' Sometimes I like to cut people loose early to go do things." At the same time, he is very demanding. "I take a very hard line at a certain point. When people don't meet their goals, I will drop the hammer. When they get out of line, we have a hard meeting. The health and mind of each person comes first, their families are second, and work is third. I cut people slack when they need it but also don't mind calling someone at 2:00 o'clock in the morning if they don't have their deliverables. I don't feel guilty for calling them in—this is the sort of relationship that I have established here."

Gary's business objectives for the Shanghai Research and Development Center included transforming the team into a more innovative unit that would be able to go beyond its prior role. "I was to come into the organization and upgrade it, to add people and change direction, change the mission. I started building up a layer of trust around me, and it was about ten months before I could open up. I had to test the leaders to see if I could win them over to the new business model."

Ultimately this task involved making difficult changes in personnel. "About ten percent of the people couldn't adapt to the new dynamics of the team, which sometimes meant multitasking or changing directions on a day's notice. For the past twenty years some had been part of a manufacturing base that was using an established process or trying to copy something. The new setup requires completely different thinking; it requires innovation, and there may not be a ready-made system for that. There were people who could not get their mind around this so they couldn't stay. This doesn't happen with new graduates, but it can happen with managers from local companies—the old guard is sometimes not able to adapt. When I see my good people overcompensating for people who don't get it, that is the point where I start cutting loose. I moved a couple of people out, and it really broke through the stagnation."

Gary's leadership style seems to work well in the highly competitive Chinese business environment, where employee retention is a constant challenge and some companies have turnover rates of twenty percent or more per year. "I have had to fire twenty people in my lifetime and have managed several hundred, but have had just one staff member resign on me. People can adapt and flourish under my style. I use humor and a sense of family as well as recognition. We have two hundred people here now, and have lost no one that we wanted to keep after the first eighteen months. We started from the ground up."

Gary notes that over time his role has broadened beyond R&D. "You are an ambassador, representing the company. Everyone is looking at me to see what it is like to work for this company, so you are representing the company both internally and externally. I'm also an ambassador back to the U.S., where there are preconceptions about losing jobs to China, or that the Chinese engineers don't get paid as much so they must not be as valuable. I give management in the U.S. data to garner respect and appreciation, and often bring key people over to spend time in Shanghai. I also bring data back from the U.S. to compare with the China teams. I always carry this toolkit with me so that I can bring it out in planning sessions or conversations."

Gary has come to value some of the behaviors he sees in his Chinese team members. "I'm sometimes disappointed with teams in the U.S., which tend to think by the fiscal quarter. Here, we need to think by the year, or three to five years. We tend not to let details move us off our targets. Things are so dynamic in the States. People don't get as excited in China about not meeting quarterly goals perfectly, and this makes for a much calmer business environment. Also, a major communication tool is text messaging rather than a long voice mail or 'Reply All' emails. Text messaging is a brief and convenient form of communication. In the U.S., I couldn't imagine sharing a text message with my boss. We sometimes overdo communication there. Now that I've been working in China, I've begun to feel, 'Don't waste my time calling me or emailing.' People in China are frugal. When presented with a problem, they don't waste resources but find ways to reuse what they have or to do things as cheaply as possible. In the U.S., we waste so much. If you don't spend your budget, then you lose it. There's a real difference in this mentality in China."

Adapt and Add Value

The behavior *adapt and add value* means to balance adaptation to local practices with finding the best places to assert a different perspective or to act as a constructive change agent. Leaders' tasks often include driving a change agenda, which calls for setting a new direction and introducing a fresh set of objectives. Change agentry and action orientation are the hallmarks of great leaders. However, as Gary Ashmore's story underlines, global leaders must learn to temper these attributes through scrupulous self-awareness, a heightened sense of judgment and restraint, and adaptation to local circumstances. At the same time, they must demonstrate their ability to make a valuable contribution to employees who may question their authority or the costs incurred by their presence. According to one interviewee, "You still need to prove you are an expert who can add value to the leadership task. If you're not doing that, you're not needed." It is sometimes necessary to teach as well as to learn, to push as well as know when to hold back. Getting this balance right, both in terms of timing and content, is critical to long-term success. Leaders who adapt too much are unlikely to accomplish their goals, yet those who are overly hasty in their attempts to add value or who introduce new objectives that are unsuitable to the business environment may find themselves living on an island, shunned by local colleagues.

WAYS OF ACHIEVING BALANCE

Our interviewees suggested numerous ways of trying to achieve the proper balance between adjusting and contributing. These include building a foundation of mutual respect and inquiry, and patiently investing the time to learn about the new environment before initiating something new. They also stressed the importance of asking questions, challenging the status quo, and introducing different perspectives.

> "In Mozambique, one of the critical points for a leader is to understand the context, the history, what people have lived through, their emotive point of view. You have to invest in the foundational things like relationships, trust, credibility—really listen and understand where your employees are coming from, valuing their perspective and creating a venue to hear it. If you have this, then you can push back with the international standards that perhaps go against the local culture, and they will understand and respect this decision."

"You're only in your role for a short time. Don't march in and make decisions or kick off projects too quickly. It's good to learn a broader perspective on everything. To really get embedded in a country takes a minimum of six months."

"Make no decisions initially. Don't talk too much immediately; be quiet and listen. The local method is sometimes more correct. And when the planning is done, they execute better than we do. It's a judgment call that requires time and thought. You need to be patient but not a slow wheel."

"I am very results- and performance-oriented and we should not give up those points or we would be ineffective, but being aware of the planning and time needed to get the correct understanding and answers the first time is essential."

"Try to manage within the social context and adapt, but also question the status quo at the same time."

"There is always the question of whether I bring my own perspective or adapt in what I am bringing to the table. I have learned that I add value because I have a different perspective. How can you choose between the two things? It really varies as you go. It is easiest to do what everyone else is doing culturally because it gets results, but sometimes there is a need for difference to enrich the end result."

POSITIONING THE LEADER'S ROLE

An important consideration for global leaders is how they position themselves in driving initiatives. The specific role that a leader will take obviously depends upon the nature of the initiative and the capabilities of the people in his or her organization, but our interviewees generally favored an approach in which they contributed expertise without imposing it. They were positioned in a strategic role to structure and guide the process while incorporating various forms of local knowledge. This definitely does not mean forever walking on eggshells or avoiding problems that must be addressed in favor of getting along well with others. They supported and accelerated efforts across many time zones and made difficult choices when necessary. In some cases a leader may actually need to move faster rather than slower.

"You have to be able to educate and share your knowledge without imposing."

Insights from Global Followers

We have some idea of what executive salaries are, and we know that we could hire five or six very high-quality people in this market for the same price the company pays for one executive. So a person in a global leadership role had better be able to show us that they can add some real value or we will be disappointed.

People on this team have rather contradictory attitudes. On the one hand we expect our team leader to listen to us very carefully and to incorporate our ideas into any solution, and we aspire to gain more authority over time. On the other hand, our team members want to be able to learn skills from the leader that they haven't yet mastered, and to have somebody who is willing to take responsibility for risky decisions that go beyond what we have done before—although they are less likely to admit this directly.

We also expect that our team leader will convince headquarters to understand the needs of our customers here, even when the product delivery times and quality requirements are different, and customers are very demanding about specifications and price points. When there is a problem or a mistake, we expect him to help us get the resources we need to resolve the issue.

"My advice is to not come across as if you know everything, but you have to prove that you can add value."

"Critical analysis is key, because people want to see the value that you add. This value need not necessarily be technical. Position yourself based on an evaluation of your strengths and what you can add."

"Strategic thinking and decision making can help you gain credibility. As an outsider, it is sometimes easier to make tough decisions, to take in information and act.... You can add value in this position."

"Leadership comes from respect and credibility. You earn it by respecting the diversity of others' opinions. Listen and try to understand but also be very explicit about your standards. You need the ability to make hard decisions; sometimes people don't want to do this because they are afraid of hurting others, but you have to do this for the benefit of the organization in a fair and respectful manner."

"You must deliver results. You don't have much time to build your image in this culture. I tried to work to get results quickly, and had a 'hundred-day plan' with results visible to everyone. If you don't know the environment, on the other hand, you need to practice patience and go slowly—plan realistically considering the local culture."

Core Values and Flexibility

Gary Ashmore and other leaders such as Hannah de Zwaan, whose profiles we have featured earlier, note the appeal of certain values held by their counterparts from other countries. Learning the values of a different culture is an important part of building meaningful relationships. "You need to find the values in the new culture so that you can be respectful and use this knowledge to build relationships with the people you are leading." Another step involves learning to "style-switch," or to actually change one's behavior in order to function in a way better suited to the local environment. However, the leaders we interviewed have also gone beyond style-switching, a term from the intercultural jargon that implies a tactical adjustment with no real shift in one's fundamental values. Most of them have incorporated other ways of approaching the world into their own personal belief systems. Taking a long-term approach, being frugal in the use of resources, or avoiding nonessential information exchange and discussion—commonly held values in some cultures—have now become a part of their expanded worldview as well as their own behavioral repertoire, and will probably remain with them as they move into new leadership roles. Such flexibility, which means not only seeing the merits of values once viewed as foreign but also being open enough to adopt them, has helped to make them successful.

> "Even if you know about the other culture and become an expert, you still need to be flexible enough to embrace some of the true values of the culture. Understanding and being flexible are two different things. The ability to adjust at the level of personal values is more challenging."

As with *adapt and add value*, the previous behavior described in this chapter, there is another side to this equation. Many of our interviewees, especially those with experience in the developing world, insisted that it is essential for leaders to identify their own values and to know clearly which have the highest priority. "Core values" in this sense does not signify an extensive laundry list of items, but rather a critical few that the leader is prepared to defend at all costs, even when they run counter to standard local business practices. Such values could be personal in origin, or they might be deeply embedded in an organizational culture or a national legal framework.

"When you are in someplace really different, you need to understand your own values, including which ones are above the cultural context and non-negotiable. Otherwise you can lose yourself pretty fast. . . . It is important to immerse yourself and then to separate your core values from what you are open to changing."

"There comes a certain point where you need to adhere to the values of the organization."

"The best preparation was my faith life and engagement with the church in Moscow. The church affiliation means having people in your camp; you don't feel alone, and it's easier to get your mind around going to a new culture with new values and norms."

Core values may permit more superficial style-switching, but only to a point. Inflexibility is a surefire recipe for disaster in a global leadership role, but our interviewees reported that consistently upholding a few closely held values tended to elicit respect from foreign colleagues. In the meantime, leaders in a global context must also learn to exercise flexibility with nearly everything else.

"I try to tackle problems from a variety of angles while adhering to core values."

"You can develop social relationships, but don't compromise basic principles. This has been successful for me. People respect you in every difficult situation, and you gain respect in every culture. It is critical to my success as a leader."

"You need to ask, 'How do I get results in this cultural context?' The path may be different, and you need to be open to learn the skills to get there. You have to recognize if the path is in violation of those vital few values, and if not, go for it."

"If values are too closely linked to style, it is very difficult to lead globally. Values need to be broad enough, but if you don't have them then it will be a struggle."

DEALING WITH CORRUPTION

Among the difficult challenges that global leaders face are bribery, corruption, and more venal forms of exploitation and gross transgressions of basic human rights. Resisting such practices is neither popular nor easy, but some of the leaders we interviewed testified that they had to take a stand due to deep conflicts between their values and the circumstances in which they found themselves. Having a precise grasp of company policies and national laws is also advisable—these may be more or less flexible than one's personal values.

"When dealing with corruption, it took a lot of patience and a lot of time to establish my reputation as someone who wouldn't do unethical business. Early on, people were testing us, looking for bribes and kickbacks. We consumed a lot of time by not playing this game—we were delayed because we didn't pay. But over time, we established a reputation so that the other party wouldn't waste time either. After this, the vendors knew there was no point in waiting it out. This front-end investment was key. You either do this or pay for it forever after. I decided at the beginning that I didn't want to be corrupt, and that my actions needed to follow my words for a sufficient length of time so that I wouldn't have to go through the same process again."

"There is a dance between sensitivity and the delicate balance of maintaining core values. You cannot be entirely a chameleon but you must be enough of one to adapt. You have to know what your limits are. There is so much corruption here, where are your boundaries? There are some things I just will not do. The key is in knowing my core values and when to hold the line, and also in knowing what is not core, what is just preference and not important."

"We really have to learn to respect and work with cultural norms. Yet as leaders of international organizations, we are often pushing those norms. An example is our policy of zero tolerance for sexual exploitation. In an African setting, the understanding of sexual exploitation is not the same as in the West. As an international organization, we have to be very clear about what that means. Even if such exploitation is acceptable by local cultural standards, we have to be clear and demonstrate the policy in our behavior. If an employee in this country engages in inappropriate behavior, you have to call him on it even if it is within his cultural norm as well as the other person's cultural norm. I have to spend time with the staff to explain and then give them the chance to develop real trust. I have to be very clear, take time to do that, put it into policies, and demonstrate it. You cannot make one exception as a leader, and cannot make an exception for yourself."

Insights from Global Followers

One of the principles that the leader of our business has been very firm on is what she calls "integrity"—for her this means a prohibition of bribery in any form. Although at first we didn't understand what she meant, this is a big issue for her, and she fired or reprimanded several of our senior employees who were giving gifts to government bureaucrats responsible for interpreting and enforcing regulations covering our industry in their province.

Actually, in my country bribery is not commonly seen as an ethical issue, especially when you are providing gifts to officials to build relationships and to encourage them to expedite our company's business without doing anything illegal themselves. In this country, gifts are given to others in return for favors at every level of society, including top government officials. It is often impossible to get things done through the front door, and people who can get things done through the back door are seen as skillful and well-connected. Even my family had to learn to get things done through back-door connections in the past in order to survive through difficult times. Although our legal system officially prohibits bribery for some purposes, in practice there are many gray areas and the laws are violated by everyone. The government uses the legal system to punish their enemies or those who have gone too far. For ordinary people here, integrity and ethics have more to do with social relationships: how loyal and generous you are to your own family and friends, whether you respect and care for seniors and elderly parents, and your daily conduct in giving face or preserving the face of others while resolving difficult situations.

When our leader began to enforce her new policy, at first everything took longer and it was difficult for us to get even standard permits approved. However, the government officials eventually accepted that things are different with our company, especially because we worked out ways to donate equipment and training classes to local schools that are a priority for each province, and we have located facilities in places where the employment opportunities are very welcome.

Our employees are gradually becoming proud of this policy. They also like to work here because they know that within the company you aren't going to be promoted just because you are a friend of the boss and have given your superiors nice gifts or have done favors for them. We still do some of our work through contractors and I'm not completely sure what happens when they take government officials out to dinner, but the overall situation has changed quite a bit because the business head has been firm about this, and we are beginning to see some advantages of her policy.

CORE VALUES: EXAMPLES

Core values come in many forms. Interviewees brought up examples such as fairness, integrity, respect, honesty, effective feedback, openness, allegiance to common goals, rational allocation of organizational resources, and adherence to the law.

"When I was in Sri Lanka, there were many ethnic tensions. Although this happens in the external social context, it manifested itself internally as well. I couldn't be seen as biased; I had to give equal time to all perspectives and had to speak about the situation with integrity."

"My values are honesty, effective feedback, and openness. Feedback was initially very difficult."

"As program director, it is not my job to make everyone happy, but I have let them know that I am aware of their feelings. There is a common goal and we have to move towards that. If in achieving that I make you unhappy, I care about that, but we still need to achieve this goal. We cannot compromise the goal, but I see and am aware of your feelings."

"There were differences about allocation of resources based on pressure from the government. I was trying to do my job and respond to the government. If you uphold the values of the organization, this may not be seen as in the national interest. You can be influenced through security people, harassment. When I refused to do what an official asked, he came in with his security people, asked me to leave, and confiscated records from the office. A minister wanted certain castes to be favored, and there was the threat of expulsion if we didn't comply. They want you to allocate resources to people who are their allies."

"In this part of the world, laws don't exist. You can be surprised. People won't say anything but will try to do what they want anyway, whereas in other countries if you break the law you go to jail. Our corporate culture has very strong values related to following the law."

The core values of a skillful leader can become a rallying point for the team as a whole, even when they are not entirely consistent with local norms. "You need to build core values that bring people together, specific values that govern work and help you to achieve your vision." At the same time, for general values such as "respect" or "honesty," especially when people from different cultures assume that they mean the same thing, it is useful to discuss what each value means in terms of specific behaviors. What appears to be a demonstration of respect in one location—for example, asking questions during an executive presentation—may be regarded as offensive in another. Leaders who truly immerse themselves in the countries that they work with will probably find that their personal values and their understanding of how these are best defined and demonstrated gradually evolve over time. Embracing the strengths of other cultures can provide leaders with a broader perspective even regarding their own core values.

SUMMARY AND REVIEW: **QUESTIONS FOR LEADERS**

1. Can you manage effectively within different cultural contexts while also raising good questions about the way things are normally done?
2. How do you balance learning and teaching? How do you incorporate the ideas of colleagues and customers from other locations while also offering new information and ideas?
3. How would you identify the right moments to add value and/or drive change in a foreign business environment?
4. Are you able to both listen carefully to the views of colleagues from other cultural backgrounds and make tough decisions when needed?
5. What are the key personal and corporate values that you are willing to defend at all costs?
6. In addition to maintaining your core values, how flexible are you about adapting your approach to achieve organizational goals so long as these values are preserved?
7. Are you an effective advocate for key personal and corporate values, even in other locations where these differ from local norms?
8. Have you adopted values from other parts of the world based on your experience in different locations? If so, what values?

CHAPTER **SEVEN**

Establishing Solutions

However wide the gaps might be between their home context and the global business environment, leaders must sooner or later produce results. The global leadership behaviors outlined thus far provide a road map for how to engage employees around the world to elicit their best possible contributions in resolving complex issues, including ones that span multiple boundaries. These behaviors take into account real differences while enabling the leader to add value and to remain true to key personal or organizational values. In this chapter we focus more specifically on the act of creating solutions. *Influence across boundaries* and *third-way solutions* represent essential aspects of this process.

Global Leader: Khalid al-Faddagh, Saudi Aramco

Khalid al-Faddagh is from Saudi Arabia. Arabic is his native tongue, and he speaks English and some French. Saudi Aramco, his employer, is the national oil company of Saudi Arabia. It is the world's largest oil company with about 55,000 employees, and it supplies ten percent of global oil demand and constitutes approximately seventy percent of the Saudi economy. "Aramco" is short for *Arabian American Oil Company*, which recalls the days when Standard Oil of California still had a substantial interest in the company. Starting back in 2003, Khalid was assigned for four years in the Philippines as the president and CEO of his company's joint venture operations there. These are owned by both Saudi Aramco and the Philippine government, with the remaining stock publicly traded. Upon his return to Saudi Arabia, Khalid was assigned to Corporate Planning to lead the team responsible for strategy development and the five-year business plan for this global giant. Subsequently he was again promoted to become the company's General Auditor.

During his more than twenty-five years with Saudi Aramco, Khalid has served in various roles. He started in a specialist capacity based on his doctorate in Mechanical Engineering from the United Kingdom. Since then, he has worked in central engineering, consulting services, quality control, facilities planning, and oil production, holding a number of leadership roles. Khalid describes his leadership style as one that balances people skills and technical skills. "Technical knowledge is important, but people skills have also been quite critical when dealing with the many people reporting to me during my different assignments. I have an open-door policy, with not much formality. The balance of skills varies depending on which department I am in. When working with the top consultants or "prima donnas" in the technical arena, I use a different style than with a more field-oriented assignment, where setting certain targets and tasks, checking on progress, and assessing the impact and implications of recommendations including their bearing on cost becomes more critical. When I had a chance to manage the maintenance programs at a major oil facility, I had to be clear with the superintendents reporting to me about the objectives, and more assertive and clear about expectations, because we don't want any interruption to oil production. Things are much easier in the field because the objective is clear: no breakdowns to critical equipment. All other strategies and initiatives are aligned around that."

The best preparation that Khalid had for his leadership role abroad turned out to be special projects to which he was assigned. "Not only the standard assignments but special projects that I got involved with developed competencies and skills that really helped in later assignments. I led one special project with highly technical people to conduct plant integrity and safety assessments of five major Saudi Aramco refineries. I formed a team of thirty-plus specialists to develop the methodology and systematically assess the integrity of the plants in question. The Senior Vice President of the downstream business fully supported this assessment in order to determine whether field behavior matches the written procedures and process controls. This leadership role required me to go into ambiguous but exciting situations to try to find the right answers. I also chaired, on other occasions, major plant safety assessments and accident investigations. On the Human Resources side, I participated in many pilot programs to compare how Saudi Aramco would score. The experience gained from these special projects became very handy at a later stage in my career. You're on your own, with no previous friends and colleagues, new team members in a new situation, and a lot of unknowns. This builds the system in your mind for how to approach an ambiguous situation, a skill which is critical while on assignment abroad. It was not the typical command-and-control role, in which you can achieve operational excellence through direct intervention and hands-on involvement. You really have to rely on your people skills, compelling your counterparts with articulation and charm, and not just telling people what to do. In the international arena you need totally different approach and competencies."

In the Philippines, Khalid found that he was challenged in some very different ways than he had been accustomed to in Saudi Arabia. He had to draw upon all of his prior experience, including his time in the United Kingdom as well as a year and a half living in the United States, and from his travel experience in other parts of the world. For the two years before his assignment to Manila, Khalid served on the board of directors of the joint venture, traveling there four times a year. This allowed him to get to know the people, to go out into the city, and to begin to understand local sensitivities and culture.

Khalid comments that all of these experiences were very helpful, and that after arriving in Manila as an expatriate, "I discovered that I had things in me that I had developed and could actually display and use in this totally different environment. Execution skills are standard in Saudi Aramco, as are other core management skills. But different things became critical in Manila. People are people, with the same basic aspirations, and the simple things that humans want—family, a decent living, good schooling, etc. But you also have to learn cultural sensitivity very quickly. Thanks to my previous experience, I tuned in quickly to the fact that everything you say or do as a leader has a huge impact. You have to start finding the things that really matter.

"The perception in Saudi Arabia is that most Filipinos work in the service industry as skilled labor and domestic helpers. However, when you live in that country you realize how intelligent they are, like in any other nation in the world. If you go there with the wrong perception, then you can expect to have huge problems. You have to submerge yourself in the culture in order to be effective in leading people, and what really matters to them is that you treat them with respect. You need to spend the time to get to know them personally. Family ties are very strong in the Philippines. It is best to talk with people one-on-one, to eat with them without an aloof attitude. You can appreciate the culture without compromising your leadership or who you are. This doesn't get taught in books, and receives very little attention before such an overseas assignment."

He also points out significant communication style differences between the Philippines and other locations. "In the U.S., you go straight to the point, but in the Philippines people don't like to confront; they will tell someone off to a third party or do it in private. This is so critical. You will have the whole organization against you if you embarrass someone in public. When there is a conflict, you can disagree but do it tactfully without showing disrespect to the other side. We really don't pay attention to the soft skills necessary, yet they have so much impact on everything that you do during such an assignment. I would not have achieved favorable results if I had tried to do this outside of cultural norms. In the Philippines, issues related to style and culture matter a lot. If you are too execution focused, and want everything done in your own time, you will get stonewalled, nothing will happen. . . . My advice is not to come across as if you know everything, but rather to look for ways to show that you can add value. Try to imagine yourself in the opposite position, as someone coming from the Philippines to head up Saudi Aramco. For the first four to six months it would be advisable to listen and engage people, to understand the cultural sensitivities and adjust your style accordingly. This period will give you some pointers about the right questions to ask. It is much better not to exert undue pressure and make drastic changes during this initial period. You simply need to prove that, as partners, we can add value."

Over time a global leader can emerge from this listening profile and begin to reach out to talk about strategic direction, both internally and externally. For this, Khalid says, "You must be visible and know your strategies, know about the company's core business, its growth potential, and have a clear message for the market analysts. Moreover, you need to know how to articulate the elements of your strategy and offer directed and focused public relations. That kind of leadership role is vital."

He emphasizes the importance of relationships and a personal touch as well. "You have to pay attention to the little details, such as sending a note to someone whose mother died. We had six or seven thousand dealers who operate gas stations. Can you make yourself visible and show sincerity and appreciation even to the dealers in remote locations? These people are your face to the public. Go there and have your picture taken with them; this sends such a good message. While communicating a clear message regarding the company's strategic direction is important, it is equally important to use your soft skills to send a clear message about who you are as a person by appreciating people who are doing a great job. Show up for ceremonial occasions, including funerals. This goes a long way with the families, and matters a lot at all levels of the organization. They don't teach you these skills before your assignment, and this is not the way we operate back home. In the Philippines you have to live it and display such behaviors."

Khalid compares his expanded role in the Philippines with his subsequent post in Saudi Arabia in Corporate Planning, noting that his assignment required a set of skills that may not be necessary back home. "You need a strong financial background to excel during such an assignment. I attended an executive program that really helped. My role expanded, and the bottom line is the company's financial performance. In Saudi Arabia we are shielded, because we have a bigger organization to support us. In the Philippines, as an expatriate, you have to keep things afloat yourself and provide convincing answers to your shareholders. You need to know about financial performance not just in a purely technical way but on a strategic level—not balance sheets but what the analysts are looking for when viewing the company. Another thing that is critical is facing the media. Sixty percent of my time there was public relations. You need to be articulate, show passion and sincerity, attend functions, present a good marketing campaign, and speak with conviction to the stockholders, the public, and financial analysts. There are many functions and events to attend to, which could be pretty stressful. You are often put in public situations where you have to make a speech on the spot in front of smart and influential people, and you also have occasions to speak in front of banks and creditors. You have to lay out key messages, be a diplomat, act as the face of the company, and build credibility. We are shielded from the media in Saudi Arabia, but in the Philippines if the public gets upset with the rising gas prices and you have a poor company image, there may be protests in front of your building and you get all sorts of threats. You have to recognize your limitations. A reporter may well confront you with a microphone and start asking about price increases which you cannot disclose before receiving government approval. Full awareness of good corporate governance and confidentiality practices is essential. The legal implications and potential damages to the organization are just huge. A lack of the right public relations skills could ruin your reputation and the company's. Such awareness and skills are indispensable, as you could easily end up in jail through ignorance."

Khalid's greatest test in the Philippines turned out to be leading the joint-venture company through a huge crisis. "There was a major oil spill while I was there. One of our contracted fuel tankers sank and spilled two million liters of fuel oil, polluting the sea and the beaches. The chairman of the company was a very influential Filipino, and we had government agencies working with us, but we still had to face the hostility of the media and citizens. We were called every name in the book. Criminal charges were filed against me, the chairman, and other company officers. If someone is ignorant about cultural sensitivities and thinks the company or themselves are untouchable, then they are wrong. We formed a crisis management committee, and we spent all day in a big conference room, or the 'war room,' following events as they unfolded. One thing that helped was that I immediately started thinking of the crisis management case studies I had learned about during my executive management program at Harvard. I had to be up front, apologize publicaly, make clear commitments to repair the damage. We deployed people immediately, cleaned over 140 kilometers of polluted beaches, contracted with a high-tech company to siphon oil from the sea, created a livelihood program for the fishermen, and dealt with political pressure. The president of the Philippines visited the site twice; the Chairman and myself were present to report on the progress and assure the company's commitment. We created support programs for thousands of families, and built a school and library as a gesture of good will. The financial analysts were all over us to assess the impact of this spill on our financial results. This was eight months in hell with an end result that had a sweeter taste... At home in Saudi Arabia when we have a crisis, teams get formed and someone else always takes care of it. But in the Philippines, I was on my own at the front line, with no one to protect me or to deal with it. Things normalized towards the end. I made a presentation back home describing the crisis and our structured response. We received a lot of praise and support both at home and in the Philippines for the outcome. It was a whole new lifetime of experience in the Philippines...."

In retrospect, Khalid remarks, "I learned a lot about myself. I didn't know that I could deal with the media and learned that I could do a good job at handling a crisis and with public relations. I had to display these skills or fail and disappoint many people around me. At home I don't need these competencies." He also comments that he returned to headquarters with a new perspective on the company. "While I was in the Philippines I had to look at Saudi Aramco from an outsider's perspective, and saw many opportunities to improve our global message. You have to ask yourself, 'What is important to those who are receiving the message?' They are concerned about topics such as how secure is their oil, and whether we are developing the hydrocarbon resources responsibly.... We often overwhelm others with details that don't matter. A key skill is to be able to articulate a message that is relevant. What would a fund manager want to know? You need to give them the bottom line points and be clear about your strategies for growth and sustainability. Leadership makes a difference, and the difference is in these things. How do you excite people and the market about your company? To be successful, you have to step outside your own head. The definition of leadership is entirely different on the global scene than within the country of Saudi Arabia."

Influence Across Boundaries

Khalid al-Faddagh underwent a huge role expansion in a crisis situation. Suddenly he was the face of his company toward the entire Filipino public, and he had to draw upon all of his experiences and inner resources to handle the crisis effectively. Although his story might seem like an anomaly, many of our interviewees had similar stories to tell. Fernando Lopez-Bris, portrayed in Chapter 3, found himself handling a severe flood shortly after arriving in Kansas from his native Spain. Others were pressured or even threatened by government officials to favor one internal faction or another. Some tales were less dramatic, but the consistent theme was that these leaders stepped into significantly wider responsibilities in roles where they had to find new ways to exert influence.

The "Leadership Pipeline" concept of Ram Charan and his colleagues, mentioned in Chapter 2, portrays an unfolding telescope of expanding responsibilities and complexity from one stage of a leader's career to the next. However, the authors do not seem to fully account for the fact that a role with global content, whether it involves being a team leader or running an entire business unit, can be significantly more complex at any stage in the pipeline than if the same role is confined to one's domestic market.

A drawback of our research approach was that we were not able to objectively compare the role expansion that occurs in moving to a global posting with the role expansion that occurs with any upward step in the leadership pipeline, whether global or domestic. Taking on global responsibilities, particularly on an international assignment in which one is heading up a subsidiary or a region, can mean vaulting one or more levels beyond one's previous organizational position to deal with new challenges as a bigger fish in a foreign pond. Based upon the testimony of our interviewees, we would claim that the scope of responsibilities in global roles tends to be significantly greater than in their domestic equivalents. Working in a global job appears more comparable in many cases to what Ram Charan describes as the multifaceted role of an entrepreneur running a growing company who must handle numerous leadership tasks that in a larger enterprise would normally come at a higher-ranking career stage.[1]

Role expansion while working in a global context was a persistent theme in nearly every interview, and not simply in terms of official responsibilities. Global leaders must often contend with a dearth of the support systems that are available within a company's home market, and yet they face constant pressure to get things done across internal and external boundaries. In many cases they need to create solutions without having direct authority, finding ways to influence others across the organizational matrix.

A person who has worked in a global role can return home and be promoted to a domestic job that appears to be at a higher point in the leadership pipeline yet turns out to be less challenging. In fact, some of our interviewees who had already completed their assignments abroad and had returned to headquarters reported with regret that even though their new jobs at home involved promotions to a higher rank within the organization, the scope of their job responsibilities was actually narrower. This may be one of several factors behind the poor retention track record that many companies have with employees who have completed global assignments.

THE AMBASSADOR ROLE

Many interviewees used words like *ambassador* and *diplomat* to describe their role, both externally as well as within their organizations. They often had to represent their enterprise to the government, the media, or to industry associations, and therefore needed sufficient political acumen to be cognizant of corporate governance and confidentiality concerns along with the interests of contending parties.

> "As a leader you are likely to find yourself working in community and public relations activities that may not have been involved in your home-country role. I meet with the government here in Australia whereas I would never do that in my same role at home."

> "If you look at the local context, political acumen can really influence your work. There is a social context with a strategic impact. It starts with the history, and you need to look at the present as well. You need to listen to both internal diversity and external views; otherwise you can easily be influenced by a certain group in an area where you're working. Each group has its own interests, and can give you advice, but they may have primarily their own interests in mind."

These leaders were also closely scrutinized by employees who had never been to headquarters and who viewed them as an exemplar of what it is like to work for this particular firm: "Everything you do is seen as what everyone in the company does." This is very much a front-line job without the support or buffer functions that others might provide at home.

> "Global leadership is broader in that it touches all aspects of who you are in the country: you are an ambassador, viewed as being from headquarters or the mother ship, so there is a higher responsibility to walk the talk, to be an example. Everyone is watching. I had to be more cautious in how I acted, behaved, and responded because they would perceive it all as corporate culture—the beliefs and values of the company and its leadership. In the domestic role, no one is looking at you as an ambassador. In an international environment, you are the company's face. This can be detrimental or beneficial."

> "You need self-confidence because you represent something that is unknown to the people you are living and working with. They see everything through the lens of you. The company is viewed through your behavior; this is a

115

tremendous responsibility. You need to be the first one in, last one out—a real role model."

INFLUENCING ACROSS FUNCTIONS

Whether global leaders start in a top executive role or work in a particular functional unit, they must be able to drive collaboration across organizational boundaries in order to craft real solutions. People who are based in R&D will soon find themselves working with manufacturing; if their particular expertise is in marketing, it is likely that they will soon need to learn about sales and product development as well. Going back to the concepts of adding value and frame-shifting, some roles may require leaders to demonstrate that they have the subject matter expertise to make effective contributions in several functions; other roles may call for the leader to step back and orchestrate cross-functional collaboration in a more strategic manner without becoming enmeshed in the specifics. The constant refrain in all of this, however, is that a global leader must orchestrate the process of generating solutions across functional boundaries, and if he or she does not, nobody else will.

> "Your role gets expanded: you play the role of human relations, international business strategy, retail—it's a crash course, with no time to go to school. You learn by hard knocks."

Insights from Global Followers

Our current country director is from headquarters, and has been here now for two years. She has longer experience in the company than anyone else and knows all of the top executives. We see her as a kind of model, and listen carefully when she is talking on conference calls or holding a meeting with employees. As a woman, I find it inspiring to have her here as a leader because it is rare for women to rise to such a high rank in my country. The country director's leadership style is different from most of the local leaders here. Even though she does her best to fit into the local culture, she is still more direct in her communication style in a way that people sometimes find surprising, and she stays very focused on the business tasks. She comes into the office by 7:00 in the morning and leaves about 8:00 P.M. It is hard for me to imagine a whole build-ing at headquarters filled with people like her. I'm not sure that it would be a very comfortable place to work because I like to take a bit more time to catch up with people and prefer to avoid conflicts, but I definitely want to learn more from her.

"You have to work outside your functional area, and have a greater breadth of communication within the organization and across functions."

"If you cannot think beyond your function to a multifunctional job, you will have a problem internationally. Generalists tend to do better in a leadership role outside their home country because they can cover more functional areas."

"In the U.S., you can just come in based on your title and function. It takes more work abroad to hit the ground running; you need to show some functional capability. I had functional managers look for evidence of capability from me in their areas in order for me to have credibility as a leader. I learned more than I would have otherwise needed so that I could have influence there through my depth in their functional areas. They expected me to be knowledgeable in every area."

"In a foreign assignment, you cannot work in a silo. You have to communicate cross-functionally as a team."

FREEDOM TO EXPERIMENT

With the weighty responsibility for driving solutions comes a measure of freedom, too. Global leaders who are working away from headquarters frequently discover that they have opportunities to make decisions and try out new ideas or products that would receive much closer scrutiny in a larger organization. A significant degree of anticipation, analysis, and advance planning are required to set the right course.

"One of the great benefits for me in working overseas is that I have a lot more autonomy and scope to do a broad range of things. It has provided me opportunities to experiment, a lot of freedom in what I do. I have to be accountable but am able to engage many more facets of the job, from management to implementation. I really learn so much because I am not focused on one specific pocket, but I have a whole range of opportunities. You have to be accountable and responsible, but it is always an incredible challenge and I have learned a lot through this. You can take a holistic perspective and really pick and choose where you want to focus. You do not have someone telling you what to do all the time. There is a lot of flexibility in roles."

"You need to be able to read situations and predict scenarios, to think ahead—forethought is very useful. You play a lot of roles. No one will tell you what will happen tomorrow so you have to look at trends, analyze the situation, and get a good sense for what is going on around you. I have to have acumen in terms of feelings and undercurrents in the organization, and need to keep my finger on how things are changing in society and in the office."

CREATIVE RESOURCEFULNESS

Our interviewees also noted that they encountered many dead ends—and still had to find another way. The experiences they described are not for the faint of heart, and the situations demanded a rapid learning curve along with tolerance not only for ambiguity but for failures along the way. These global leaders went through a process of toughening or tempering that made them more resourceful and better able to find solutions using the assets available to them.

"Necessity is mother of invention—there was often nothing I could do, and at that point it gets down to survival. It's ridiculous to throw a fit, and if I can't do something, I need to redirect my efforts. There is a realization that this is the way it is, so I need to think of another approach. Try to find different angles to approach a problem. There is not always just one way."

"There is no better experience than international, but you have to walk in with your eyes open. You won't be afloat the whole time; this experience is not for everyone. There is real risk, without much time to learn to swim. You will swallow water."

"I became more resourceful in my work and emotions, in my ability to work through difficult things. This resourcefulness includes being able to stand outside a problem and get to the essence of what needs to be done. It requires a distance from the emotions of it—an ability to build systems and concepts. I initially had nothing to work with. But I now know that I can get there eventually. Look for what you have and build on that . . . you need that mindset as a global leader."

Third-Way Solutions

Third-way solutions draw upon all of the behaviors that have been outlined already, and therefore in a sense this term signifies the ability to put everything together to generate real solutions. Each of the ten behaviors summarized in Figure 7-1 can be utilized by global leaders every day on the job to move toward constructive solutions with maximum engagement of global employees.

Seeing differences	**C**losing the gap	**O**pening the system	**P**reserving balance	**E**stablishing solutions
• Cultural self-awareness • Invite the unexpected	• Results through relationships • Frame-shifting	• Expand ownership • Develop future leaders	• Adapt & add value • Core values & flexibility	• Influence across boundaries • Third-way solutions

FIGURE 7-1   Global Leadership Behaviors: An Overview

Neuroscience and Culture: Multiculturalism and Creativity

A study published in the *American Psychologist* empirically demonstrates that exposure to multiple cultures enhances creativity. The research found that one's degree of exposure to multicultural experiences was positively related to both creative performance, such as insight learning and idea generation, and to creativity-supported cognitive processes, such as retrieval of unconventional knowledge for idea expansion. Individuals with significant multicultural exposure are more likely to come up with novel combinations, see the same form as having multiple possible meanings, have access to alternative forms of knowledge, and seek ideas from diverse sources. Significantly, an individual who has been exposed to different cultures is more able to take discrepant ideas from two cultures and integrate those ideas in a novel, or third, way.

The researchers found that these creative benefits were also dependent on how participants gained their cross-cultural exposure. The connection between multicultural experience and creativity is most visible in individuals who have deeply immersed themselves in foreign countries (living versus merely traveling abroad), and also varies depending on the degree to which the individuals adapt and open themselves to these new cultures. Researchers attribute this distinction to the fact that short-term travelers rarely need to change their actual thinking and behaviors, whereas this is almost always required for those actually living abroad. It is not enough for individuals to simply be exposed to foreign cultures; they must make concrete cognitive and behavioral adaptations and have an open mindset that welcomes new experiences to obtain a tangible creative benefit.[2]

In the more micro, problem-solving context in which a leader seeks to address a specific issue, there is also an application for many of the behaviors we have described. Figure 7-2 illustrates a set of steps commonly taken in creating third-way solutions, referencing leadership behaviors that contribute to various phases of this process. Other behaviors, such as *developing future leaders* or *core values and flexibility*, shape the overall climate in which viable solutions can be reached.

An easy way to remember this sequence is with the label BRIC(C): **B**racket, **R**elate, **I**nquire, **C**ocreate, and **C**ommit. Although the steps follow a logical sequence and are roughly parallel with the stages depicted in Figure 7-1, they can all occur to some extent in tandem with the exception of the final one: commit to implementation.

The role of the global leader in this process will depend upon the capabilities and maturity level of participants, but ideally leaders position themselves as a "catalyst" for creating the best solution rather than as an "advocate" for a particular point of view. This requires confidence in what will emerge from honest dialogue and a shared focus on finding the optimum solution for the

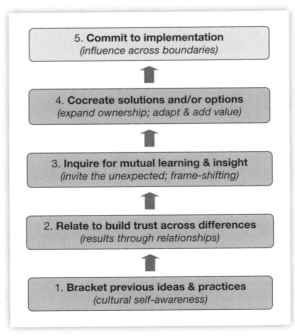

FIGURE 7-2 Third-Way Solutions: The BRIC(C) Process

organization. Often it involves the cultivation of an experimental approach, with freedom and anticipation about trying new things. Leaders who seek to become an effective catalyst should consider the following short checklist of questions related to each element of the BRIC(C) model:

1. **Bracket:** What would I normally advocate in this situation based upon my cultural background and experience, and am I willing to question that and/or set it aside for the moment?
2. **Relate:** Does everyone involved in this process know each other, and how can we develop a foundation of personal trust and mutual understanding across cultural differences?
3. **Inquire:** What do each of us not know about this situation that we need to know, and how can we work together to find out? Are there aspects of my style or strategic approach that I should consider changing to better support our global work?
4. **Cocreate:** Who are likely to be key global players influencing the decision and implementing the outcome—even those who haven't previously been decision makers—and how can I involve them in creating the solution? How can I both learn and contribute?
5. **Commit:** Does each person who participated in the process feel that the final outcome is their own, with some pride of authorship? Have we fully leveraged the global, local, and functional resources available to us and our freedom to experiment in this location?[3]

TRANSPARENCY

Our interviewees stressed a couple of additional features of their role in creating shared solutions. One was to be transparent about their assumptions and expectations as well as consistent in their actions. Leaders may set the ground rules for a discussion or define a result that is nonnegotiable, but they also need to make their own preconceptions clear enough to themselves and to other team members so that these can be called into question. Implicit assumptions do not translate well across cultural boundaries, and they often wind up in conflict with the unspoken beliefs of others.

> "I had to become vastly more articulate. When working with shared implicit meanings, you don't need to be so specific. But the minute you shift out of your home context, you cannot do this anymore. You have to be explicit about your expectations."

"You have to be consistent and transparent. Transparency can get confused with confidentiality issues, but you can be transparent without violating confidentiality. Consistency means actions and words lining up to generate trust, for people to know that you will not play favorites. I hold myself accountable for what I say because I am holding others to that as well. I am asking people to be self-reflective constantly."

ACTING AS A BRIDGE

The diplomatic skills described earlier in this chapter for influencing across boundaries are vital for generating solutions. At times, as Gary Ashmore described in the last chapter, there is even a kind of "shuttle diplomacy" that the global leader must engage in back and forth between headquarters and other locations to increase understanding and collaboration from all sides. Setting expectations, providing information, coaching, explaining, linking corporate and local objectives, introducing new players, obtaining resources, quelling misunderstandings, solving cultural conflicts, gaining buy-in—all of these are aspects of the global leader's bridge role.

"There are many people wanting things from you but you are dependent on them. Keep headquarters informed very thoroughly so that they understand your situation. Sometimes they just want results—communicate to enough people and in an appropriate way so that you can balance expectations with headquarters."

"Don't lose sight of corporate and local objectives and how to weave those two together."

"A person from headquarters turned to a person from another country at the break and said, 'I hope this will open your eyes up to doing it *our* way . . .' I ended up chatting with the department head about making everyone feel like part of the company."

"If I see that people have been marginalized in a situation, I will specifically bring them into the circle, inviting others to participate in making decisions in matters involving them."

"I have to practice open-mindedness every day in explaining U.S. actions and company style to colleagues in Germany to build bridges with the corporate culture. I use these bridge-building skills daily. I am a cultural interpreter for colleagues, explaining differences in cultures. The higher you climb, the more you have to find solutions to very tricky clashes. A large amount of time is spent solving conflicts—the majority of them are related to culture. In every company it is like this. The easy stuff never gets escalated; only very complex problems come to the top."

"Communication with headquarters was essential, because all the resources were there. I was really struggling between headquarters and our U.K. acquisition, working as an ambassador, representing the company, and in the middle trying to get all sides to understand how the other works, and what we need to focus on. It's important to get this buy-in from all sides and balance this with getting the job done. There was a lot of push back from headquarters to 'just get it done.' I was dealing with a company that has been successful in one market... but they don't understand the other market."

CREATING VIABLE SOLUTIONS

Overall, our interviewees were less attached to the specific form that solutions took than to the process of getting there and the fact that the solution was ultimately achieved. Their focus was on integrating the various parties involved to discover common ground and to generate real solutions, without being so concerned about where the solution ultimately came from.

"Sometimes I end up with a completely different solution because I listen to all players, a solution not even related to what I originally thought. Sometimes I push through my thought process and get them to adapt... but generally I end up with something different."

"My approach has been to integrate people from different walks of life, respond to different interests and peoples, and bring together a diverse set of goals, interests, and perspectives to focus on common denominators. This informs my entire approach: making compatible diverging positions, trying to get people to work together. Perhaps early on this approach was for reasons of survival. I saw the benefits of making people feel they are pushing in the same direction, the benefits of being together and relying on each other. I was also gaining an increasing awareness of failures of other organizations that could not work as a team—these observations pushed me in this way. I saw many of our partner organizations fail because they were not integrated. I learned from this."

So, third-way solutions can assume a number of possible forms. Global leaders who have demonstrated the other nine behaviors described in this book will find that they have a reservoir of trust to draw upon, and that employees around the world understand and expect that their leaders will want to explore a full range of solution options. There is sufficient goodwill to engender support even for the occasional top-down directive during difficult times, in part because employees know that a good idea generated anywhere in the world has the chance to be adopted by the whole company.

Figure 7-3 illustrates a set of solution options, and the following list includes brief definitions of each. Experienced global leaders are likely to find that they use every option available to them over time. A viable process for creating *third-way solutions* always places the needs of the organization and its customers front and center while welcoming and building upon worthwhile input from any source.

Insights from Global Followers

We all want the most practical solutions for the company. Of course, we are going to advocate what we believe to be in the best interests of our local customers and employees—this is part of our job. But we understand that you can't have a different IT solution for every country or ten different systems for financial accounting. It's more about the way in which initiatives are introduced. If the leader shows us some respect, asks for our opinion—even about the best process of implementation if it's a company-wide mandate—we are much more eager to support it than if there are a lot of incorrect assumptions made about what is good for us.

We trust our current leader to ask the right questions of the right people, and to be as flexible as he can in the process of discussion and implementation. We also know that even if this time we're implementing a standard global solution, next time it could be different. Recently we were very excited when he took an idea for a new service that we had created for this market and introduced it to another country; a whole team traveled from here to that country's subsidiary to share the idea. This made us feel really proud, and we also learned things from seeing that other market.

FIGURE 7-3 Potential Third-Way Solutions

- **Standardize:** Establish a single policy at corporate headquarters that is applied uniformly worldwide.
- **Select:** Work with local managers in each country to choose and apply the elements of a corporate-wide initiative that have the most relevance for their operations.
- **Adapt:** Alter the form or packaging of a particular change to make it more readily acceptable to local employees or customers.
- **Combine:** Seek out a felicitous combination of ideas from headquarters and local sources that will work better than a one-sided approach.
- **Integrate:** Fuse different contributions from diverse participants into a synergistic result that exceeds the sum of the parts.
- **Adopt:** Identify an idea from a nonheadquarters location and apply it in other markets where it offers potential benefits.[4]

SUMMARY AND REVIEW: **QUESTIONS FOR LEADERS**

1. Do you work successfully across different functions to accomplish global business tasks?

2. Are you seen as an effective ambassador and role model both inside and outside the organization?

3. How could you be more creative and resourceful in leveraging limited resources to deliver new global solutions?

4. How do you persuade people across geographies and organizational lines to get the job done in a matrix environment?

5. Are you sufficiently transparent that colleagues from different cultures understand your expectations?

6. How could you bridge headquarters and subsidiary perspectives in a way that enables both sides to better understand each other and to share a common sense of purpose?

7. Have you created a process that incorporates the ideas of team members from different backgrounds to create the best solutions for the organization?

8. Can you convert cross-border disagreements into innovative business outcomes?

CHAPTER EIGHT

Training the Ten Behaviors

Global leadership training programs perform important functions and will play a valuable role for a long time to come. In particular, the face-to-face connections and network-building that take place between high-potential leaders from around the world are usually well worth the investment. Participants often remark afterward that, thanks to their new network, they are able to solve problems in a day that would have previously taken months to address.

Program Design: Going Global?

Contemporary leadership program designs typically involve anywhere from twenty to forty participants, and their content includes elements such as:

- Preparatory work:
  - Invitation and messages from top executive(s)
  - Readings on leadership
  - Completion of self-assessment and/or multirater instruments
  - Kickoff of coaching relationships
  - Face-to-face or virtual meetings to orient participants to the program agenda
  - Review of global business data
  - Webinars by expert speakers
- One or two weeks in an important emerging market location, featuring:
  - Feedback on self-assessment and multirater tool results
  - Visits to customer or supplier locations
  - Interaction with local leadership and employees through presentations, tours of facilities, and shared meals
  - Observation of retail outlets and consumer behavior
  - Dialogue with customers and/or community members

- Unvarnished views from local industry analysts
- Cultural experiences such as visits to historical or religious sites and art exhibits
- Presentations from experts on leadership, innovation, industry trends, national culture, and the local marketplace
- Activities in support of corporate social responsibility (housing construction, environmental cleanup, donations and visits to schools, etc.)
- Daily debriefing and discussion of participant reactions to new experiences
- Kickoff for action-learning projects with multicultural teams
- Action-learning projects that continue during a several-month interim period through virtual coordination between team members
- Ongoing one-on-one coaching for each program participant
- A final week together at headquarters for:
  - Presentations by top executives
  - Informal interaction with company executives and other headquarters counterparts
  - Simulations to cultivate leadership capabilities in areas such as business acumen or crisis response
  - Reports on action-learning project findings and recommendations
  - Wrap-up of coaching relationships or planning for next steps
  - Application of program material to one's own job
  - Personal career planning
- Post-program networking, follow-up on project action steps, tracking and assessment of results, ongoing self-development based upon training and coaching experiences, and alumni events

Although this kind of program design has many virtues, it usually contains inherent flaws as well. Most of the leadership models shared by executives, academics, and consultants—even those explicitly labeled as "global"—are shaped in unacknowledged ways by Western and largely U.S. cultural perspectives, including the classic works represented in the "best-seller" list in Figure 8-1. But what about, for example, considering Chinese approaches to leadership that have a pedigree of more than 2,500 years?

Examples of frame-shifting in previous chapters showed how leaders steeped in the more egalitarian and consultative leadership styles that are regular fixtures of such program fare sometimes need to adapt to different cultural contexts. Such leadership models also tend to be individualistic, emphasize very direct communication techniques, and highlight tasks and execution.

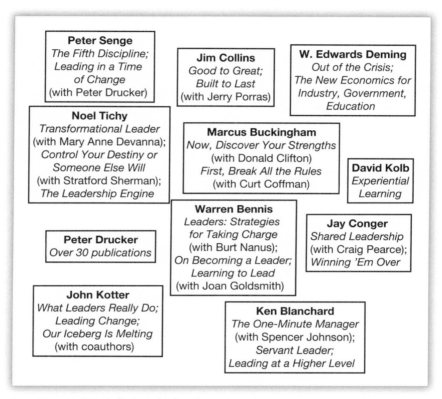

FIGURE 8-1 "Best-Seller" Leadership Theorists

They are less likely to prepare leaders to operate effectively in the cultures that comprise the majority of the world's population and are profoundly collectivist, hierarchical, and relationship-based, with very different approaches to time and to task completion.

There is a potential hazard that leadership development programs, although global in name, will replicate and reinforce the limitations of an organization's current state rather than cultivate behaviors that can take it into the future. Common flaws of existing programs include too few participants from emerging markets due to a real or perceived scarcity of "high-potential" personnel from these locations, and Western participants who dominate discussions based on factors such as assertive communication styles, language facility, and prior exposure to the program contents. For companies trying to grow in emerging markets, having a preponderance of Western participants doing most of the talking and referring to models that derive from their own cultural background—especially in presentation-heavy programs that involve a lot of sitting and listening—is not the best way to challenge participants to think and act differently.

Often there are participants with firsthand knowledge of emerging markets whose voices, perhaps more tentative or less fluent, have the potential to transform the dialogue and to create a fresh sense of mutual learning. These voices, combined with meaningful opportunities for participants to see an unfamiliar market with their own eyes and to hear directly from customers and local colleagues, can spark genuine inquiry and jaw-dropping new insights. The following are examples of comments made by leadership program participants from emerging markets that have set off serious reflection and intense debate.

"Customers like us because we are foreign."

"Our prices are too high by a factor of ten for this market segment."

"We could become the leading foreign company in this market, although the government will always favor local firms."

"The average monthly wage for workers in our factory is around $200."

"The footprint of our leading product is much too large for the typical office space in this city."

"The technical standards and environmental practices of our national monopoly firm are better than those of many major multinationals."

"Our largest competitor is based in this market, and their revenue is growing by about thirty percent per year."

"The average employee turnover rate here is twenty percent per year, which means a company can have close to one hundred percent turnover in five years."

"The communications infrastructure installed in this city over the last few years is more advanced than the infrastructure in London or New York."

"This city has several million illegal internal migrants from the countryside."

One means of generating a learning environment that deliberately leverages such perspectives is to introduce some or all of the key global leadership behaviors described in this book and to craft a venue that enables participants to begin to apply them. For example, four behaviors that are easily linked with the objectives of most programs and with standard leadership competencies are *results through relationships*, *frame-shifting*, *expand ownership*, and *develop future leaders*.

Training for Results Through Relationships

The global participants themselves represent the program's greatest asset, and it takes a major investment to bring them all together in one place. Years after a leadership program is complete, memories of expert presenters and their frameworks, the market data, and the seemingly endless PowerPoint slides often fade away. What lives on most vividly are the recollections participants have of each other, captured and maintained by digital images, along with the personal networks they have created. Lasting relationships form sometimes almost in spite of a program's content. If participants are left to their own devices, however, they may gravitate toward small clusters of people with shared cultural and linguistic backgrounds. It is a good idea, early in the program, to get participants focused on regularly reaching across their own mental boundaries to get to know people they would otherwise be less likely to meet. When this becomes the norm rather than the exception, the excitement of real discovery often begins to occur.

RELATIONSHIP-BUILDING EXERCISES

There are various techniques for accelerating the growth of interest, interaction, and conversation among program participants. Members of a leadership development cohort usually have bios of the others in the program, but they can benefit from knowing more specifically what others have to offer to them, and what they bring that others find valuable. One simple warm-up exercise called "Give and Get" can be facilitated using the instructions on the next page. This exercise works best if the leaders involved are from business units or functions with global responsibilities and therefore have a business need to learn about different markets.

For a roomful of people of different nationalities in the first blush of a leadership program, the most difficult part of facilitating this "Give and Get" exercise can be convincing them to stop! With smaller groups we have also successfully used a variation of this exercise that we call "Exponential Networking," in which each leader is asked to think of two or three other people in his or her personal network who could be of use to other leaders in the group. They write down the person's name and role, and place it on a map of the world in the appropriate area. Then the participants each describe in turn the contacts they have selected and why. Afterward they are given time to circulate informally and ask more about the people in whom they have a special interest. This exercise serves the dual purpose of expanding the group's network of relationships beyond the people in the room (names and contact information can be

RELATIONSHIP BUILDING EXERCISE:
GIVE & GET

STEP ONE: Please take a few minutes to consider the business needs and interests of others in the room, along with your own leadership goals.

- Identify one thing that you can *give* to others that will help them achieve their objectives. Write it on a Post-it note and place it on the world map in a location that seems appropriate. Be sure to include your name.
- Identify one thing that you would like to *get*, or to receive from others in order to achieve your own objectives. Write it on a Post-it note and place it on the map in a location that seems appropriate. Be sure to include your name.
- After you have finished writing your own notes, spend ten minutes looking at all of the notes on the map.

STEP TWO: Find a person with whom you may have something to exchange (either give or get) and initiate a conversation with that person. After ten minutes, change partners and repeat.

"Give" and "get" examples: A local contact, a best practice, a technical application, market knowledge, a suggestion or an idea.

Materials needed: Post-it notes and a large map of the world, drawn on a whiteboard or across several flip-chart pages, that demarcates major business regions.

recorded and provided as a program takeaway), and of positioning participants from emerging markets positively with other members who can see readily the value of the network they bring.

Training for Frame-Shifting

There are many ways within a training context to approach the behavior called *frame-shifting*. With respect to communication style, for instance, there are video resources and role-playing exercises that demonstrate common differences and teach new skills. Leaders can also learn about frame-shifting on the more strategic level from formal case studies with information that challenges their assumptions.[1] Most effective of all, however, especially when it comes to shifting one's leadership style, is the structured sharing of anecdotes and examples between leadership program participants from divergent cultural backgrounds. The experiences of Gina Qiao, described next, touch upon most of the global leadership behaviors discussed in this book, but they include particularly compelling demonstrations of frame-shifting.

Global Leader: Gina Qiao, Lenovo

Gina Qiao is the chief financial officer for Lenovo in Beijing. Before this job she was based in the United States and was director of Human Resources for her employer's global computer business. Gina is originally from Dalian, an industrial port city in northeastern China. She has lived abroad on assignment in New York, Singapore, and in Raleigh, North Carolina. Lenovo is China's largest computer company—it emerged as a major player on the global business scene through its acquisition of IBM's personal computer division, and it is currently the world's fourth-largest computer maker in terms of revenues.

Gina's early roles with Lenovo were in marketing, and these experiences have strongly influenced her leadership style. "This time really trained me. I broadened my writing skills, communication ability, and organizational skills, and learned how to inspire my own team. I started out with a small team and then developed it into a very large team, working with a number of different products. We did a lot of big product launches, so this time taught me a lot about team motivation and nurturing a team. This was a key training ground for me. The company saw that I did well in this role, and based on this, moved me into Human Resources, where I needed to learn how to motivate even more people, and how to better organize work within the company internally."

She did receive some global management and leadership skills training while in China. However, she notes, "The real focus was on how to manage within a Chinese organization; how to communicate effectively with those above you, below you, on the same level as you; how to navigate the different layers [above and below]; how to create team cooperation; how to work towards goals and to motivate others. I received training on all of this in a Chinese context."

Gina's initial experiences abroad were challenging, but she learned a great deal from them, including how to prepare. "The assignment that I had in Singapore for one year, and then before that for a half-year in New York—these were very tough assignments. The three years in Raleigh, North Carolina, compared with these two initial assignments, were not as hard because I had already adjusted so much from these first two assignments. I think an important reason that the stays in Singapore and New York were so difficult was because I never received any kind of preparation, no basic training for my assignment or what to expect. I just went. So during those first two assignments I felt uncomfortable in many ways: getting off the airplane and trying to find the location, with no one picking me up; trying to use a credit card and not knowing how it worked; showing up at a meeting and not understanding anything or being able to express myself. But after these assignments, in preparation for moving to North Carolina and because of these past two experiences on assignment, I arranged a lot of training before moving. This training included information about my assignment country's religion, history, working style, culture, and the areas that I needed to really pay attention to because of differences. We also included a daily life section in the training, covering what is important in daily living in addition to what is important at work. The three-year assignment to North Carolina allowed me to improve a lot and to correct my previous mistakes. Such training really improves your efficiency in a new work environment. Also, the training helps with your mental and emotional state, or the way that you feel while you are there."

In terms of her communication style as a leader, a key learning experience for Gina was to be more open. "I have learned to become more direct. Before, in China, if I was in a meeting and had a conflicting idea, I would like to agree—not just me but any Chinese—both within the meeting and after the meeting. We like to quickly agree, without necessarily a lot of thought, for agreement's sake. But while on assignment, I saw that in meetings you could say directly that you disagreed and no one minded. In a meeting in China, if you want to say something or express a thought, you have to consider the system, the organization. You have to think clearly about what you want to say and how to say it, and carefully assess the value of what you are saying, including its impact on you, before speaking. In the States, I saw that people spoke without any hesitation, just spoke their thoughts. There wasn't this pressure that I saw in China related to speaking out. Americans were much more direct and willing to speak up. They felt comfortable even if they didn't really have anything to say in meetings, still speaking out just to interject their opinion. In the U.S., hearing everyone's voices is how they measure if people are engaged or not. Are you willing to participate in this meeting, are you adding value? You always have to prove this."

"In China, people emphasize that you need to have everything that you want to say completely prepared in your mind before you speak; you want it to come out in a very clear way and for everyone to think, 'Hey, this person deserves a gold medal!'—that they are really well spoken. If you don't come across eloquently and intelligently, then you might as well not say anything. You want people to think well of you and be impressed by what you say and how you say it. You almost have to have a complete thesis prepared in your head before you feel that you can say anything. In the U.S., I saw that people would add their little bit and then another would add their little bit and this would build, and in the end you would have something that was good. I learned a lot from seeing this process and how it functioned."

Gina also reports discovering different approaches to risk-taking, particularly risks related to strategy. "Another area where I learned a lot from the different working styles that I found in the U.S. and China was in attitudes towards risk. In

China, people like to consider for a long time, thinking things through and getting a lot of clarity before they can start doing something. The planning process is a lot longer, including strategy creation. When we were working on company strategy, we would spend two to three months out of the year creating these strategies, and had to make sure that the plan for the coming year was extremely clear. This was also true on a day-to-day basis—you always needed to think very clearly before starting to do something. But in the U.S., I realized that from small things like creating a PowerPoint presentation or planning a meeting, to big things like creating a strategy, they would first just do it and then if it didn't work, they would change things. It was an environment of constant planning, constant motion, a constant moving forward. These things were ongoing and continuous. There wasn't a certain period set aside for them. This was a big difference."

Gina also encountered major contrasts in attitudes toward hierarchy and authority. "In China, there is always a head and he is always the one with the authority. For example, if there are three department heads working together, there is always one head with the authority among these three, and everyone recognizes this; he is the one whose position is highest.

But in the U.S., the authority or the head isn't always the person with the highest position. It could be that within the organization, there is just an average person who is given the task of being the facilitator or coordinator, and this person has the authority in a certain situation. Also, these two words—'facilitator' and 'coordinator'—we don't have any good translation in Chinese to express this type of role or policy. The way of thinking about this is very different."

Contrasting approaches to hierarchy are linked with methods for resolving conflicts, as Gina discovered to her own chagrin. "When I was working in HR in North Carolina, I would always go to my boss with any issue that I had because this is what you do in China. If two employees have a conflict, you go to the boss to help you resolve it. In this way everyone can save face, because maybe I have an issue with someone, and then I go talk to the boss, and the boss may think that my position isn't logical and just tell me, and then I will drop it. The issue may even be with a good friend, but the boss will know how to resolve it. This is better than two people trying to resolve a conflict who are at the same level. So in North Carolina, anytime I had a situation with someone in which I didn't agree with them, I would just go straight to my boss. At that time, my U.S. boss thought that the problem must be really extreme and he asked me if we couldn't just resolve this directly between the two of us. And according to the American way of thinking, this was a major insult from the standpoint of my other leadership team members. Their reaction was, 'Why would you go to the boss and tell on me? You had a conflict with me and you went to speak with our boss about this?' So at that time I thought that I had done the right thing, but my colleague was really upset that I hadn't just gone directly to him to resolve it. He saw it as me complicating the situation by bringing in someone else. I had difficult relations with a lot of people because of this."

Gina points to deep-rooted social causes for such organizational culture clashes, and notes that her time abroad has caused her to incorporate different values, and to change her own approach in some cases. "In China, if as children we have a fight, we always seek an adult to sort it out for us. But my U.S. colleague told me during our training program that he sends his kids into another room and says, 'You work it out yourselves!' In the States, the boss is more like the parent telling kids to go work it out themselves. So even at a household level this difference is really instilled in them.

It's funny because now I have adjusted so much to the American way of resolving things that I no longer take a problem to a superior for resolution, but I haven't yet been able to adjust back to the Chinese way.

I am shocked now in China when people come to me to resolve an issue, and I tell them to go resolve it themselves. They act this way in China because the boss is really involved at this level of things on a day-to-day basis, seeing everything that goes on. We recently had an incident between two departments and the VP came to me to tell me about the issues that they were having and I said, 'If you have problems, you can't just be coming to me to resolve them.' But before in North Carolina I was the same; I wanted the boss to hear me out and to judge whether I was right or not and give me feedback. I completely understand their thinking . . . but now I have gotten used to the U.S. way and so I come back here to China and I think, 'How can they be using this method to resolve a conflict?'"

As comments like these suggest, Gina has adopted the habit of self-conscious reflection on the nature of leadership and what is required to succeed in a global context. "Before you go abroad, you really need to understand what your unique strengths are. What are you bringing to the table? Many people, before going on assignment, say, 'I have been very successful in this area by doing these things.' But then when they arrive in the new country, the same steps do not lead to success. Their success was culturally dependent. So you have to take a real honest searching look at yourself and ask yourself what are the true abilities that you are able to bring into a new country. What is your original area of strength and how can you bring this into play in your new environment?"

Gina emphasizes the importance of being able to adjust leadership styles to accommodate new circumstances. "The most vital skill for leaders is the ability to style-switch, to use different language with different people, to be able to use a different style that matches with the style of the people whom you are with and to have flexibility as a leader. When working with people from a different culture, you must be able to look at things using their value system, to see things through their eyes, to adapt in each country to the best, most effective way of working in that country."

She provides examples related to a variety of activities from decision making to workplace hours in which leaders may need to either shift their own established patterns or recognize that others have equally effective ways of getting things done. "I think that some differences lie in a leader's policies. For example, one leader may have a certain policy that is very hierarchical when it comes to decision making, but another leader may emphasize consensus and talking matters through to reach agreement. Or to give another example, in America, everyone is very results oriented, but flexible. So maybe you have a private phone conversation here and there during the day but if in the end you get things done, then everything is okay. But if you go to China, the value system is really about working very hard and being seen as working very hard during the workday, not leaving to go home right on the dot. So if you are working on 'American flex time' in China, and leaving work early, people's estimation of you will definitely be very low. In America they are very relaxed about this; you can leave or come when you like as long as you get your work done. So in the U.S., some people I know would leave at three o'clock to pick up their kids from school, but then they might go back home and work all evening after that. This style is not recognized in China. So these sorts of things you might need to change when you go abroad."

Gina has also thought about similarities between successful leaders regardless of nationality, and how to best bridge differences between cultures and organizations. "There are similarities between leaders everywhere. The similarities lie in the fact that all leaders want to be successful and do a good job, to get the job done. Also, everyone needs motivation and encouragement from a leader. Everyone wants to win, and wants to be a part of an organization that is constantly moving ahead toward success. And we all like to work for a good boss, a boss who is knowledgeable and able to provide resources. Employees like it when there is a clear strategy and everyone is working hard together to achieve that. One of the key differences for a global leader is that you must embody an understanding of all the different nationalities that you work with. So if global leaders are managing Chinese, Russian, French, and German subordinates, they must know: What does successful leadership mean in Germany? What is the perspective of my German report? Where is he or she coming from? And a global company working with an Indian company or a Chinese company must know that relationships are very important and very useful in these places. If you are just a Chinese leader or an Indian leader, you might just think that, 'This is who I am and this is my style and it's fine like that.' But if you are a truly global company, you need to have leaders who understand the differences in these countries, and what areas are not the same.

"The first thing that a global leader needs to know is that styles differ across cultures. Then they need to learn those styles and adapt their own style. Another part of becoming a global leader or a truly global company is to understand the overarching goal, the overarching strategy, and how to build trust with others. Because if you need to go to each country to learn their style and to adapt, this is actually quite difficult, so you need to learn how to build trust and credibility across all these countries, creating a sense of trust in each location. Then you can leverage these trusting relationships toward developing the business."

Gina observes that both she and Lenovo have changed substantially as a result of their global experiences. "Lenovo is now a merged entity, so these differences have become really important to us, and it is important for me to spend time thinking about them. If I could describe our style, it is half thinking and half doing. Before going on assignment, I wasn't really aware of these differences and had not run into them before or understood them: things like going to a meeting and people just speaking right up or people jumping into action without spending time to think. When you first encounter these things, your initial psychological response is to disrespect the other person and their way of doing things. But now I feel that I can understand all these approaches.

"When I am leading both Americans and Chinese, I feel like I have become a mixture of the two cultures in my leadership style. I try to take the strengths of both cultures. So, for example, with regards to planning strategy, I say that we should use the Chinese style and really thoughtfully plan and think about these things very deeply, not just show up at a meeting and draw some things on a flip chart and send everyone away to give it a try. In this area, we should study the Chinese style of careful strategic planning. I do this with my American team and teach them the Chinese style. Then when I am back in China working with my Chinese team, I encourage them to jump into new roles and be a project leader, to practice leadership roles within the team. And I encourage them to talk about things and to express their ideas freely. With this team I try to get them to cross boundaries within the organization and not be so stuck in hierarchy or in their roles, to take initiative and try to take on a project and make it work, regardless of whether it is part of their official role or not.

"Our company chairman once came to the States and no one went to pick him up; then he came to the company and no one knew who he was when he first arrived. And even worse than this, he came to attend a meeting and realized that he didn't have a seat. In China, they would have asked him where he wanted to sit and given up their seat for him and provided him with anything that he wanted. Now, in meetings in the States, they agree that he doesn't have to have a special seat, but he at least needs to have a seat! Our company is actually very good. I feel like the Westerners have also learned a lot about Chinese culture and have really made an effort. So we've become a mix of the two cultures. And now in China, we know that although we have to leave an extra seat for the boss, it doesn't matter so much where he sits.

"These were all things that I learned, ways that I changed, and this was also a time when I improved my understanding of different people. My colleagues feel that my working style has grown a bit, and I have more thoughts or resources for how to do things. I have also become a bridge between Americans and Chinese. If we are having a meeting, I know the points at which my Chinese colleagues must have thoughts or opinions on an issue and are not saying anything, and I will urge them to speak. So these are the new leadership methods that I have learned and taken with me."

A leadership development program that taps into the experiences of participants such as Gina Qiao has the potential to induce deep insights and to initiate behavioral changes on the spot. It is not easy to bring such voices into the discussion for reasons that Gina herself describes: culturally based communication standards for carefully considered and eloquent expression, or concern about hierarchical factors that may be present in the group. Language skills are another variable—imagine participating in a leadership program held in Chinese, Japanese, or Arabic, three of the world's most difficult languages! And not every program participant has the self-awareness, flexibility, or willingness to share his or her own sometimes painful experiences. Gina has been remarkably adept at both adjusting to different cultural environments and sharing what she has learned in a way that informs and inspires others. Those who design and deliver global leadership programs need to seek out, model, and cultivate channels of mutual inquiry and exchange that draw upon participants like her.

One way to stimulate discussion about the cultural basis for leadership styles is to create mini-case scenarios for group discussion. Here is a sample case related to Gina's experience that can help leaders consider together when and how to engage in frame-shifting if they are working in an environment that includes people from various backgrounds.

MINI-CASE: **RESOLVING A CONFLICT**

A Chinese executive felt there were problems with a project initiative that one of her fellow leadership team members was running. She went to the top executive who headed up the team and the organization to describe the problems in the hope that the boss would handle the issue from there.

- What is the "Why" behind this behavior?
- How might a Western colleague (mis)interpret it?

A Western executive felt there were problems with an initiative that one of his fellow leadership team members was running. The executive went directly to that team member to raise the issues and to make a few recommendations based on his own experience. The team leader, the head of the organization, was kept out of the discussion.

- What is the "Why" behind this behavior?
- How might a Chinese colleague (mis)interpret it?

Training to Expand Ownership

Companies seeking to enhance their global leadership bench strength normally have positive examples within their own operations that are not widely known or recognized. Leadership programs can serve a useful purpose by identifying and disseminating such best practices. Participants react to internal examples in various ways because these are close to the world they know—they ask questions, challenge the facts, recall similar examples, admire and perhaps envy the people involved, and feel challenged to generate best practices themselves. Practices that hold up to participants' scrutiny and also serve to illustrate one or more global leadership behaviors provide a memorable and convincing impetus to adopt such behaviors. The story that begins on the next page provides one such example.

It is hard to imagine a better example of the global leadership behavior *expand ownership*. The Kohler VP and his team have enhanced the responsibilities of their global counterparts through process adjustments, face-to-face interactions, and altering the organizational structure of the project to give greater responsibility to a manager who is closer to the new facility's site. Most importantly, instead of handing off projects that are mostly complete and therefore difficult to impact, his team has increasingly taken the approach that is "global from the start."

BEST PRACTICE EXAMPLE:
KOHLER FACILITIES CONSTRUCTION

Kohler is a famous manufacturer in the midwestern region of the United States, with its headquarters in Wisconsin. Founded in 1873, the company is best known for the products of its Kitchen & Bath Group; other business units include Interiors (furniture, tiles), Global Power (engines, generators), and Hospitality (luxury resorts). It has more than fifty manufacturing locations worldwide. Kohler has gone through a remarkable process of globalization in the past decade, transforming itself through acquisitions and organic growth from a primarily domestic company to one that now has 18,000 of its total 32,000 employees—well over half—located outside the U.S.

As the company's employees and business reach have become more global, it has also needed to reevaluate and revise systems that have traditionally been centralized in Wisconsin. One of these is the system for new site development. With the demand for its products increasing around the world, Kohler is now building manufacturing facilities in places like India and China, where it has a large and growing presence. The company's vice president for Corporate Operations Support[2] describes the work of his site development team along with the significant changes it has made to work more efficiently on a global scale.

"Construction Engineering Management is the group that goes out and works with the business to find the site, and then, depending on the manufacturing process, we design a building to fit that process and do the construction. There are three different phases in the design: first there is the concept design, then there is the detail design, and the last is the finished design, including the construction drawings.

"Historically, we've had a large group of facility engineers who reside here in Wisconsin. These engineers would do the concept design through the detail design, which meant the building design would be seventy to eighty percent complete. Once that design work was complete, we would send it overseas and our counterparts there would work with their local design institute to finish the design and do the construction drawings.

"It is commonly understood that in the product design process, once a product is designed, eighty percent of the cost and eighty percent of the quality are locked in at that point. So when we talk about manufacturing process improvement of existing products, we are really working on a twenty percent window. To improve quality, we've worked a lot on moving our improvement activities up into the process so we have input from all parties before we get that design locked in. We're doing the same thing with buildings now.

"India was a great learning experience for us. One of my sayings to my organization is 'We don't know what we don't know.' In the area of working cross-culturally, most of the time, we don't know what we don't know. We think we do—we go in with our paradigms, our mental images and models we have always relied on, but they probably aren't useful for this purpose. India was a very tough project to complete on schedule, at the right quality, and at the right cost. What we found is that the way we had always done the design and construction management process wasn't working. Fortunately, we really dramatically changed not only our approach for India but for all businesses. Now the design group here in the U.S. is only doing fifteen to twenty percent of the design, and then it goes over to the in-country designers, where they do the other eighty percent. What we've learned is that this gives the in-country design team the opportunity to have real input on the design that is going to impact the schedule, cost, and the quality of what we get.

"Our engineers used to complete the design and send it to the in-country design institute for their twenty percent. After that in-country design institute completed their twenty percent, it would be returned to the U.S. design engineers and they would find issues or mistakes. This would then require the U.S. design team to go back to review the changes with the in-country design institute to try to get the design right. So we'd have probably two or three redo loops. The old process took about seventeen weeks. With the new process, our engineers design the twenty percent, and then the design team travels to the in-country design institute to ensure not only that the design intent is clearly understood but also for both teams to meet face-to-face to establish a working relationship and open lines of communication. Once these lines of communication are open and the design intent is understood, the foreign design firm has freedom within that framework to really design the building. Now the design is completed in about ten weeks instead of seventeen. This means about a forty percent reduction in just calendar time, and it's also about a forty-five percent reduction in hours spent doing the design phase. So we've made significant improvements in saving cost and time, plus the frustration of doing redo loops—we're now doing it once, doing it correctly, and we also have a superior product.

"Our colleagues in other countries now feel that they actually have an opportunity to influence and to have an impact. If I had been in their shoes with the previous system, I think I would have been pretty frustrated. I really wouldn't have felt like I had an opportunity to influence and change the thinking, because they had been sent drawings that were already eighty percent complete. I'm not sure if they were sending us this message but my gut tells me they were—there were some times where we would take the drawings and we'd do our eighty percent, which was about six hundred drawings. We'd send it to them, they would work on it for their four weeks, and when we got the packet back there were only thirty drawings. We'd ask them, 'What did you do with all of our drawings and design?' I think their response was basically, 'Well, there's nothing we can really do with this so here are your thirty drawings back.' I think they were giving us that message, but we were just not hearing it.

"I find that as soon as you have the concept, that's when you get on the plane and get in front of them at their desk and start talking. This way they have input into the concept and it's not so complete that we have to say, 'Well, we do it this way, and I'm sorry but the train has left the station.' It's really taking the concept and going to them to get that mutual understanding and input as early as possible. After we have had the face-to-face meetings, it is then that we can start having the conference calls, which will be much more meaningful and productive. First take the concept and hold a face-to-face meeting to get a clear understanding. As I've been taking this approach and doing it over and over again, I have learned that it doesn't matter if it's at the plant manager level or at the country president level—I'm just amazed at the acceptance of some of the things we want to do."

Kohler has also made dramatic organizational changes to support the new process. Before, for instance, there were supposed to be U.S. and Asian teams working in parallel, but the reality was that the Asian team was taking instructions from the U.S. team. So the VP asked the U.S.-based engineers to create plans for mentoring and developing their Asian counterparts to enable them to work at an equivalent technical and managerial level. Now an Asian project manager is taking the lead.

"With the newest project, we have the project manager in Asia—he drives the meetings, he drives the agenda. We put in videoconferencing in China and in the U.S. because it's a little harder for him to be the project manager if others are in a separate room but he doesn't see them when he's talking on the phone. We use technology to facilitate the conversation. And then we took all the other team members, including those in the U.S., and they are reporting to him. When I first put this forward, people said, 'It won't work because of this, and it won't work because of that.' So I asked, 'What about the development plan you were telling me was going so well? Either we have a problem with the development plan, or maybe we just need to have some faith and let them step forward while we support them to be successful.' Again, there was resistance to it—our paradigms get in the way often."

These steps have had a dramatic impact on the level of acceptance and engagement from their global counterparts, although there has also been resistance from some at headquarters who must now become accustomed to letting go of certain tasks. Expanding ownership on a global scale also turns out to have a bottom line impact, with hundreds of thousands of dollars in savings as well as better project results from this one example.

Not all best practice examples are quite so compelling. In relation to cases like this one, however, participants in a global leadership program could benefit from considering the following questions:

- What are the key success factors present in this example? Are there weaknesses or ways in which it is still incomplete?
- Are there similar practices that exist already in your organization that could be leveraged?
- Are there aspects of this best practice that could be applied to your area?
- What specific steps would you need to take as a leader to implement the global leadership behavior *expand ownership*?

Training to Develop Future Leaders

Although the need to develop future global leaders seems obvious, knowing whom to select and how to develop them is less readily evident. Many companies still depend upon a cadre of "global leaders" who are all from the same country or ethnic background, whether they are the head of Asia Pacific, the Americas, or Europe, the Middle East, and Africa (EMEA). This same pattern is often evident in the top several layers of the organization chart for each major business unit or function. Chapter 5 noted the natural tendency for leaders to evaluate most positively those who look like them, and to misjudge leadership potential based upon candidates' lack of fluency in a second language or their use of communication and leadership styles that depart from headquarters norms.

Participants in a global leadership training program can benefit from considering whether the process for selecting future leadership candidates in their own organization provides a balanced view of each person's leadership potential. Such balance is usually best achieved by incorporating multicultural perspectives in the assessment team. Beyond the selection process, current leaders are often focused on how to accelerate the development of high-potential subordinates from around the world so that these individuals can step into roles with greater responsibilities. When speeding up talent development in the organization is among the top priorities for participants in a global leadership program, it can be valuable to provide a structured session that enables them to exchange ideas and to generate development plans together in regional, business, or functional groups.

There are a number of training and development opportunities that should be systematically considered for employees who have been targeted for their future leadership potential. One way to begin planning the development of global leadership capabilities is to weigh the degree of difficulty and the degree of difference presented by any opportunity in connection with the candidate's present state of readiness. The objective over time is to work with each future leader to arrange a series of increasingly challenging "fish out of water" experiences, as illustrated in Figure 8-2. These continue to test the candidate's potential while better enabling him or her to quickly find firm footing and

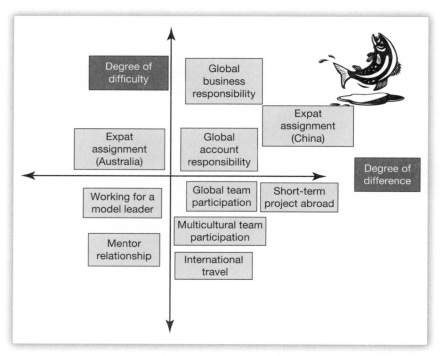

FIGURE 8-2 Developing Future Global Leaders: Sample Development Path for a Candidate from Europe or the U.S.

accomplish business objectives even when presented with radically different market circumstances.

Leadership program participants often have creative ideas that are unique to their business and industry for how to develop future leaders within their organizations. It is helpful for them to be able to share and build upon such ideas with each other. In addition, the following list identifies some standard practices for cultivating global leadership skills that can stimulate discussion and concrete planning efforts.

- Hiring people with previous successful experience of living and working abroad
- Traveling on international business
- Attending global conferences
- Traveling with short-term immersion in local markets or operations
- Mentoring from a model global leader
- Reporting relationship with a model global leader
- Training and development opportunities with global content
- Hosting of visitors or employees on assignment from abroad
- Rotating assignments among global functions or businesses
- Working on or leading a multicultural team
- Handling regional versus domestic responsibilities
- Managing subordinates from other countries
- Working on or leading a global/virtual team
- Working on a short-term project assignment abroad
- Assuming global responsibility for a product or service
- Taking an expatriate assignment
- Running a global business

When training is being conducted for a group of leaders who face similar dilemmas in planning the next developmental steps for their employees, another learning device is to provide them with brief case examples to consider together (see pages 147–148). They may arrive at proposed solutions through original ideas that emerge from discussion or through the application of practices from lists like the preceding one.

The beginning of this chapter noted the danger that leadership programs may replicate culturally embedded styles of learning and leadership that some participants are already comfortable with, while those from emerging markets may be less engaged even though they have much to contribute. An antidote for

CASE #1: **CAN'T RELOCATE NOW**

Jean, a headquarters-based mid-level manager with significant growth potential, knows she needs to develop multimarket and global skills, but she won't be able to relocate for at least five years. The biggest market opportunities for the business Jean is assigned to will be shifting to India and Brazil over the next five years. Jean has unique technical knowledge about the brands that are critical to this business's growth outside the domestic market in which she works. She is willing to travel, but she has never lived abroad and can't move now for family reasons. What would you do if you wanted to develop Jean's potential as a future global leader?

Possible responses: Travel with short-term immersion; mentor relationship with a global leader; global team and/or project responsibilities.

CASE #2: **REGIONAL MARKETING CANDIDATE**

The head of marketing in Russia, Andrei, has been identified through succession planning as a potential candidate for a regional job based in Brussels. The regional role is a developmental post that colleagues are rotated through to gain cross-franchise and multimarket experience. This job needs to be filled in three months. Andrei has identified a successor with high potential from his team in Russia to step into his current role, but the employee won't be fully ready to take on Andrei's job for at least one year. Russia is a critical market, with many logistical and regulatory complexities, and significant new product launches are scheduled for the next six to nine months. Andrei is very talented and is able to relocate to Brussels at any time. He also could be a retention risk if he doesn't see career growth relatively quickly. (He has already turned down two outside job offers.) If you were the director of Marketing for Europe, what would you do in this situation?

Possible responses: Andrei takes on the regional role while still based in Moscow, with frequent travel to Brussels; accelerated mentorship and coaching for Andrei's successor; additional talent is hired in Russia to support upcoming product launches.

CASE #3: **IT INNOVATION**

Your company is growing rapidly in key global markets. There is increasing pressure on the IT function to innovate in order to meet internal customer needs. Business units are asking for new IT products and services. The existing headquarters-centric organization, with limited work implemented abroad, cannot adequately meet these needs from a cost or customer service standpoint. IT employees must now collaborate more effectively across numerous global work sites (including Bangalore, Singapore, Manila, and Moscow). People who have been "implementers" in the past will now have to contribute at a new level in a global network. IT has strong pockets of global expertise, but needs to be able to disseminate this expertise across the entire organization to increase efficiency and effectiveness. What changes will you implement to enable your organization to serve its internal customer needs more effectively?

Possible responses: Short- or long-term rotation of high-potential employees between different sites; global projects that allow employees to take on new responsibilities; a structured knowledge transfer and mentorship initiative that sends current experts to key global locations to provide training and development; clear communication of globalization strategy to address fears of headquarters-based employees over potential job losses.

this tendency is to have program participants begin to apply global leadership behaviors such as *results through relationships, frame-shifting, expand ownership,* and *develop future leaders* to their own thinking and conduct during the session. In a more expansive vein, beyond stretching to incorporate new behaviors into their personal actions, participants can also be challenged to foster these behaviors in subordinates and potential successors. Analyzing the development needs of others and nurturing their growth will help the leaders themselves to more fully absorb and integrate new patterns of action. A final recommendation for encouraging the growth of global leadership behaviors within a training context is to have leaders apply these behaviors not only to themselves but to other potential leaders, as in the following learning exercise.

EXERCISE: **DEVELOP FUTURE LEADERS**

INSTRUCTIONS:

- Identify two or three of your own direct reports and/or colleagues who you feel have the potential to take on more responsible global leadership roles. Are you missing any global colleagues with real potential?
- For each person, what are his/her current strengths and areas for improvement related to the ten global leadership behaviors?
- What specific development steps are you taking or could you take to help them better leverage their strengths or address their areas for improvement?

Seeing differences	**C**losing the gap	**O**pening the system	**P**reserving balance	**E**stablishing solutions
• Cultural self-awareness • Invite the unexpected	• Results through relationships • Frame-shifting	• Expand ownership • Develop future leaders	• Adapt & add value • Core values & flexibility	• Influence across boundaries • Third-way solutions

FIGURE 8-3 Global Leadership Behaviors: Five Stages

149

CHAPTER **NINE**

Coaching the Ten Behaviors

Global leaders work on the forefront of globalization for their organizations at the inflection point between strategy and execution. It is at this pivotal juncture that executive coaching becomes a powerful lever to help leaders develop global capabilities. This chapter features examples of the ten key behaviors in the context of executive coaching. It will examine the viewpoints of the coaches as well as the global leaders they coach.

Executive coaching is a one-on-one development process that increases the capability of key talent to achieve targeted business objectives and specific leadership skills. Coaching is a short- to medium-term, goal-focused form of learning for executives who wish to improve their performance by working through organizational challenges and change initiatives with the help of a skilled partner.

There are many models and frameworks for coaches to choose from in this work. Most often we find that coaches use a mixture of techniques other tools that depends on the client (coachee) and the situation. From our perspective, frameworks such as Appreciative Inquiry, Ontological Coaching, GROW (Goals, Reality, Options, Will),[1] and Brain-Based Coaching are all useful in working with global executives. Gifted coaches can pull from their toolbox the technique or combination of techniques that fits the needs of a particular coachee.

As Figure 9-1 illustrates, most of these coaching models involve bringing clients to their own insights through a structured listening process. The coach focuses intently on the other person, reflects his or her comments, further draws out thoughts and feelings related to an issue or opportunity, encourages the coachee to generate options for action, and then seeks a commitment to act on a chosen direction. Coaches may augment such structured listening with a continuum of techniques, including feedback, suggestions, instruction, challenge,

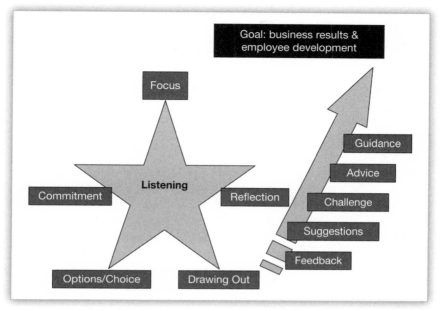

FIGURE 9-1 Common Coaching Steps

advice, and guidance. Though it is sometimes said that executive coaches do not need to have an intimate understanding of a client's business to be effective, all of these methods are more impactful when the coach is equipped with a solid understanding of the leader's business objectives, potential obstacles, and organizational context. To the extent that the leader's objectives and challenges are global ones that involve working across cultural or other boundaries, the coach can use the ten key global leadership behaviors to accelerate development.

Coaching at Citi

To test the efficacy of the ten key behaviors in relation to coaching, the authors worked with a group of executive coaches at Citi[2] who were interested in learning more about coaching across cultures, the global leader's role, and the use of this new framework in their work with executives. The coaches attended training sessions on coaching across cultures and the ten global leadership behaviors, which they then put into practice with their current coaching clients.

This chapter examines some of the coaches' formative experiences in working across borders and how they used the ten behaviors themselves to become better coaches and leaders. We will also look at common difficulties that their coaching clients faced and how the coaches used their knowledge of culture and the global leadership behaviors to support them more effectively.

We were pleased to work with Citi on this research because of the breadth and depth of its global presence, its well-established internal coaching practices, and its commitment to developing global leaders. Citi has a huge global operation. The company does business in 160 countries, with a physical presence in over 100, and employs 259,000 people globally. In recent years Citi has gone through its share of challenges related to the financial crisis, including changes in leadership, strategy and organizational structure. However, Citi has been able to pay back the TARP loan from the U.S. government, redesign its business model with a focus on banking as a core competency, restructure its remaining businesses and functions into a blend of centralized and globally dispersed operations, and return to profitability.

In addition, the leadership team has focused on key competitive differentiators that are difficult to replicate in today's market. Its post-crisis global strategy, shown in Figure 9-2, defined a path forward for the company as well as the specific skills its leaders would need to execute.

This strategy signaled a need to change the organizational culture within the company. For the Executive Development group at Citi, the top priorities became global mindset, customer-centricity, responsible finance, the development of leaders capable of directing the change, and cultivating other leaders for key next-in-line roles in the organization.

Recognizing that critical inflection point between strategy and execution, Citi saw an opportunity to accelerate its leaders' global capabilities by training their coaches on the ten key leadership behaviors. "Citi Coach" is the in-house branding for the Center of Excellence (COE) that provides thought leadership

Business Drivers	Skills to Execute
■ Leveraging globality: capitalize on competitive global footprint	■ Ability to work across functions, geographies, and products
■ Market focus: leverage global trends and socioeconomic and geopolitical forces affecting our business	■ Global mindset and systems thinking
■ Organic growth and innovation	■ Customer- and client-centricity through collaboration and cross-selling

FIGURE 9-2 Citi's Global Strategy and Skills

and oversight for the seventy executive coaches comprising the internal coaching practice. The Citi Coach cadre is composed of mostly Human Resources practitioners who, beside their "day jobs," which include coaching, take on an additional forty to fifty hours of ongoing professional coaching development each year. The coaches are nominated by the regional senior Human Resource officers who preside over HR for a business or region. The coaches work their way up the "coach pipeline" through a combination of training, supervision, and job experience.

The Citi Coach COE provides a centralized approach to the coaching philosophy, criteria, competencies, training, certification, and performance management of coaches. Implementation is done regionally, with local variations predicated on the developmental needs of individual clients and the resources that are available. Coaching at Citi is seen as an accelerated development intervention for high-potential talent, with the ultimate objective of increasing a leader's ability to manage change, guide people, and execute on business strategies.

Training Event for Coaches

One aspect of the training curriculum for the coaches is the annual Citi Coach Conference, which brings the coaching community together for a three- to-four-day development event at the company's training center in Armonk, New York. The main theme of the most recent Coach Conference was enhancing the coaches' understanding of how the company's new global strategy translates to the developmental needs of Citi's leaders. The sessions were designed to build the coaches' cultural self-awareness, their facility with global leadership behaviors, and their hands-on skills for using these in their coaching engagements.

Two of the central training modules of the four-day conference were "Coaching Across Cultures" and "Coaching Global Leaders." The Coaching Across Cultures session highlighted the dimensions of culture, cultural self-awareness, and skills for bridging differences between nation states, functions, product lines, and geographies. For this segment, the coaches filled out the *GlobeSmart®* Assessment Profile, which plotted their work-style preferences on six dimensions of culture. They compared their own profiles to those of other cultures and program participants, and learned techniques for bridging differences between themselves and clients from other parts of the world.

The Coaching Global Leaders session was centered on the ten key behaviors described in this book. For this module, the coaches were given the *Global Leadership Online* survey, which they completed as both a self-assessment and

153

a 360-degree evaluation, inviting key business partners to rate their global leadership performance. The results of the multirater survey, comparing self-assessment results with feedback from coworkers, were used in the session, which also included case study analysis and role playing. The objectives of the training modules were to build the coaches' understanding of global leadership as well as their skills for increasing the global leadership competencies of their clients.

Three months later, we met with the coaches to ask how they were using the ten key behaviors in their practice, and what, if any, new insights and behavioral changes they were helping clients to attain. All of the coaches interviewed work with high-potential executives in large, matrixed global businesses. The coaches themselves have global HR roles, are multilingual, and have many years of experience working in various companies and countries.

Coaching in a Global Context

The coaches we interviewed found the frameworks from the training—the dimensions of culture and the ten key leadership behaviors—useful both for their own professional development and in working with their coaching clients. With respect to their development as coaches, they noted that these frameworks had provided ways of better understanding and applying their prior experience. They felt that in the role of coach they needed to be more aware of their own cultural preferences in order to be effective in coaching clients from other cultures, and that their understanding and use of the leadership behaviors was critical for them as coaches and HR business partners.

COACHES: PERSONAL LEARNING EXPERIENCES

Each of the coaches we spoke with had a long history of working in other countries and with a culturally diverse client base of globally minded executives. These experiences made them predisposed to learning how to be more effective in the global arena. The *Global Leadership Online* multirater survey provided the opportunity for the coaches to assess their own facility with global leadership behaviors as well as gain feedback from others. This exercise made them more conscious of their own strengths and skill gaps as global leaders. The coaches spoke at length about the need for a global mindset as a prerequisite for their success in coaching across cultures. They most commonly cited *cultural self-awareness*, *invite the unexpected*, and *frame-shifting* as critical behaviors for their work as coaches.

Cultural Self-Awareness

Larissa Durant has been in Human Resources since 1994, working mostly for U.S. financial institutions in Switzerland, England, Belgium, and Denmark. Today, she is a regional HR business partner for Citi in EMEA. Larissa is from Brittany, where she says that the confluence of Celtic and French cultures formed her earliest lessons regarding cultural self-awareness. Early in her career, beginning in Geneva, Switzerland, she worked for another large financial institution.

> "Being French and French-speaking, I went to Geneva confident of our com-
> monalties, but had completely underestimated the differences in mentality,
> culture, and behavior. I alienated a lot of people in the office by using 'tu'
> [the familiar form of address], as we had in the French office. I used this
> for everyone, and the senior bankers were not impressed. I had not earned
> the right to be familiar with them. No one would tell me. I found out by
> accident. No one felt they could give me this feedback. I was twenty-eight
> years old and quite young to be heading up the HR practice. It took three
> months to recover. In the end my stay there was a success, but it started as
> a disaster."

When Larissa moved from Geneva to the London office, she observed instances when she and others would err in the opposite direction, attributing too much meaning to cultural differences. Her own self-awareness has continued to evolve along the way, helping her to understand not only which kinds of issues may be cultural in origin, but also which are not.

> "I initially thought that everything was due to cultural differences, and then
> thought maybe very little, and now I am more balanced in my approach. I
> realize that global leadership always calls for different approaches. Today,
> on my own team, I have to be very culturally self-aware. I have people
> reporting to me from many different places. I cannot make assumptions
> about what they want from me and how they want me to deal with them.
> I have to have flexibility, especially when I think about developing my own
> people. I want to develop HR leaders from places other than the U.K. or the
> U.S. because our presence in Eastern Europe and Russia is growing. We
> have to think about the competency model we are using in our organization.
> Does the framework need to change to address the realities and needs of
> where our employees will be coming from in the future? Moving from one

region to the next means dealing with such ambiguities, finding different solutions, and making sure that you absolutely understand your colleagues and clients—plus listening and clarifying to a much greater degree."

This was a common theme among the coaches. They all said that it was critical to not make hasty assumptions about their clients' cultural backgrounds or work experiences. Similarly, the coaches consistently said that they had to be vigilant about not imposing their own cultural assumptions on their clients.

Abigail Kwong, a regional HR partner for APAC, is a native of Taiwan working in Citi's Singapore office. She has also worked in South Korea, China, and Taiwan and speaks Mandarin, English, Cantonese, and Taiwanese. She described how she learned that so-called common sense can vary from one location to another.

"When I first started working globally, I thought that there was black and there was white. Then I began to see that 'right' has many different shapes. There are different standards, not one set of standards. Working globally, it is all relative. What is acceptable in one society is not the same as what is acceptable in others. The client's values must be understood. For example, I was coaching a leader from mainland China during the time when private enterprise first started there. For me, pricing was straightforward; there is a value, in monetary terms, for almost all objects. To him, there was no so-called market and, therefore, the valuation of an object was a big task. We take for granted what is common knowledge, but where this person came from, everything was starting from scratch. My 'common sense' could not dominate the discussion. This seems trivial, but the principle behind it is that 'common sense' is not common in other environments."

Brian Goodman, who works in Executive Development for Citi in New York, has been an executive coach for five years, working mostly with North American and Latin American clients. Brian previously lived in Mexico City for nine years, where he learned Spanish. Brian's early lessons have also had an important impact on his role as a coach, even when it comes to how to view people within the same cultural group.

"As a coach, one needs to be really cautious in making any assumptions. When you look at a bell curve, differences between two groups are often less than the differences within the groups. Just as there will be someone who epitomizes the culture, there will be someone who does not. I try

156

to understand people on their own terms. I have to constantly ask myself when coaching across cultures, 'What am I bringing to the table?' and then challenging those assumptions by asking myself, 'Are there other ways that individuals can be thinking about this?' I have to be aware that I am interpreting through my lens."

In any new coaching engagement, forming a relationship takes time, but the Citi coaches were quick to point out that coaching across cultures requires even more time and careful focus on getting to know the client. As Brian pointed out, "I am from a task-orientated background, so I have a high need to show that I am adding value. Now I realize that I have to open the space for clients to fill in as much as they would like to. I have to get to know people in a different way, being careful and respectful of their life history."

Learning about how one's cultural background influences coaching is a lifelong process for coaches. Larissa Durant, who already speaks Breton, English, and Danish, offered this anecdote.

"The feedback that I got back from my 360-raters when they completed the *Global Leadership Online* survey was extremely beneficial. I had selected raters who were colleagues outside of the U.K. office because I wanted frank feedback. What they told me was that I needed to make progress around cultural self-awareness. This was so striking to me, as I didn't think that I could get more self-aware. I saw myself as a fully formed global leader. But actually I can, and I will do a lot more work in this area. This prompted me to put myself in the shoes of someone who wants to learn about another culture, and so I have begun learning German. Curiosity and lust for learning are global leadership traits. It is really a never-ending journey of learning."

Invite the Unexpected

Abigail Kwong's early experiences working for a large U.S. multinational in Korea taught her the value of understanding her cultural assumptions as well as inviting the unexpected to be able to better anticipate difficulties. As the country HR leader at that time, she was called upon to work through union issues during an acquisition of the company's Korean business partner. In South Korea, where the union was very strong and an integral part of the country's culture, the negotiations were difficult, and she was surprised and chagrined by what happened next.

"We ended up with a strike on our hands for sixteen months. This was a very good learning experience for me personally. I realized afterwards that there were things we could have done to make this deal smoother and to have avoided the strike. I had to learn how to win the hearts and the minds of business leaders. To form the strategy, you have to work with the employees from the top to the bottom."

Having encountered this very unexpected event in a previous phase of her career, Abigail was able to put her knowledge and experience to use elsewhere.

"In another company, working in Taiwan, we were merging with a local bank and I was able to apply the lessons and the experience from Korea. There were many showstoppers for this deal that put HR directly in the center of the negotiations, which took two years. We were able to dissolve the labor union in this case. We had better due diligence. Being mindful of the cultural differences and how that impacts strategy was what made the difference. The merger experiences in Korea and Taiwan helped me to understand the importance of the society, the mentality, and the values of the people I am working with."

Abigail is now trying to more consciously integrate the behavior *invite the unexpected*, into her coaching practice with every new engagement.

"'Invite the unexpected' puts a label to something that I was doing subconsciously. Learning about it at the conference, it now comes to the conscious level. I realize that sometimes I search for the answer rather than listen for the unknown. This is intuitively contradictory. How can you know what you don't know? How can you listen for something that you don't know is there? I believe that, when coaching someone from another part of the business or another country, you must pay attention and be aware of the fact that there are some things you cannot know. You must cue yourself to ask, 'Is this an area I don't know about? Where is this person coming from? Why is he bringing that up?' Coaches must help themselves to shape the context for this person so that they can then work with that context. Even people within the same culture or society cannot assume that they know one another. Every coaching experience is a learning experience. I learn about the business. I learn about the person and appreciate the differences between two people.

This is what makes coaching so interesting. Every coaching experience is a mind-challenge."

Frame-Shifting

Brian Goodman cited differences in communication style that he experienced early in his professional career to illustrate how he learned to play a useful role in facilitating *frame-shifting* between cultural groups.

"I was a translator for an oil company. One of the clients was a brokerage planning a joint venture with a company from the U.K. The U.K. company sent a global head of operations. He came into the Mexico office and needed to make things happen in a culture he didn't know well. He decided to keep me on to help support him and I became his chief of staff, acting as a liaison between the North American, Mexican, and U.K. offices. I was coordinating between these countries, arbitrating selfish impulses, misunderstandings, and judgments from all sides. It was a very important learning experience, straddling these cultures. I tried hard to create positive working relationships between New York, London, and Mexico City executives. Each group had its own biases that would become apparent during the negotiations. For instance, the Mexican team would have a very hard time saying 'no' and had a strong desire to please. The U.S. and U.K. teams were very straightforward, negotiating in a linear fashion, making concessions in response to what they thought were past concessions from the Mexican team. Then later, when the deal was nearly done, the Mexicans would reopen the negotiations. These became sore points that would flare up in future discussions. I started to recognize that an outside perspective was valuable, and that I could make an important contribution by staying 'outside' and giving my views on the situation. This was where my experience has been most rich—pulling together initiatives with diverse groups."

Pio Arcuni was a credit analyst and trader at other financial institutions before joining Citi in 1993 as a foreign exchange trader. He continued on the business side until 2003, when he became the human resources officer for Italy. Today, in addition to his coaching responsibilities, Pio is the HR partner for Western Europe working out of the Milan office. He speaks Italian, English, and basic French.

As we have seen from previous chapters, leaders must continually adapt their styles to the local environment. Pio has run into the need to frame-shift with respect to his own assumptions about the stance a leader should take regarding input from team members, and how this affects the efforts of the coach.

> "I was working with a business manager in Eastern Europe, and I did 360-degree stakeholder interviews with his team to get their input. You would think that the team would see his transparent approach as a gift. But some of the senior team members said, 'He is the manager; he should know how to deal with things and not ask us.' This was a surprise for me."

Jane McGill works in the New York office for Citi as a senior leadership training manager and executive coach. Jane's father was a diplomat, and she spent her childhood in a succession of locations across the world: France, Cypress, Lebanon, Turkey, Pakistan, London, and the Philippines. Jane notes that although this kind of thoroughly international experience may help her and people of like background to calmly encounter differences that others find shocking, it does not exempt them from the need to challenge their own paradigms in order to lead in a more inclusive way.

> "I know from personal experience that living and traveling in very different cultures can lead to tolerance, acceptance, and a decreased possibility of being shocked or dismayed at some of the more drastic differences one observes. However, that openness does not necessarily translate into the kind of inclusiveness we know matters in building global effectiveness in an organization. I think there may be a pitfall for global leaders who think that because they have lived outside their home country they are automatically inclusive, without putting the true thought and work into that paradigm shift. As a coach, I need to remind myself that merely having lived in other countries does not lead to the kind of inclusive leadership behaviors we encourage and that, in fact, some people with this kind of life experience may become complacent and make less effort than is required because they give themselves, in essence, a 'pass.'"

Larissa Durant links frame-shifting with another global leadership behavior, *core values and flexibility*.

> "'Frame-shifting' is a competency that I really like and use. This is also linked with 'core values and flexibility.' I am inclined to build my coaching practice

around this ambiguous place: What are the coachee's core values and beliefs and how does this inform their perspective? With this as my frame of reference, I am in a position to help them come to a good decision. I think that, for me, frame-shifting means broadening my horizon in terms of understanding human behavior and human nature. It is about how we approach leadership—being aware of our own leadership style. Coaches have to be able to do this consciously. Clients bring you problems, and you may have your own solution, but frame-shifting for the coach is about putting your own solutions aside and going with the coachee on a journey to find his or her own solution. This may not be a solution that comes from your values, but one that you have to accept is right for them."

COACHES: SUPPORTING GLOBAL LEADERS

Since the Citi Coach Conference, the coaches have also been using the ten key behaviors as a framework for coaching in their work with business partners. *Results through relationships, adapt and add value, influence across boundaries*, and *third-way solutions* were among the behaviors they cited most often. Their clients are sophisticated global leaders in their own right, and the coaches noted that they are lifelong learners, too, eager to continue developing their leadership skills. As Pio Arcuni commented:

"My clients are problem solvers who can make the matrix work, who have good connections and know how to motivate people outside their responsibilities to make something happen. The common denominator is eagerness to develop themselves further and a commitment to coaching as a tool to get there. The important differentiator for global leaders is their commitment to lifelong learning."

Results through Relationships

Pio's clients are mostly chief country officers (CCOs) and regional heads who represent the bank in local markets. His CCO clients must be able to work within the constraints of the local market while still meeting the demands of headquarters. They share the common challenges of needing to quickly establish credibility with not only the local offices, but with governmental officials, clients, regulators, and other outside constituencies. Obtaining results through relationships is a common challenge for these clients.

"In one set of stakeholder interviews for a CCO from Southern Europe, the employees said of the manager, 'He is so remote and reserved; he is missing important signals and relationships throughout the organization because he is perceived as distant.' I told him to go and meet more with the people, ask them what they need. This tells you something about perceptions. I encourage them to be aware of the culture and to understand the impact they are having on the environment."

Pio cited another example of an executive who was able to achieve his objectives through adroit focus on relationships in the initial stages of an assignment.

"I worked with a client once who had to do some restructuring. This leader was technically proficient and knew the market very well. He was thrown into the local culture where it is difficult to get support and to be recognized as a leader due to strong leadership styles and personalities. The risk is in needing to make changes but having the local managers say, 'Who are you to come here and make these changes?' He took the time to listen. He was approachable, open, and caring. He had to talk to the people, build relationships. He had immense pressure to immediately focus on the task at hand, but was clever enough to stop and invite the team's feedback first. On the other hand, if the leader had shown a lot of interest in the people but then had not taken action for them, this would not have been good. I coach my clients to show openness but to follow with action, to make good on promises, as this is also inherent in the relationship. If not, you lose credibility. This is leading through relationships."

Adapt and Add Value

As in the previous example, leaders not only need to get started on the right foot and take the time to build relationships, but also demonstrate the value they bring and ultimately take action. *Adapt and add value* is a common challenge for these leaders, as Pio continued:

"They need to understand the environment first. It is risky to make changes without first understanding what is going on and creating common ground from which to implement your changes. The leaders must have an open agenda from the beginning, to the extent that this is possible. They must learn to build bridges with the local team, be approachable, think about what scares people and deal with their anxieties from the very beginning, creating a secure environment. You make an impression in the first thirty seconds but it can take a lifetime to undo it if it is not right. I coach my clients that it is important to establish that you know what you are talking about from the very beginning. Yet these initial steps also require a lot of humility in order to understand the environment. The locals are always asking global leaders, 'Why do I need you?' The leader needs to make clear, 'This is the help I can provide to you and the help that I need from you.' They need to enter a contract where there is an exchange."

Brian Goodman provided another example of such trade-offs, which may mean working long days to establish relationships and to respond to the professional development needs of subordinates while still pushing for performance.

"I was coaching a client from the U.K. in the Hong Kong office who has worked in several countries over the years. There were six people waiting to see him outside his office door. He asked me, 'How do I spend my time here as a manger in Hong Kong? Face time with the managers is so important; it requires that I really think through how to orchestrate my day. I feel sometimes, however, that they are very aggressive and demanding about their own development and advancement, but they drag their feet on the things I am asking them to execute.'

"This leader wanted to be respectful of local protocols but also push hard to get them to perform: 'I tell them that I am in this role because of my subject matter expertise and what I have been able to accomplish. I want them to be open to new ways of working, while still being sensitive to their expertise and needs.' We worked together on ways that he could shift his values and get comfortable with other ways of working while still being effective, but he continued to put in very long hours."

Influence across Boundaries

Bandwidth, which in this context means the leader's ability to exert influence across organizational functions and layers, is another common challenge for the global clients of our coaches. Abigail Kwong described it this way.

"One has to be more politically savvy when working globally. You get pulled into different layers and discussions, especially in an organization the size of Citi, with so many matrix lines. In a global role the bandwidth is wider and global leaders therefore need to be able to process a wider spectrum of data. They need to be able to 'play checkers' better. The playbook is much bigger and the requirement is for a broader and deeper understanding."

Larissa Durant noted that this bandwidth challenge also involves both ambiguity and complexity.

"The global leader has to deal with ambiguity in terms of the problems, which tend to be a lot more complex, spanning countries and businesses matrices."

Pio Arcuni described the need for local, regional, and global influence, and the capacity to serve as an ambassador between different locations.

"It becomes essential for the global leader to have links with regional centers and help the local people who don't understand what is happening at this level, and who maybe don't know who to go to in order to get things done. I once coached a leader who had never lived outside his home country. His direct reports were saying that he needed an international assignment to expand his network because they believed that his weakness was in being too insular. We got him into a training program in the States as a part of his development plan as well as travel to other offices to establish relationships face-to-face. The leader has to have the ability to be an ambassador to the other regions and to headquarters. Even if it is not in the person's job description, it is essential."

Third-Way Solutions

The coaches all said that they were impressed at how their clients grappled with *third-way solutions*, constantly walking the line between accepting the mandates and business drivers of headquarters while being open to new ways of doing business that would benefit the local office.

Pio described the daunting challenge of bridging different matrix priorities and perspectives in an even-handed way, which requires leveraging a global network of relationships while working within the context of a particular organizational culture.

"I was working with a client in Central Europe once who was originally from India. He needed to leverage relationships across product lines and regional centers to get more support for the local office. Sometimes people get bogged down with local requirements and don't prioritize these relationships with the other offices and businesses. I have noticed that people on assignments spend most of their energies locally, but I tell them that they need to work with the matrix and regional centers and have good relationships across boundaries; otherwise, they cannot make things happen. The leader needs to make the regional stakeholders aware and get their support. We all need these relationships to navigate the complexity in organizations today. I coach them to have regular one-on-one calls with these remote managers. The ideal country manager is someone with local and international experience, with good knowledge of the matrix. They must have local relationships but not be driven by the local culture. You don't need to be a dictator to be a leader in Russia, but you need to be aware of the culture. Knowing the matrix, knowing the company culture, and knowing how to resolve issues and gain credibility across these different 'boundaries'—all of these are needed. Company culture is another culture that you must be aware of, and it may be the most important because that culture is the glue, the common denominator in a company."

Larissa Durant talked about different functional orientations and the crucial need to create third-way solutions among the company's silos.

"A global leader coming from a background that is very structured and process-oriented struggles more with third-way solutions than others in finding a way to be creative and still meet the objectives of the client and company. When I think in terms of innovation, this is a competency that we are trying to develop much more in our senior management team. There are cultural differences among businesses as well. There is a difference, for example, between the functional culture of the Operations and Technology [O&T] group and the investment bankers in this regard. Coming from a technology or an engineering background, O&T leaders are more black-and-white and process-oriented, and therefore finding third-way solutions is more of a challenge for them than for those in perhaps sales or banking. I think that our functional culture is changing. We are working hard to make this happen and are now are seeing an improvement in creativity and third-way solutions without compromising our relationship with our clients. We are dealing with ambiguity in a more effective way."

Brian Goodman also spoke about developing integrated solutions, even across silos and functional subcultures.

> "There are cultures within cultures in the bank. My clients are highly evolved leaders, but their success is intertwined with these environments, and these interdependencies are so embedded. It really comes down to a virtuous cycle or a vicious cycle. In my coaching, I encourage the virtuous cycle: getting the coaches to check all stakeholder needs first before developing solutions."

Brian works with clients to help them to both frame-shift in terms of communication style and signal to others that they are willing to strive for solutions with collective benefits.

> "I was coaching a client from South America who was working in the Miami office, with Latin America [LATAM] responsibilities. Each country in LATAM is so unique; there are cultures where hierarchy is more pronounced and politeness, gentility, and formality are very important. This person's strengths were her clarity of thinking, incisiveness, and an analytical mind. Many of the cultures had an issue with her delivery, her directness, and they said that she did not appear to respect their competence and expertise. Then link this to being part of a company with its headquarters in New York, and there is a complex interplay of all these cultures that she has to navigate. Sometimes the question of bridging across boundaries is a matter of signaling intentions. If she wants to move up, she will have to move beyond herself and the team's interest and think about the larger, collective 'we.' She will need to get better about knowing where and how she adds value and how to leverage these strengths."

COACHING PRACTICES

The Citi coaches portrayed in this chapter indicate a number of ways that they have incorporated the ten key leadership behaviors into their work with clients to better grasp their challenges or to help them achieve their goals. The following more specific examples, based upon previous executive coaching work, were presented to them during their training conference. Analyzing these vignettes can help coaches from any organization augment their preexisting coaching repertoire by diagnosing and addressing the need for particular global leadership behaviors.

EXAMPLE 1: **THE DRIVER**

Client A is a real driver. He likes to get things done, and he will run over people, if necessary, to do it. In his mind, the tough management approach that he takes reflects the company's corporate culture, and employees either need to learn to deal with it or find a different place to work. He tends to speak very directly and forcefully to people, with little variation depending upon whom he is speaking with. Some of his company colleagues and direct reports, particularly those from Asia Pacific, say they prefer to avoid him because they are uncomfortable with his temper. In addition, he frequently misinterprets positive-sounding messages as indicating agreement or commitment, when others are simply trying to please him but do not necessarily agree at all; this has led to further misunderstandings and confrontations. Most seriously, he has developed adversarial relationships with two other functional groups that his own team needs to collaborate with smoothly in order to be effective—in both cases he was critical of the other groups for not delivering results they had allegedly made a firm commitment to provide.

Possible Interpretation and Coaching Strategy: The colleagues and direct reports of this team leader—most notably those from Asia—are likely to have a less direct approach to communication and be put off by his forceful communication style. Their indirect approach to communication might also be the key to comprehending the missed deliverables. They could be saying "no" to project deadlines in a way that cannot be heard by the leader, who is taking their silence or positive-sounding messages to signify assent. The team members avoiding him because of his temper might also be those who shirk from anger or other demonstrations of strong emotion in favor of at least the display of outward group harmony.

This client could benefit from learning all of the ten key leadership behaviors, and he is unlikely to be successful without them. An effective coaching approach would probably combine concrete feedback based upon solid evidence with an invitation to learn more about global leadership in order to advance to the next career step. *Cultural self-awareness* would be a good place to start. This coachee seems to assume that his personal communication style and values are in line with the company values and therefore are universal. He is coming to premature conclusions about the level of agreement he is getting from team members and the capabilities of other groups. Scratching the surface of polite head-nodding might yield a different result. For instance, asking his colleagues in a more open-ended way about the extent to which they have the resources and time to meet commitments would be a good way to discern if "yes" really

167

means "yes" or rather "I hear you." Cultivating *frame-shifting* and a balance between *core values and flexibility* might also be among the subsequent steps for this leader; the coaching dialogue with him could include questions about what is most important to him in the workplace and what he is willing to let go. He may discover along the way that he can start to build more reciprocal communication that leads to new discoveries, and that there is more than one way to accomplish the same objectives.

EXAMPLE 2: **THE SUCCESSFUL EXECUTIVE**

Client B is a relatively high-ranking and successful executive. He set several key objectives for himself six months ago that he has now achieved. As you speak with him today in your coaching session, you notice that he seems to be very pleased and satisfied with the progress he has made, and does not express an urgent need to do further work on the areas that you have discussed thus far. His sense of satisfaction begins to make you wonder to yourself whether you have come far enough in this coaching relationship to bring it to a conclusion. However, you also know from speaking to some of this executive's direct reports in Central Europe that they feel he is not sufficiently well-informed about market conditions there—he seems to assume that these markets are similar to other markets that he has already encountered. Meanwhile, several rapidly growing local competitors have become very nimble and innovative in meeting customer needs. To expand his line of business, a next step could be to develop a more differentiated set of product offerings for this region.

Possible Interpretation and Coaching Strategy: This client may be overly complacent in light of the market situation in Central Europe. While congratulating him on his success to date, the coach could also ask whether he is fully satisfied with the situation in Central Europe, and inquire how he might find out more and take action if necessary. There are many ways for the coachee to determine whether serious concern is justified: spending time on-site to see and hear for himself; seeking out fresh sources of competitive data; and/or cultivating deeper relationships with employees, customers, or outside advisors who are willing to speak frankly. The most crucial factor is for him to deliberately consider if he should *invite the unexpected* and then to listen carefully to any data that emerge. If the client decides to take on this challenge, knowing that the situation in this market could be different from what he has been accustomed to, the result might be a new-found sense of urgency about competitors and product offerings.

EXAMPLE 3: **THE PEOPLE PERSON**

Client C manages a fairly large functional unit, and she has a strong reputation as a "people person." When you first met with her, it seemed to you that she had a viable plan for leading the group and developing its members. Her objectives included working with several experienced direct reports to help them take on greater responsibilities so that she herself could take a more strategic and forward-looking role. Now that you have met her a second time, you observe that although there is still some distance to go, she has indeed made good progress in the direction of developing key people in her group. As you speak with her, she comes up with several new ideas for further accelerating this development process. The primary limitation in her leadership development activities to date seems to be that she is most focused on developing reports who are in close physical proximity to her own location, or with whom she has the most regular interactions; she has placed less emphasis on identifying and cultivating high-potential future leaders who are more remote.

Possible Interpretation and Coaching Strategy: This client appears to be quite self-aware and proactive, and she has significant strengths. One area for improvement that would extend her preexisting strengths might be for her to *develop future leaders* who are in other locations. It is easy for leaders to unintentionally neglect dispersed team members—those who are "out of sight and out of mind"—in favor of people whom they encounter every day. This is especially true when cultural and linguistic differences mean that greater effort is required to communicate and to coordinate tasks with others at a distance. Because this client already has good people instincts and is evidently eager to develop her subordinates, the coach could focus on questions that encourage her to further examine and address the leadership potential and developmental needs of employees who are working at distant sites: "Have you designated any of the managers working for you in other locations as 'high potential'? How well do you know them? Are you confident that their capabilities have been accurately assessed to date? What are their primary developmental areas? What are you doing now to cultivate their skills? How can you ensure that people in remote locations have growth opportunities of the same caliber as those for the people who are colocated with you? Are there other forms of developmental support for people elsewhere that could augment what you do in your leadership role? What kinds of next steps do you think would make sense? What are you willing to do?"

EXAMPLE 4: **THE PROJECT TEAM LEADER**

Client D is a managing director from Denmark who has accepted a long-term project assignment to get a new customer up and running across many product lines for the company. Given the number of departments and subject matter experts involved, there are six people reporting to her from the United States, the United Kingdom, Denmark, and Singapore. These individuals are at various levels in the organization: VPs, directors, and managing directors (MDs). About two weeks into the project, your client got a call from the English regional MD, who was very angry and told your client that he will not work with the U.S. VP on the team because he is steamrolling the group, making decisions before including others' opinions, and not taking direction from him, the regional MD. This MD from the U.K. had spoken with the U.S. VP, who said he was following instructions that he claimed to have received directly from the project leader. Your client, the Denmark MD in charge of the project, is anxious to make a great impression in this stretch assignment but has told you that the issue between the UK MD and the U.S. VP seems to be a standoff that will impact the due dates and deliverables that have been promised to the new customer. Your client wants to know what you think she should do.

Possible Interpretation and Coaching Strategy: The client must first be able to draw upon her *cultural self-awareness.* Is she assuming that an independent, egalitarian style should be the norm for accomplishing tasks in this team? What has she done to gauge the culturally based predilections of her team members? Based on the evidence presented so far, it seems that the UK MD could have a more hierarchical leadership style than the U.S. VP, who is more egalitarian in his approach. If it is the client's intention to *expand ownership* among team members, another question for the coach to ask is whether and how she might be more explicit about roles and responsibilities on the team. This could mean specifying when team members are empowered to take independent action and when they are not, or looking for ways to bridge different styles and to build shared norms for sharing information and arriving at decisions together. If the team's decision-making structure contradicts traditional lines of authority or assumptions about the regional MD's sphere of control, the client needs to be explicit about the change and her expectations; this will give both the U.S. VP and the regional MD the opportunity to *frame-shift* more effectively. Finally, given the complex nature of the project and the fact that many different company units will be working with the same customer, the coach could bring to her attention questions related to *influence across boundaries.* Are her team members already able to work fluidly across a global matrix, or is more effort needed to engage vital stakeholders? Is she allowing her team members to make decisions about the rollout process or what is best for the customer without consulting sufficiently with one another, or can she help to create a more virtuous cycle of mutual consultation and input in preparation for the project launch?

Although in this chapter we have used the terms "coach" and "client" (coachee), the applications are much broader than a formal coaching relationship with an external or internal coach. Nearly every executive who seeks to foster the growth of future global leaders must assume the role of a coach, identifying both the strengths and skill gaps of possible successors along with other high-potential talent, and working together with them to develop new capabilities. The ten key behaviors provide executives, too, with a practical roadmap for evaluating and developing future global leaders that they can use in their day-to-day coaching work. This framework is also applicable in more structured formats such as *leader-led action learning*, which will be discussed in Chapter 11.

CHAPTER **TEN**

Teaming the Ten Behaviors

Leveraging the Leadership Behaviors for Shared Vision

A great deal has been written about the tactical challenges of leading global teams, especially in the areas of virtual communication technologies and cultural dynamics. For the global leaders involved in our research, however, the most significant challenge is creating and maintaining a shared focus. In this chapter, we will explore how several of the global leadership behaviors outlined in earlier chapters can be used to create and implement a common sense of direction in a global team.

How can a team leader create a common vision and shared goals when leading a team that spans boundaries of geography, culture, and function? Our interviewees acknowledged that aligning the work of team members is difficult even in a domestic team, but emphasized that global and virtual dynamics add significant complexity. In spite of long, successful track records in high-level domestic leadership positions, even the most senior executives struggle to create a shared vision within their global teams, citing it as their key challenge.[1] So what is being lost in the translation of this key leadership capability from a domestic environment to a global one?

Differences in market environments and commonsense assumptions about how to do business are more pronounced for members of global teams than for teams whose participants work in the same domestic environment. In our work with hundreds of global teams, a lack of knowledge-sharing systems has been cited as one of the key obstacles to implementing shared goals. Global team members typically lack sufficient insight into their colleagues' skills and potential contributions. This fosters isolation and duplicate work, and sets up obstacles to the exchange of best practices, preventing team members from working collaboratively toward a common goal.

Global organizations also typically have a matrix structure in which it is quite common for individuals to belong to a number of teams simultaneously. This matrix dynamic means that team members are linked with a variety of "stakeholders," each bearing competing priorities that reflect the needs of different functions, business units, and geographies. For all these reasons it is more difficult for the individual members of a global team to consistently identify how their efforts fit into the "bigger picture," and a shared vision becomes both more essential and more challenging to create and maintain.[2]

Virtual communication challenges further contribute to the issues global leaders face when trying to create a shared vision and goals for their teams. Our interviewees indicated that a clear sense of direction, even in the midst of tremendous complexity, is a crucial factor in the success of globally dispersed teams. Their comments are supported by others with special expertise in this area:

> "Successful leaders of virtual teams clearly articulate team goals and direction and continually revisit these over time so team members have a shared target. Although important to any kind of team, clear team goals are especially crucial for members of virtual teams because the members are given a sense of purpose and meaning that sustains them when they are working alone or without regular direct contact with the team leader or other team members. Clear goals also help to unify the actions of a globally dispersed team and keep the team members focused on execution."[3]

While recognizing the heightened importance of establishing shared direction within a global, virtual team, the more traditional team literature seldom speaks of the distinct skills required to accomplish this in a global environment. The global team leaders in our study stressed the unique nature of their roles and the inadequacy of domestic leadership models to prepare them to be successful in a truly global environment.

Leadership Behaviors for Global Teams

Which leadership behaviors are the most critical for achieving a common direction within a globally dispersed team? All ten behaviors play an important role in the success of a global team leader, but our research suggests that the most important behaviors to leverage are:

- *Invite the unexpected*
- *Frame-shifting*
- *Influence across boundaries*

While we will look at each of these global leadership behaviors individually as they relate to creating and implementing a shared sense of team direction, they are actually interconnected and mutually dependent.

INVITE THE UNEXPECTED

What does a global team leader need to know to create a vision and goals that will resonate with team members from around the world? Team leaders must of course carefully consider the complex functional, market, and regulatory factors already cited, including how these issues will influence the ways that team members interpret and implement common goals. Moreover, the leader must take into account other factors, such as what motivates team members as well as the best means to tap into this kind of vital information. As one interviewee working in Brazil told us:

> "When dealing with individual team members and what they respond to in a global context, it requires a bigger tool box because people are motivated very differently. There is a much broader range of what motivates my team members in Brazil: they like feeling part of a team, they are interested in learning more about our industry, and so on. It is more challenging to learn my team members' interests because those interests are much more diverse. The motivational goal of earning money is less valued in places such as Brazil or in France. My team members in both these countries come from more of a socialist culture. So appealing to folks to work hard in order to make money for the company shareholders does not motivate them. They do not value capitalism for its own sake as a key driver. I had to really work to understand their motivation and create a development plan that allowed them to see how our work was meeting their motivational drivers. As a team leader, I needed to broaden my skills in order to motivate along a broader set of interests. Even finding out about their motivations requires a different approach than in a domestic context. In Brazil, those conversations cannot start in the office. I had to earn trust over meals, away from work. I had to use a different way of getting to know people and employ a broader range of drivers than I did in North America."

One of the greatest obstacles for leaders and team members working in a global environment may be what they think they already know. Past successes have produced a level of confidence in certain approaches and the assumptions

Global Leader: Birgit Masjost, Roche

Dr. Birgit Masjost leads the technical development team at Roche, a major pharmaceutical company, and is based at Roche headquarters in Basel, Switzerland. Her first language is German, and she also speaks French, but she works primarily in English with her team members.

Birgit's technical development team is a subset of Roche's overall development team, and her team members are based across the globe, representing all of Roche's global sites for technical activities. These sites include Germany, Japan, Switzerland, and four sites in the United States—Boulder, Colorado; Nutley, New Jersey; Florence, South Carolina; and Palo Alto, California. She is also working closely with Chinese team members from the company's new development center in China. Within the Basel, Switzerland, site alone, her team members represent a diverse group, hailing from the United Kingdom, Germany, France, and Italy. As the technical development leader (TDL), Birgit also works broadly across several departments and teams located around the globe.

With so many different sites and cultures involved, a primary challenge for Birgit is creating alignment around a shared vision. Her job is further complicated by the multiple time zones in which team members reside and a virtual communication environment. Most of Birgit's team members, including Birgit herself, speak English as their second or third language, and misunderstandings are common. In addition, team members working at various sites and partner companies often have different organizational systems in place within their respective environments. For example, Birgit's U.S. colleagues work with a unified approval process for trials of new drugs under the U.S. Food and Drug Administration. This contrasts with Europe, where every country has its own health authority and requirements. Birgit's team must create technical procedures that work for all these locations and their different needs. She says, "Some people have different systems in place in their environment, but others don't have the context on that system. Team members should have a chance to explain the context and what they really need. Typically it is very important for teams to communicate a lot."

The circumstances under which Birgit leads her team could easily become fragmented, clouding the team's vision and slowing down the team's progress. Their overall goal is to bring drugs and medical devices through the trial process as quickly as possible while meeting all legal requirements, and thereby gain a competitive advantage in the market. To prevent fragmentation of their efforts, it is crucial for Birgit's team members to each "know what they don't know" so they can have the essential context for understanding their colleagues' different systems and requirements.

Within this global, virtual environment, Birgit has tapped into practices that help her to *invite the unexpected* as a means of gaining alignment. Fundamental to these practices are strong relationships. Birgit believes that these relationships are impossible to build through email, and thus insists on a face-to-face meeting to start things off. She wants team members to know one another and to have the chance to bond through team-building exercises—during one off-site retreat, for example, they learned to row a boat together. "No one knew how to do this, so we had to learn it together and work together. We could see the impact if one person was doing something different, and the impact of different styles." Thanks to such events, subsequent communication with one another improves immensely in their normal virtual, dispersed interactions. Through the initial face-to-face meetings, Birgit has also created a shared sense of meaning that influences her team's work patterns even when she is not present. "It is part of the team's culture now to always ask for a lot of input from fellow members before moving forward: 'Is this aligned with your system? Is this a strategy that you would like to follow?'"

As the TDL, Birgit herself gains insights into her team members' different working styles through these face-to-face meetings, understanding their questions and needs better in light of this knowledge. For example, when working with her Japanese colleagues with the company Chugai in Japan, Birgit often struggled with how to include them in the team's decision-making process. When she would address an issue during a meeting, her Japanese colleagues would often remain silent. Even after she asked them directly for their opinions during the meeting, her Japanese colleagues rarely spoke up but would then come back several days later to express their disagreement with her. By learning her colleagues' working style, Birgit now knows to wait a couple days after the official meeting before rolling out a solution in order to receive this feedback. And after she had met with her Japanese team members several times and had built a relationship with them, they also better understood her working style and became more comfortable providing her with direct feedback.

For important team decisions, Birgit does her best to ensure that everyone is on board to encourage thorough discussions and to prevent unanticipated problems. "Our decision-making process is mostly consensus based. My experience has been that if this is not the case, the topic will need to come back on the table at some other point. Usually we come up with a compromise. In a very few cases, we need to escalate an issue to the management decision board. This doesn't happen often, as we tend to agree on the most reasonable thing. By discussing and explaining our reasons to each other, we gain understanding. People want to be involved or else there is resistance. It is better to involve more people in the decision to prevent this resistance."

Birgit also leverages several knowledge-sharing practices as a means of addressing the "unexpected" aspects of her team members' diverse contexts. When working with the different sites, a TDL often does not know the standard procedures in other countries. However, it is essential to navigate these regulations for a successful project. Birgit has learned the procedures by making short-term visits to the most important sites for the team, staying three to four weeks at each. "As a team leader," she says, "it is essential to understand the background of what my team members are saying and be able to make sound judgments on that basis." Birgit also sees the value of this for her team members and ensures that the team's face-to-face meeting sites are always rotated, so that it is not always the regions traveling to headquarters. This allows team members the opportunity to gain firsthand experience of others' working environments.

In addition to Birgit's personal efforts, Roche has set up a successful one-year exchange program between Japan and Basel, Switzerland, that has allowed both Japanese and European employees to spend time working in one another's environments. Roche also hires many Chugai employees directly into positions in Basel as a means of instilling their knowledge within company headquarters. Because systems such as governmental procedures for doing a trial are so different for each country, colleagues begin to get a real sense of the challenges faced by their team members and consequently are able to anticipate their unique needs. Thus, these exchanges have made it much easier for Basel to deliver the things that Japan needs in order to get approval for a study.

Birgit has also been able to overcome some of the challenges of the "unexpected" by participating in a knowledge-sharing system specifically created for her twenty-two fellow TDLs. This group meets once every two weeks and has workshops twice a year. The meetings feature one or two TDLs sharing their experience with a project along with any new discoveries. The TDL group uses the workshops to invite presenters from other parts of the company to share interesting developments and gain a holistic picture of the organization's work.

Birgit is enthusiastic about these practices. "We have a great knowledge-sharing system. We exchange experiences that we have in Tech Dev with our colleagues. We exchange all sorts of technical experiences, communicated very well. If I know that I have a problem, I will look up who has had a similar issue. We use the workshops to invite people from different parts of the company and then there are two days just for knowledge-sharing presentations. In my staff meetings I also have one or two colleagues talk about their projects or new information or experiences. This is working very well. We have an intranet for our department, and all our information goes on this website, too."

> Birgit has access to a broad range of knowledge across the organization's diverse sites and functions, has created hybrid processes for exchanging views and making decisions, and is committed to building strong relationships with team members regardless of their location. These practices have helped her to foster a shared sense of direction among team members while enabling them to overcome their challenges together. As a global team leader, she strategically positions herself and the entire team to *invite the unexpected*, ensuring that her team members have a shared sense of meaning and common goals across their various functional, geographical, and cultural borders.

on which they are based. But if the practice of creating a shared vision, for example, involves "unearthing shared 'pictures of the future' that foster genuine commitment and enrollment rather than compliance,"[4] global team leaders need to take special care to elicit viewpoints that contradict their own or take a different tack entirely. And all the members of a global team must learn how to engrain the custom of inviting the unexpected on a regular basis.

The pharmaceutical industry provides a good picture of the intricacies involved when working across borders—Birgit experiences a degree of complexity that is a reality for a number of different industries. Team members hail from a wide range of professional and educational backgrounds, including pharmacology, chemistry, physiology, biology, and marketing. And by design, drug-development teams represent diverse market perspectives, thus ensuring a sound development process in each location. So the functional perspectives present on the team must be integrated effectively with all the market and regulatory environments. How can a team leader build a shared picture of the future when heading up a team that holds such enormous diversity of perspectives and will rarely meet in person? The rich array of methods used by Birgit's team for inviting the unexpected are worth keeping in mind:

- Face-to-face kickoff meeting to build personal relationships
- Regular solicitation of information and input from team members regarding their local context
- Broad involvement of team members in decision making
- Waiting for feedback after meetings before rolling out solutions
- Short-term site visits by team leader
- Rotation of team meetings between different market locations to promote broader team member awareness

- Longer-term people exchange between key locations
- Hiring of foreign partner employees into headquarters positions to supplement a workforce that is already highly multicultural
- Knowledge sharing system between team leaders: two meetings per month; biannual workshops with presenters from different parts of the company

Such a list might take on a different form for another industry or corporate culture, but what is striking is the sheer number of practices that Birgit and her team have integrated to ensure that they are systematically learning from one another and from people in other parts of the organization.

There are additional ways for global team leaders to *invite the unexpected* by asking the right questions of team members and listening with a new intensity. Figure 10-1 provides a sample list of questions that leaders can ask to elicit key information from team members in a highly matrixed environment. Like the knowledge-sharing systems created by Birgit's technical development team at Roche, these questions will help to develop a shared sense of meaning and context from which to create a common vision and goals. The questions will also elicit key practical information to ensure that the team's goals can be implemented. The more concrete details all team members have about similarities and differences between their markets and those of others on the team, the easier it will be for them to collaborate for mutual benefit in achieving their business objectives. The Nobel Prize winner Naguib Mahfouz wrote,

---

Organizational Questions

Where do you fit in the organizational matrix?

Who are your key stakeholders and what do they expect and require of you?

What would a future picture of this team's success look like for you?

Do you have objectives related to this team already? How do your objectives fit with the overall organizational vision?

What are your current work priorities? What is the priority of this team's activities compared with the other teams you are on?

What functional or departmental differences do you need to bridge in the overall organization?

What other parts of our organization do you interact with? Are your current objectives aligned with or in conflict with those of any other part of the organization?

What else do I (the team leader) not know? What questions should I be asking to get more information?

FIGURE 10-1 Invite the Unexpected: Questions for Team Members (*continues*)

Local Environment Questions

What is your history with the organization? Is there any historical context that might impact your participation and your goals on this team?

Who have you worked with previously? To whom do you report locally, either in a direct line or by matrix?

How is our organization structured locally and how does this impact you?

Are there local resource, technical, or infrastructure constraints that could impact your ability to meet team goals?

Are there any particular local circumstances—customer needs, supply base, laws, internal or external politics—that the team needs to take into account in setting and implementing its goals?

What is your preferred mode of communication? Are the same methods available outside the "business day" if you are communicating from home?

What expectations do you face outside your team based on local culture, customs, or law?

What else do I (the team leader) not know? What questions should I be asking to get more information?

Personal Experience Questions

What is your understanding so far of this team's vision and goals? Is there anything missing? What would you like to add?

What motivates you personally in your everyday work? What aspects of the team's activities do you find most interesting or inspiring?

What particular knowledge or experience do you have to contribute to the team?

In the best teams you have participated on before, what were the standard team methods for:

- Getting to know each other
- Sharing information
- Meetings
- Decision making
- Identifying and resolving conflicts

Were there any best practices by a previous team leader or the team as a whole that you would like to see used on this team?

What are your expectations of me as the team leader?

What hours do you normally work? How do you try to balance your work and other parts of your life?

What are the most important holidays or family events for you?

How well do you know the other team members personally? Have you ever met any of them face-to-face?

Do you have any other specific hopes or concerns about your involvement with this team?

What are your professional development goals and how are they related to the direction of this team?

What else do I not know? What questions should I be asking to get more information?

FIGURE 10-1   Invite the Unexpected: Questions for Team Members (*continued*)

"You can tell whether a man is clever by his answers. You can tell whether a man is wise by his questions." Our interviewees agree that for global team leaders, the questions they ask of team members are critical, particularly in the early stages of team development.

Many of these questions can also be used to structure conversations between team members themselves as they are getting to know one another. It is important for the team to retain and build upon not only the formal exchanges between team members, but also the conversations that happen more naturally. Geetha, a global team leader working for an Indian IT services corporation, described how she tackled the challenge of knowledge sharing within her team by integrating both formal and informal conversations.

"In the Indian context, which is also my own context, a lot of dialogue and knowledge sharing happens informally, before or after a meeting. This was my biggest challenge in leading a dispersed team. Our meetings were only from ten until twelve... but what happens before and after the meeting, capturing this was the greatest challenge. We dealt with this in several ways. I set up frequent dialogue points between all the participants so that they would have multiple opportunities to share with one another. I also wove a time for informal talks into our meetings by creating an agenda item specifically for this and making a window for it to come out to the whole team: 'If you think that something relevant has come up from your informal conversations this week, here is the time to share that.' This made them think about their informal conversations and become conscious of how much information they were sharing informally. It also really built trust among the team as they were able to bring their informal conversations into the group setting and add value."

FRAME-SHIFTING

The global leaders interviewed in our research each encountered the unexpected in a variety of ways. As the organizational, local, and interpersonal circumstances of team members became more evident to them, these leaders were able to put themselves into others' shoes more readily and to shift their approach. Frame-shifting, as discussed in Chapter 4, can occur on several levels: communication style, leadership style, and strategy. The creation and implementation of a shared sense of team direction can be positively impacted by frame-shifting on all three of these levels.

Geetha, the global team leader from India, noted that she had to frame-shift in terms of her communication style, even though she was working with other native English speakers on her team. Working in India, Geetha was most comfortable relying on a very verbal communication style. However, when she took on a team based in both India and Australia, "verbal communication was where we went wrong the most." The familiar adage that the U.K. and the U.S. are two countries separated by a common language seems to hold true for India and Australia as well.

> "To deal with this, I stipulated that from an operational standpoint, anything which needed to be communicated must first be communicated in writing and then team members could call to clarify, if necessary. I told them, 'If you feel you understand something differently, pick up the phone, but the first step should be email.' Then I also pulled in an Australian counterpart to work with me to review all the communication so that it translated well on a cultural level, to ensure shared understanding."

Birgit Masjost also altered her communication habits to better incorporate the input of Japanese team members into decisions. She learned to wait for their post-meeting contributions, allowing this to occur in a more private exchange rather than in the general team meeting. In addition, she invested time in building closer relationships to foster more direct communication at an earlier stage. During our interview with her, she outlined other measures a team leader can implement to ensure good communication among virtual team members.

- "Make sure that you are all talking the same language. Clarify jargon and abbreviations, always clarify terms, clarify language and meaning. Plan to schedule longer meetings than normal. If people are speaking in a second language, it takes longer for them to express themselves.
- "Write a draft agenda and ask people for agreement and input and then implement it during meetings.
- "Try to find out the most convenient meeting times for team members before scheduling one. Rotate meeting times as well.
- "Ask people frequently if the meeting process is okay with them. How many meetings would they like to have? How many face-to-face meetings do they want to hold? What about meeting length? You can also give your opinion as well. It's important to know others' preferences first so you know where the difficulties might come from."

In terms of leadership style, Birgit positions herself as a learner. This provides her with vital information while also allowing her to serve as a model for other team members in an information-intensive environment. She seeks to establish a team culture wherein each team member is trained to ask about and incorporate local constraints and processes before creating project plans. In addition to modeling a learning posture, Birgit also takes a facilitative approach to leadership, seeking to elicit the views of team members. The overall goal of her team is clear: to bring new drugs to the market quickly while ensuring product safety and compliance with local laws. Her technical development team needs to establish work flows, policies, and procedures that support this goal, and she actively solicits team members' ideas on how the team can best meet its targets.

Birgit's consensus-building leadership style appears to work well for the types of teams that she heads up. As with any style, it is based upon a set of assumptions, which in this case are probably something like, "The participants on my team are experienced professionals who expect to contribute to the team's vision and goals and are both motivated and qualified to do so." However, if a team leader with similar assumptions were to take on a different type of team and embark upon a more formal vision-building effort, asking team members to help create a "shared picture of the future," he or she could meet with a surprising response. For example, members of other global teams have expressed the following views.

Team Member Perspective #1: The team leader is from headquarters and knows the company well, and those of us on the team are younger and have less experience. Why is she asking us for our opinion? It would be better for her to just tell us what to do and teach us the skills we still need to learn.

Team Member Perspective #2: When the team leader asks for our input, it is always the same few people who speak up and dominate the conversation, even though they don't know this market well. This process is a waste of time.

Team Member Perspective #3: We have a perfectly good set of goals for our country operation already that our country director has provided and that the previous team leader used. We do not need a new direction for the team—this is too confusing.

Team Member Perspective #4: Our team leader wants us to have a shared vision, but the whole idea of vision is a fashion introduced by smarty-pants consultants who don't know what it's like to work in a real company. We don't need a fancy vision; we just need to make a good plan and implement it.

Faced with these kinds of views, a facilitative, consensus-building team leader must choose between attempting to persist with a style that team members are not yet accustomed to, or at least temporarily turning to a different style that might be more directive, tactical, or technically oriented. Figure 10-2 illustrates alternative styles that team leaders can use. Not every juxtaposition of terms in the figure is a set of precise opposites, nor is the list complete. Other forms of frame-shifting might include teaching versus learning, or being an agent of stability versus an agent of change.

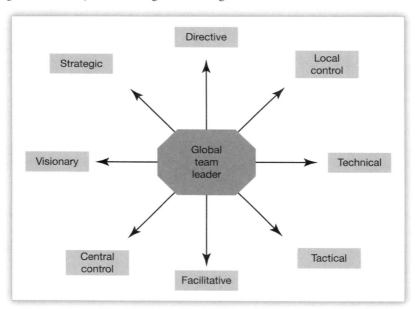

FIGURE 10-2 Team Leadership Styles: Frame-Shifting Options

As for strategy, frame-shifting typically means modifying products, services, processes, supplier relations, and so on to fit the needs of different markets. For example, this is how Birgit describes the work of her team in a developing market location:

"We have a research center there which is still being set up. The country has very different governmental procedures and it is very difficult to do a trial there. By working with our local colleagues, it became easier to deliver the things that they need in order to get approval for conducting a study. This country is still in the early stages of developing its drug approval process, so we have to plan for more than a year of approval time from the authorities for a clinical trial. There are infrastructure issues, and it is also difficult to find the study centers that can perform to the quality standards that we require."

Based on the circumstances in this country and the relative newness of the company's operations there, Birgit as team leader has to ensure that her local counterparts receive the specific kinds of data the government authorities require, plan for a longer approval process, deal with a lack of infrastructure, and identify—or more likely develop—study centers with adequate quality standards. Because each of these steps is different from what a more mature market would need, including her own native country of Germany or in Switzerland, where she now works, Birgit must frame-shift as the team leader in order to generate real solutions.

In our work with clients from a variety of industries, we have had success with a very simple strategy-building tool which lends more structure to the kind of process that Birgit has experienced. As shown in Figure 10-3, the frame-

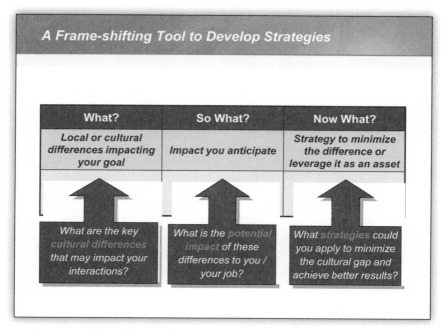

FIGURE 10-3 What? So what? Now what?

shifting approach involves (1) identifying differences in the local market that may impact the implementation of the team vision, (2) analyzing the business impact those differences may have, and (3) strategizing about how the team may need to frame-shift and modify its implementation plan in response to the identified differences.

A similar approach is recommended specifically for global drug-development teams.

"The process encourages drug-development teams to meet early in the development cycle to articulate a shared vision: the team members try to put in words on paper what it is they hope to be able to say about the drug product when it enters the market. We asked certain heuristic questions to facilitate this process. . . .

- "What *Issues* are likely to confront the product, to hold up its development, cause safety problems, raise costs, delay delivery, or result in a product that is unable to gain a market share?"

- "What *Responses* does the team propose for addressing the issues?"

- "What *Support* does the team have or need to gather? How and where will the data, rationales, and arguments be marshaled in support of the application?"[6]

These techniques are examples of ways in which team leaders can cultivate frame-shifting to successfully implement team goals. By using such methods, team members are better able to develop new and innovative approaches to fit different global business environments, even when those approaches diverge from standard practices at company headquarters.

INFLUENCE ACROSS BOUNDARIES

Both *invite the unexpected* and *frame-shifting* support a third behavior that is critically important for global team leaders: *influence across boundaries*. Leading in complex, often matrixed, global organizations calls for skillful influence and collaboration across the various "boundaries" within the organization and the team. These boundaries may be national, cultural, linguistic, functional, or organizational. When a leader is working to bring a shared sense of direction to a team, crossing these boundaries becomes essential.

Our interviewees stressed the need for global team leaders to "keep their finger on the pulse of changes" and the ways those changes may impact their teams. When working across boundaries with an unfamiliar set of environmental cues, it is important to be able to read situations accurately and to predict future scenarios. Two areas have proven to be especially worthy of attention: engaging key stakeholders and effectively facilitating the flow of knowledge and information across boundaries.

Engaging Key Stakeholders

As mentioned earlier, most team members are simultaneously involved in a number of different teams at any given time. It is critical that the team leader know both what other teams his or her team members are a part of and how those teams fit into the overall organizational context. Without this holistic picture, team leaders will not know whom to influence or why. They will not be able to grasp the origins of competing priorities pulling at their team members and impacting the team's success. Global team leaders have to work much harder in this matrixed environment to create and maintain alignment. At the same time, the imperative that they do so is far greater. As a corporate executive cited in one study commented:

> "When I'm working with a matrixed team, I always start by emphasizing that they have to be clear and aligned on the strategy, goals, structure, and rewards; and most importantly link their goals to [those] of their key stakeholders. They have to understand how what they want to do affects others."[7]

Ian is a global IT team leader for a large financial services corporation based in London, with team members in New York, Japan, Singapore, and Taiwan. He struggles with his Singapore-based team members whom he has never met face-to-face.

> "Basically, they are missing deadlines and not getting the work done, but I see them working online late into the night. I can't seem to get a sight line to what other things they are working on. When I call to ask about their workload, they tell me everything is fine. If I don't know what is on their plate in the first place, I can't take things off it. At the same time, my project deadlines are suffering."[8]

Ian's Singapore-based team members are likely struggling to balance the priorities of his team with conflicting pressures in the Singapore office. Given that the hierarchical structure of their local office has the largest daily impact on these team members, the local "hidden" stakeholders probably have more influence than does London-based Ian, whom they had never met in person. Proactively seeking to understand the priorities of all key stakeholders both acknowledges the daily realities of team participants and simultaneously helps to address barriers they may face in implementing team goals.

The Stakeholder Mapping chart in Figure 10-4 can be used to identify and begin to influence players who might otherwise remain in the background. Team leaders should work with participants to analyze:

- Who are the people outside the team that each team member feels responsible to satisfy?
- What are each stakeholder's requirements or priorities in terms of team outcomes?
- How do stakeholders' priorities, including those unrelated to the team, support or conflict with team goals?
- Does the team need to reprioritize or modify its own goals to better serve stakeholder requirements?

For teams that are in the formative stages, it is even better to anticipate the needs of at least some key stakeholders and to reach out to them before the team's labors begin. For instance, when there is a matrix relationship involving team members who have reporting lines both into the team leader and to an

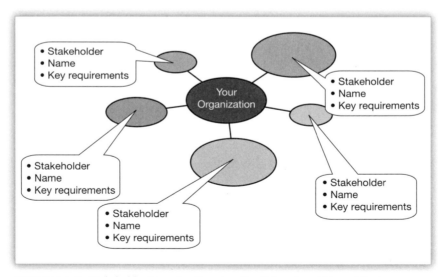

FIGURE 10-4 Stakeholder Mapping Exercise: Key External and Internal Customers

executive based in another country, it is wise for the team leader to gain that executive's buy-in to the team's objectives in advance to ensure that local team members are not getting mixed messages.

Although this outreach can be initiated directly by the team leader in some cases, with counterparts from places where respect for hierarchy is a significant cultural value, care should be taken to avoid the perception that a more junior team leader is contacting the executive and telling him or her what to do. The preferred approach for gaining alignment in such situations is usually to reach "up and across," as is illustrated in Figure 10-5. An executive at a higher level in the team leader's organization who is sponsoring the team's activities may be best positioned to contact an executive counterpart, gain mutual alignment about team objectives, and make the proper introductions. Sometimes there are several levels of hierarchy and rank that must be considered.

Facilitating Knowledge Sharing across Boundaries

The knowledge exchange supported by Birgit Masjost of Roche also helps her team to exert greater influence. It is important to stress that such exchanges need to take place across boundaries of all kinds. Unanticipated stakeholders with competing priorities can often mean that team goals are seen as unrealistic

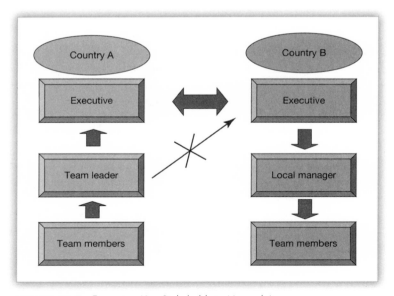

FIGURE 10-5 Engaging Key Stakeholders: Up and Across

by dispersed team members. This does not bode well for team performance. Not only do team leaders need to ensure that their own team vision takes into account local realities, but, as part of their influencing role, they also need to vocalize these circumstances to their own management and to the larger organization. Global team leaders often need to act as a "bridge" between their team members and other parts of the organization, enabling the knowledge they share among themselves to be disseminated across the company. This helps to set realistic expectations both inside and outside the team, and provides information critical to the success of a global enterprise.

Successful team leaders work to create an expanding "memory" within and beyond the team, including a mental map of who knows what in order to augment team resources and remove barriers. In the case of Birgit's technical development team, she leveraged international work exchanges, short-term site visits, and team meetings in different locations to further bolster a healthy knowledge-sharing system. Team members had the opportunity to learn their colleagues' unique culture and work environment, and brought their own expertise and best practices into this new collaboration as well. This knowledge-sharing process enabled each team member to act as a bridge person, and this system has resulted in huge benefits to the team and to the organization as a whole.

Summary

The challenge of creating a shared team vision, goals, and sense of alignment among team members is increased when leading globally. A number of factors contribute to this, but our interviewees indicated that the primary differences when leading globally versus domestically include:

- Larger gaps in the understanding of how each team member fits into a holistic vision of the team
- Less everyday knowledge sharing between the team leader and the team members and among team members, which inhibits the exchange of best practices
- More "unexpected" information that can emerge due to contrasting market environments and functional perspectives that each team members represent
- Greater need, given local realities, to frame-shift or to modify the way in which the team's goals are crafted and implemented

- Lack of a sight line to determine the team's key global stakeholders, including those who are instrumental for the team's success and those who may have competing priorities for individual team members
- A heightened imperative to exert influence across boundaries when aligning team members to achieve common goals

Through the use of global leadership behaviors such as *invite the unexpected*, *frame-shifting*, and *influence across boundaries*, team leaders are better positioned to ensure the success of their teams.

CHAPTER ELEVEN

The Future of Global Leadership

Global leaders today face more imposing tasks than ever before as they work across multiple geographies, functions, product lines, and national cultures. These leaders are often managing such "multiplexity" with a toolkit better suited for navigating technical silos and corporate hierarchies than for a cross-border, matrixed, digital, virtual, and ever-changing workplace. Many leadership development programs in corporate universities and business schools have also not yet integrated the focus, content, or methodology for developing global capabilities. In this final chapter, we will examine some of the potential obstacles and solutions to the challenge of global leadership development from the perspectives of both leaders and their organizations.

How Global Leaders Learn: What's Different?

As we have seen in the many examples global leaders have shared with us, their work is different from that of domestic leaders. Global leaders must be able to scan the environment for meaningful information, events, or commercial possibilities that allow them to formulate effective strategies and plot new courses of action. These may stem from unexpected sources in another part of the company or the world, from cultural influences that shape differences in local business practices, or from combining products and services in a new way for an emerging market. Leaders, therefore, need to be able to "see" and process information in new ways, making connections between phenomena that have never been linked before in their minds. This is *systems thinking* on a global scale, broadly defined as being able to formulate patterns out of disparate data from around the world and to leverage this information to create and implement new strategies.

INDIVIDUAL TRANSFORMATION

Helping global leaders to make sense of their work experiences, therefore, means that leadership development efforts should focus leaders on "thinking about their thinking." Thinking about thinking calls for a holistic view of the leader, leadership competencies, and the models, frameworks, and methods for development. Global leadership is a *transformational* learning experience, wherein new ways of thinking and behaving occur through the fundamental paradigm shifts created by new insights. As Jack Mezirow explains, "Transformational learning refers to the process by which we transform our taken-for-granted frames of reference (meaning perspectives, habits of mind, mind-sets) to make them more inclusive, discriminating, open, emotionally capable of change, and reflective so that they may generate beliefs and opinions that will prove more true or justified to guide action."[1]

Transformational learning can have uncertain outcomes. Because of the habitual ways in which we derive meaning from our experiences, self-directed learning may even reinforce negative views of the world and cultural differences rather than foster the development of an open mind. Some organizations have learned firsthand that regionally disparate working groups not trained to understand regional, cultural, or functional differences can actually become more polarized in their values, beliefs, and assumptions about how to get work done. This can widen differences rather than help participants learn to work together effectively. As one Human Resources practitioner stated, "Because we don't teach leaders how to understand and leverage diversity in the workplace, there's the potential for a lot of damage to be done. We all know the closets that hide the skeletons of those failed efforts."[2] Those who are in the process of learning global leadership competencies can benefit from support as the learning is happening.

ORGANIZATIONAL TRANSFORMATION

At the organizational level, global leadership development has proven to be a Gordian knot of challenges and obstacles. In spite of the often expressed concerns of CEOs from all industries and countries about a deficit of qualified global talent to lead their organizations forward, development initiatives continue to lag behind demand.

The fact that global leaders learn most of what they need to know on the job means that the organization's culture has a direct influence on learning. Much has been written on "the learning organization," which refers to learning-agile firms that are quick to integrate the lessons of leaders. Such activity leads to new ways of organizational problem solving and, ultimately, to a new corporate culture. The learning that global leaders must do is, in fact, an organizational development initiative through which the culture of the organization not only impacts the ways in which leaders learn but is also impacted by that learning.

We asked the leaders interviewed for this book, "How can global leadership competencies be disseminated most effectively to a broader employee population?" A brief summary of these findings provides two important themes. First, because their learning occurs on the job, they would like their organizations to find more effective ways to support learning "in the moment." Secondly, they expressed frustration that their organizations did not appreciate or integrate their learning in any appreciable way, ultimately slowing the arc of development for the entire organization. Individual and organizational transformation appear to be interlinked: leaders who receive effective support from their organizations are able to learn more rapidly and consistently, and organizations that absorb and integrate what global leaders learn are likely to outperform others in developing future leaders.

Defining Global Competency

To better understand the organizational complexities for developing global leaders in multinational companies, one of the authors conducted a separate set of in-depth interviews and focus groups over a two-year period with senior leaders in Human Resources, Learning and Development, Organizational Development, and Diversity from well-known Fortune 100 companies, as well as with cutting-edge leadership academics and consultants. The study asked these practitioners and academics to (1) define global leadership competency, (2) identify global competency gaps in organizations, and (3) identify the obstacles to closing these gaps.

The data from these interviews were remarkably consistent. Participants unanimously noted that:

- Their firms did not have adequate global competencies.
- These organizations lacked knowledge about culture in the workplace (which was especially apparent at the executive levels).
- Siloed thinking among support functions and academic disciplines had a negative downstream impact on their ability to effectively design and support training interventions.

Though the multinationals that participated in the research did have a defined set of leadership competencies, most did not specifically address global leadership, the competencies were often vague, and they were not vetted for applicability in the national cultures in which they did business. Competencies such as "values diversity" or "leverages diversity on teams" illustrate the very general level at which many organizations qualified global leadership behaviors. Similarly worded phrases such as "bold, game-changing strategy" and "increased velocity of execution" are not only vague but also do not translate, as demonstrated by the response of one company's Japanese office:

Bold game-changing strategy: "Bold is not necessarily good in Japan. It reminds us of an impudent approach, and Japanese dislike that."

Increased velocity of execution: "Velocity is not a common English word we learn in Japan, and so it does not land well. Rushed work is not considered good. Sometimes we need to take time to make sure that we achieve high quality."

Though many of the organizations said that they did tie competencies to the strategic goals of the firm, there still seemed to be a lack of understanding as to how they linked specifically to the execution of global strategies. The companies also said they did not track, measure, or reward leadership competencies, nor were there clear efforts to test the definition of each capability as a characteristic that predicts superior performance on the job.

To develop global leaders more effectively, practitioners need to define and assess more precisely key success factors for global leaders. As suggested in the preceding chapters, there is a set of leadership behaviors that is relatively easy recognize; these behaviors are also linked with underlying traits, attitudes, beliefs, and cognitive abilities that are more difficult to pinpoint or to socialize. Practitioners should be able to understand and appreciate all of these competencies—both dynamic and stable—in order to design appropriate interventions and sustainable support systems.

The ten key global leadership behaviors described by the exemplary global leaders whose stories fill this book increase our ability to define and build global competencies in organizations. They provide a road map for understanding the conflicting data, demands, and perspectives that the global leader must continually balance, including:

- Divergent and convergent thinking
- Reducing uncertainty and managing ambiguity

- Decisiveness versus humble inquiry
- Yes/no plus both/and thinking
- Reliable mental maps versus contradictory data
- Deductive and inductive logic
- Centralized decision making and shared leadership
- Experienced senior leadership and group intelligence

The Organizational Global Mindset

Leaders in every company we interviewed cited a significant gap between the demand for globally competent leaders and the number of individuals who were ready, willing, and able to perform in a global capacity. The gap was attributed to the absence of a "global mindset" in individuals and the ethnocentrism of headquarters.

One HR practitioner summed up the sentiments of many who were interviewed when she said, "We're not U.S.-centric; we're *New York-centric!*" The organizational global mindset begins with an understanding of company culture and its relationship to the national cultures in which the company does business. The business leaders on assignments whom we interviewed abroad were well aware of corporate culture and are engaged in constant negotiations between the local culture and that of headquarters, but this concept is far more difficult to grasp for the leader who is running a global operation from his or her home country. As the saying goes, "Fish do not know the water in which they swim."

Business leaders who are responsible for mergers and acquisitions, outsourcing, follow-the-sun work teams, and even multicultural work teams in their home country tell us that they cannot easily discern the dynamic tensions between the dominant corporate culture and national cultures. And while a very strong corporate culture can sometimes "trump" local cultures inside the same company, the cultural assumptions inherent in local practices, protocols, processes, decision making, and communication strategies are still present. In fact, differences that go unacknowledged because "we are all part the same company" can become the root cause of poor productivity and missed opportunities in the workplace as well as costly friction with outside suppliers and with customers.

Leaders often do not have a framework or language to make sense of or to talk about cultural differences across corporate, functional, product line, regional, or national cultures. The HR practitioners and academics interviewed were unanimous in their views about the problems this caused and the importance of cultural training in helping to close the gap. They also cited the challenge of having very senior executives who, because of their own ignorance of culture, were unwittingly perpetuating the lack of an "organizational global mindset" at the most strategic and systemic levels of the corporation. Training alone, however, is not the answer. The authors have on many occasions completed training programs for leaders in organizations with outsourced operations in India, only to be detained afterward by executives who say, "This is all well and good, but can you go there and train them to work more like us?" Ongoing organizational support to help leaders make sense of the cultural lessons they experience on the job is what makes training a sustainable and worthwhile investment.

OBSTACLES: SILOED THINKING OF LEADERS

Global leaders must be able to think and collaborate across products, regions, markets, and cultures, assimilating and leveraging the value of each to be effective. The structure of the archetypal organization, however, is one of separate business units that have been built around accumulated technical expertise. There was a common reason for these compartmentalized hierarchies. Top-line revenue shrinks when products and services become commoditized, pushing companies to build bottom-line growth and competitive differentiation through expanding lines of products and services. As organizations grew larger, they needed support functions with deep knowledge of their disciplines, capable of high degrees of accuracy, efficiency, and productivity. Then companies went to global markets in search of new customers and lower-cost production. New strategies were formed to capitalize on these new points of differentiation and these, in turn, necessitated new structures. New strategies and structures require new people behaviors to be successful. This is the challenge that many leaders find today: trying to execute on global strategy in a differentiated, fluid organizational structure.

Many senior executives learned their leadership skills during a different business cycle, when reaching across the silos was not a vital competency. They now have mental maps that were charted for another era. This is why leaders today tell us that they need to think hard about the way they think—testing assumptions, striving to make new connections, reflecting, asking themselves tough questions, actively seeking and being open to new ideas.

Thinking about thinking is especially important at higher levels in the organization for a number of reasons. For one, senior executives have made it to the top based on a mix of skills to which they now owe their success. The idea of tossing aside that winning formula for a new set of behaviors seems counterintuitive. Being open to new ways of thinking, however, allows them to acquire new skills for a new era. This is also crucial because the sphere of influence one has within the company is much greater at the higher levels, extending far beyond formal job responsibilities. Senior leaders have the capability to enable organizational learning—or to thwart it. They can encourage or unwittingly squelch cross-border collaboration. Thus, being tuned in to the assumptions and mental maps used to formulate problems and solutions are the new points of differentiation for leaders and their companies.

OBSTACLES: SILOED APPROACHES TO LEADERSHIP DEVELOPMENT

Just as the global leader must be able to think and collaborate across boundaries in order to be effective, so it is with the various supporting departments within companies. The Human Resources leaders we interviewed consistently said that the lack of a cohesive strategy among the Performance Management, Talent, Organizational Development, Learning and Development, Diversity, Expatriate Administration, and Compensation groups was a serious impediment to the development of global leaders. Indeed, not one of the companies represented had linked global leadership development initiatives across all of these functions. Though there was great thought leadership in maybe one or two of these functions in some companies, their progress was limited due to a lack of aligned support from the other groups. For instance, a number of companies had begun to look more strategically at mapping business objectives to leadership competencies and learning interventions, and had started incorporating these into their performance measurements. Yet these organizations were still not holding leaders accountable for their performance through their compensation and reward systems. These companies paid leaders for what they did, while neglecting to reward them for how they did it.

The companies we interviewed indicated that, even with targeted talent initiatives for executive development, there was little connection between assessment, selection, succession planning, development, and reward systems. In most instances, functional support groups (such as Learning and Development, Expatriate Administration, and Compensation) did not even know one another, let alone collaborate. The complexity of the global workplace calls for leaders and practitioners alike to draw together an equally complex mixture of solutions from multiple sources.

Developing Global Leaders: Implications

We now know the key behaviors of successful global leaders, what is different about developing them, and where individuals and organizations encounter the greatest obstacles in cultivating global capabilities. What other practical steps can be taken to foster the development of outstanding global leaders? The future of global leadership is likely to involve a closer look at how global leadership development can be integrated with everyday job roles.

ON-THE-JOB LEARNING OPPORTUNITIES

Given the emergent, fast changing, and market-specific nature of the work that leaders perform in the global theater, it is difficult to imagine that a fixed classroom curriculum alone could provide enough relevant content to meet their learning needs. In fact, as we have seen from the research on large global organizations, the curricula for such programs have not even been geared to the kinds of behaviors global leaders require. There are many on-the-job learning opportunities that, if properly identified and supported, can provide a rich forum for developing the ten key behaviors described in this book while simultaneously complementing properly designed training.

On-the-job learning activities occurring in multinational companies were previously listed in Chapter 8 (page 146) and include leading a domestic multi-cultural team, heading a global/virtual team or project, leading an organization with subordinates from other countries, or assuming global responsibility for a product or service.

When properly supported through the mechanisms of nomination, assessment, selection, performance management, compensation, succession planning, classroom training, and coaching, these on-the-job learning opportunities do in fact offer powerful and effective ways to develop not only the individual's but also the organization's global mindset.

WHAT INDIVIDUAL LEADERS CAN DO

Leadership development has often been likened to the work of the alchemist who makes gold out of common materials. The raw material of leaders' jobs, mixed in the crucible of the global work environment, can lead to transformational learning experiences. The leader, however, needs to be able to see the opportunities for making gold in the moment—out of the ordinary things that happen on the job. This is not always easy in a work world that moves at a very fast pace and where leaders are constantly under pressure to move on to the next task or crisis. However, since one of the most frequently cited personality traits of accomplished leaders is lifelong learning,[3] we know that reflection is an important ingredient for alchemy. For current and future business leaders who have the discipline to be the curators of their own learning, the ten key leadership behaviors outlined in this book can provide a framework for reflection and self-development, as the following case study illustrates.

CASE STUDY: **SELF-DEVELOPMENT**

Liam is a senior executive in the high-tech industry who started in the technology field right out of engineering school. Having "grown up" in the tech world, he has worked in many different functions over the years, and has acquired an encyclopedic knowledge of his company's products and a broad understanding of the business. He had a successful track record as the operations head of a midsized semiconductor company working primarily in its home market. Last year he was wooed away from this position by a large and well-known global tech firm to become the chief operating officer of a division created to find new distribution channels and markets for existing technology. This new role requires him to work across several functions and regions in order to research, assess, design, and deploy new processes in emerging markets.

Nearly a year into this new position, however, Liam finds himself floundering on a number of fronts. The launch of two new markets, on which he has worked since joining the firm, has been pending for nearly three months and is fraught with unresolved operational issues and resistance from local entities. He is at a stalemate with key global players from whom he needs final approval to implement the plan. Feedback from the *Global Leadership Online* survey, which he took in conjunction with a leadership training event, indicates that he has particularly low scores in the dimensions of *invite the unexpected*, *influence across boundaries*, and *adapt and add value*. Some of the written comments from his colleagues helped to pinpoint the issues.

"Liam has great enthusiasm and is very smart but he charges in, pushes his ideas forward, talks over people when they are trying to tell him something, and then goes off and does whatever he thinks is best. Honestly, we ask ourselves why he even sets up the meeting in the first place."

"He came with his team to my region to speak with suppliers. He set up meetings in town, did not invite any of us on the senior team to join him, and then showed up at the office the day before he was leaving for home with a full report of his findings. He had made conclusions about the local market and what we should do without speaking to any of us."

"He emails constantly, day and night. We find the content of these emails offensive and off-putting. There is never a conversation, just a lot of directives."

"If I could tell him one thing, it would be 'you're not a big fish in a small pond anymore,' but I doubt he would be open to hearing this. He is very unapproachable."

"His heart might be in the right place, but you'd never know it. He is constantly criticizing the way things have been done in the past. I think he means well, and truly wants to make a positive impact on the company, but he does not understand that there are legitimate reasons why some things are done this way in my country."

Given Liam's past successes, the feedback was tough, to take but it gave him some important insights. In thinking long and hard about what he could do to right the ship, Liam decided that he would go to one of his counterparts in the EMEA region, a woman he'd met on a previous business trip who had a company-wide reputation of being a good partner, and who had been successful in her work with the countries that were now filibustering against Liam's plan. For over an hour she listened carefully to his tale of woe without interrupting. Liam was struck by the simple advice she gave him: "You need to be able to walk before you run, to build trust and establish your credibility before you can expect cooperation. Go and ask the two region heads that are blocking your plan what you should be doing differently."

As grateful as he was for the input, Liam was also miffed by this advice, wondering why, at this stage in his highly successful career, he needed to "establish his credibility," and why, given the obvious merits of his plan, he had to "pander" for a country head's approval. Nonetheless, Liam put his ego aside and set up a call with the chief country officer (CCO) in the Thailand office. He started the call by saying that he had received less than favorable feedback about his leadership style and approach to the launch. He acknowledged that the CCO's support was critical to the success of the program, and asked for guidance on how he could mend fences and build better working relationships. In spite of these opening gambits, the CCO seemed reticent to tell Liam where he'd gone wrong, and in fact he would not specifically address anything Liam had done or not done in the past. This was frustrating to Liam, who was trying to be patient and humble, two traits that he did not come by naturally. Eventually, he realized that the CCO was giving him feedback, but not directly. The CCO told him of the local team's aspirations for the project. He spoke about the specific outcomes that would bring recognition to the team members and their desire to be acknowledged for the group's contribution to the company. The CCO also said that the local team was very eager to work with Liam, as he was such a well-respected and important leader.

Liam hung up the phone basking in the glow of this praise and long-overdue respect, and feeling grateful for the positive characterization of his leadership. For a moment, he forgot the pique he'd felt just a few minutes ago. Then he stopped smiling. Something was not adding up. How could he feel this range of emotions in practically the same breath? He felt confused and disoriented, saying to himself:

"What just happened? Let's see: I got negative feedback on my 360, I got over it enough to make the call to find out why, I asked the tough questions, and in return I got…flattery? That is downright dishonest! That's two-faced! Wait, what did he say again? Let me review my notes one more time."

What Liam realized was that the CCO was giving him feedback, but in a very indirect way. The CCO had given Liam the keys to a more successful partnership by describing outcomes, not prescribed behaviors. Liam still had to do the hard work of backing into these outcomes by coming up with actions for achieving them. He was uncharacteristically crestfallen, thinking, "Wow, this is a lot more work than I signed on for."

Undeterred, Liam called the CCO of Taiwan. Her advice was also puzzling. It was as if she were reciting parables, not giving him clear guidance. She told him stories about situations and people without an identifiable plot or obvious learning points. She said she had heard that some of the supply chain was pleased with the ten percent increase in fees the company recently gave them and that the other contractual terms that "have been negotiated" are far more favorable than what they had in the past. She also told a story about how the current processes were developed by a group that had worked around the clock together for three months, winning a local innovation award for their efforts.

Then she talked for a while about office dynamics, finishing the narrative with the declaration that "there are people in the office who are envious of the team that attends late-night conference calls." When he hung up the phone from the conversation and read through his notes, he realized that, between the lines, there was indeed some good input, though difficult to discern at first. He wasn't entirely sure, but he thought that she was telling him that he had left money on the table when he went to meet with the local suppliers, that he had most likely struck a nerve when he'd summarily dismissed the current local processes in favor of pushing his own, and that he should host more conference calls instead of churning out so many emails. He realized that she'd not actually said any of these things and that, during a year of working with her, she had "not said" many other things; messages that would have been of great value to him had he been listening.

Liam began to compile a list of the "feedback" he'd gathered from both calls, which would hopefully serve him better in the future. This process took an inordinately long time to accomplish, given the different way that the feedback had been delivered. In an effort to put a development plan together, he then reviewed the key global leadership behaviors on which he'd received the lowest scores and mapped these to his own actions. When he reflected on the list, he was surprised at how straightforward they appeared to be on the surface, but he decided to trust the process. The exercise resulted in three goals for himself and a few actions per goal. Figure 11-1 shows an excerpt of the plan.

Liam then made plans to go back out to his regional constituents and, in essence, start over. The progress after these changes was remarkably fast. He began to actually feel cooperation and commitment from the CCOs in Thailand and Taiwan. Having been a part of both the problem formation and the solutions, the local teams were willing and able to act much more quickly than in the past, and the new processes in the two emerging markets were launched successfully. In retrospect, he could also say that he had "felt" their lack of support in the past, though at the time he was not tuned in to the physical reaction that this tension had caused him.

These lessons have remained with Liam, who uses them frequently to determine root causes and solve business issues. "I have to practice open-mindedness every day in the way I examine my leadership style and signal my intentions to colleagues in other countries. It is not something that you can do once. Building these bridges is a daily exercise. The higher in the organization you are, the more often you have to find solutions to the kinds of conflicts that come from the assumptions we make about how people think. I spend a lot of my time now solving conflicts that are rooted in cultural differences."

Global Leadership Behavior	Goal	Action/Behaviors
Results through relationships *Influence across boundaries*	Build matrix relationships	■ Ask CCOs for a list of regional/local stakeholders and subject matter experts. ■ Use email for information sharing, not communication. Pick up the phone! ■ Schedule social time, outside the workday, to get to know Asian counterparts when on local business travel. ■ Signal intentions—tell them why I am making comments and ask if my critiques are relevant or not.
Invite the unexpected	Understand local market differences	■ Extend regional business by a few days to include meetings with local stakeholders and visit local factories. ■ Devise a survey, with CCO input, to conduct "stakeholder interviews" and gain the benefit of local expertise. ■ Write up findings and ask local counterparts to verify, add, and edit.
Adapt and add value	Rework regional implementation plans	■ Partner with regional owners to develop a list of "critical-to-quality" components of the plan, based on their operations and supply chain. Verify list. Get additional input. ■ Identify all constituencies impacted and their respective top priorities. ■ Jointly devise a timeline, with milestones, for key activities.

FIGURE 11-1 An Example of a Leader's Personal Action Plan

As a global leader, Liam's on-the-job learning opportunities are not unique, and his solutions are not dramatic or fancy. What was different about his experience was his openness to learning from his earlier failures and willingness to try new behaviors. Critically important factors for Liam, which ultimately led to his change in approach, were taking the time for reflection, his astute selection of the EMEA regional head as a cultural guide, and his ability to "hear" the indirect feedback of his Asian counterparts. Equally important were the discipline Liam showed in transforming this feedback into a plan for himself and his commitment to action.

WHAT ORGANIZATIONS CAN DO

In order for organizations to leverage on-the-job learning, a fundamental shift in perspective needs to occur to best support the development of future leaders. A fixed curriculum, even if updated on an annual basis or designed to include action-learning projects, has natural limitations. Leaders convene in a classroom location to learn what the experts have deemed to be important and relevant to their work. This may be determined according to leadership competencies blessed by top executives, an analysis of aggregate assessment data such as 360s or employee satisfaction surveys, or by the prevailing academic theories. This curriculum may or may not have direct relevance to participants' jobs, current capabilities, or learning objectives. One of the main reasons learning budgets are subject to cuts is that the business leaders making spending decisions, even if they have been consulted in the definition of leadership competencies, do not see how learning is aligned with implementation of their near-term business objectives. Learning cycles and budget cycles are not coordinated, which makes learning "nice to have" but not essential in the eyes of at least some decision makers. Whereas classroom learning includes frameworks with which participants can make sense of past and current experiences, it is seldom effective in providing anticipatory tools for future learning and for changing one's approach to daily business decisions.

Alignment with the individual learner's needs is also important to consider because research on generations in the workplace and in emerging markets tells us that customized, ongoing learning is a critical factor in recruiting and retaining key talent. Career development, in many parts of the world today, is viewed as another perquisite along the same lines as job title and level, compensation, or vacation time. In fact, the reputation of a company as a "learning organization," as having a "leadership performance culture," or as employing leaders with high levels of expertise and a willingness to train their direct reports are among the top features that attract coveted recruits. The capability of a corporation to design learner-centric training interventions is increasingly becoming a point of competitive differentiation in global markets.

Leader-Led Action Learning

How can organizations incorporate these business-centric and learner-centric concepts? We propose a model for implementing the ten global leadership behaviors that can put both the learner's development and the organization's global business objectives in the center of the frame. We use the term, *leader-led action learning* and believe that, for target groups of mission-critical, high-potential talent, it may provide a meaningful path forward.

Leader-led action learning has the potential to transform corporate learning in a way that goes far beyond its standard applications, but this requires a shift in mindset and skills on the part of those who are driving it. Traditional action learning typically occurs in the context of a leadership "program" that lasts for six months or a year, structured around two or three face-to-face gatherings of current or future leaders at headquarters or in a key emerging market location. During the course of the program, corporate executives are called upon to share information about the business and its future direction, tell their personal stories, and talk with participants. In addition, such executives are often asked to propose and sponsor action-learning projects that are carried out by small teams of participants during the interim period between face-to-face meetings; later, these executives may listen and respond to presentations by project teams of their results.

However, the very structure of this kind of leadership development program places inherent limitations on the potential of leader-led action learning. Figure 11-2 outlines some common program features along with their limitations for action-learning projects.

Although these constraints are natural enough in the context of a leadership development program, what if they were removed? More specifically, consider the impact if leader-led action learning were to include:

- **Objectives:** Vital strategic projects with high levels of visibility and support; focus on key corporate objectives for business growth and performance, with complete integration of business and leadership development objectives
- **Duration:** As much time and resources as needed to accomplish the task
- **Participant pool:** Project team leaders and participants who are the best people to carry out the assigned tasks
- **Executive sponsors:** Full executive sponsorship and accountability for results
- **Resources:** Resources are budgeted to accomplish the objectives both efficiently and effectively
- **Scope:** Teams are able to design the scope according to what is necessary to ensure full implementation and lasting results
- **Follow-up:** Alignment of project outcomes with required changes in organizational systems; metrics and regular reviews are used to identify lessons learned and to ensure continuous improvement

Program Design	Impact on Action Learning
Program objectives: Focus on readying candidates for the next level in the leadership pipeline.	Learning objectives are frequently a higher priority than project-related business objectives.
Program duration: Six to twelve months.	All projects must be started and completed within the same time frame.
Participant pool: "High-potential" individuals from various countries and business lines.	Project teams consist of the best mix of people who are participating in a given program, but not necessarily the best selection of people to address the project's objectives.
Executive sponsorship: Executives identify a topic, help to kick off the work of the team, and respond to team presentations.	Executive involvement may be inconsistent, and some project sponsors lose their sense of ownership between the start and finish of the project.
Program resources: Leadership development programs operate on a fixed budget.	Project teams must work within the context of the program budget regardless of their project's nature.
Program scope: Projects tend to focus on a set of objectives that can be handled within the context of the project team, and team members ultimately return to their previous locations and jobs.	Constraints on project scope make it difficult to propose and implement broader organizational and systemic changes when this is required to achieve lasting results.
Program follow-up: Fixed duration means that project results must be handed off to others.	Once a leadership program is finished, project team members are seldom in a position to follow through on recommendations; there is seldom enough time or interest for measuring results or for continuous improvement

FIGURE 11-2 Limitations of Program-Based Action Learning

On-the-job action learning can of course occur without any formal structure at all, but learning can also be accelerated and enhanced through a structured approach that creates a project "crucible" for optimum results. The project's business objectives are more likely to be achieved because the leader and participants receive special visibility, guidance, coaching, and support. Leadership development is intensified because the team is working with live ammunition on a strategically vital project, and the team leader is doing, learning, and developing other project members at the same time.

Leader-led action learning employs a just-in-time approach to curriculum development. It is based on linking organizational strategy to specific business unit goals and then to the people skills required to execute these objectives. This form of learning puts the business, the business leaders, and their teams in the center of the learning and development frame. It also coordinates efforts among the business leaders, global talent leads, and practitioners from Training and Development, Human Resources, and Organizational Development

(OD), whose jobs are to identify the top business imperatives, the specific skills required to achieve them, and to design learning interventions.

For instance, a stated organizational goal might be organic growth through cross-selling of products or services to existing clients. At the business unit level, this involves getting a group of global account executives to collaborate across product, organizational, and geographic boundaries to fulfill the strategy. This may entail devising specific account strategies with the input of their regional counterparts, jointly determining roles and responsibilities, and organizing communications and the work of global project teams. The requisite global leadership behaviors needed for learners to accomplish these tasks might include *cultural self-awareness*, *frame-shifting*, and *influence across boundaries*.

There are key roles and milestones in the learner-centric model. Figure 11-3 illustrates how such an initiative could be conceived, piloted, and scaled up to impact a broad spectrum of leaders and accounts.

To ensure the relevance and impact of the learning project, it must be aligned to very specific and discrete business objectives that can be measured. The learning objectives are inseparable from the objectives of the business. The learning points describe the way in which the leaders need to behave to successfully

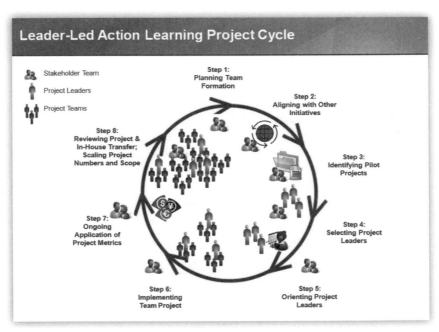

FIGURE 11-3 Leader-Led Action Learning Project Cycle

meet the targeted business objectives. The learning leader is a manager in the business unit who has demonstrated an aptitude for the identified competencies, has further room to grow, and is willing to focus on developing these skills in selected team members. The functional support groups working in a concerted and integrated team design the learning infrastructure. The steps outlined in Figure 11-3 are spelled out below in more detail:

Step 1: Planning team formation

The leader-led action-learning project would begin with identification of key stakeholders by the person within the organization who is responsible for leadership development initiatives. These stakeholders, who comprise the planning team, would include those individuals or departments that have a vested interest in the project and those that can support the learning process. In our cross-sell example, these stakeholders might be the business leader, the project leaders, the account managers, HR, L&D, OD, and Compensation.

For this kind of leader-led action learning, the role of the staff professional (HR, OD, Leadership Development, Diversity, etc.) is different. He or she is not a "trainer" or instructional designer, but a true strategic business partner working closely with executives to identify top business priorities, select projects and team members, align related support disciplines, serve as a coach for team leaders, and plan and implement needed changes in organizational systems. Everyone who is involved with this kind of action learning must be in touch with the heartbeat of the organization. Specifically, they must be able to answer at least three questions related to the health of the business:

- How is the firm going to grow and become more profitable?
- How is it going to become more efficient?
- What are its needs for global talent development?

The responses to these three questions define the business environment and the parameters for action learning, and set the stage for selecting high-priority projects.

Step 2: Aligning with other initiatives

In addition to aligning the project team members with one another, it is also important to determine, on an ongoing basis, how the efforts of the project team can be supported through related shifts in:

- Organizational structure
- Recruitment and selection
- Performance management
- Metrics and rewards
- Promotion
- Mobility: short-term and long-term global assignments
- Succession planning for top leadership roles
- Communication networks
- Informal corporate culture

Step 3: Identifying pilot projects

The pilot project, in our example, is the cross-selling of existing products to one selected customer. The objectives of the business unit that owns this product become the objectives of the pilot learning project. The project team members are in the center of the action, with staff professionals building a supportive context. Examples of other projects might include:

- **Business growth:** Exploration of new markets; possible mergers or acquisitions; new products or services; global account management; evaluation of distribution channels; alternative business models
- **Efficiency:** Cost-cutting proposals; supply chain rationalization; IT solutions; pricing; delivery time; product or service quality
- **Talent development:** Leveraging diversity; best practices for global teams; recruitment growth markets; employee engagement and retention; learning and development opportunities; knowledge transfer; bridging generational differences

Step 4: Selecting project leaders

Once the project has been identified, the relevant competencies required for successful implementation need to be confirmed. This is where the partnership between HR, L&D, and the business leaders needs to not only agree on the competencies, but also on the assessment of the best "leading leaders" to steward the learning process. Project team leaders are the ones who put the "leader-led" into action learning by developing future leaders through the course of the project in addition to gleaning their own learning along the way. It is, therefore, crucial to select the right people and provide them with the support they will need both to accomplish their vital tasks and help to cultivate a new generation of leaders. The ten key behaviors could be used as one factor in the screening of candidates along with the company's leadership competency model, to the extent that they adequately capture the necessary skills. It is desirable for team leaders to have a strategic global perspective and prior experience with a multicultural workforce. The following are some broader suggested criteria for team leader selection:

- "High-potential" designation
- Strong performance ratings for leadership capabilities and achieving business results
- Functional or subject matter expertise
- Prior global working experience
- Completion of successful cross-border assignments
- Positioning within internal company networks
- High peer and 360-degree feedback ratings
- Representation of various forms of diversity, including national, ethnic, gender, generational, and thought

Step 5: Orienting project team

Ensuring that the project team has a structured orientation can help it start off in the right direction. It is generally useful for the executive sponsor and the team leader to provide a comprehensive overview of the project and its significance for the company. The orientation should also include clear definitions of roles and responsibilities, team objectives, milestones, timelines, deliverables, and metrics, as well as relationship-building among team members that allows them to begin to establish mutual trust.

It is advisable that each team leader have a professional coach to provide support and guidance, both for carrying out tasks and for developing the capabilities of team members. The coach can be introduced during the orientation process, along with global leadership development objectives that will be interwoven with the project tasks. While many leaders are great teachers, they are not L&D professionals. Therefore, a "curriculum" composed of the learning opportunities, tools for providing feedback on the performance of the leader as well as team members, and other support mechanisms should be designed and coordinated through a joint effort of L&D and HR and augmented by the coach.

Step 6: Implementing the team project

As the project unfolds, regular contact between the team leader and a support network that includes the executive sponsor, coach, and other team leaders can help ensure rapid progress. Executive sponsors sometimes assign a liaison from their organization who is more regularly available to the team leader. A coach helps the leader consider various approaches to achieving team objectives and select the best course of action; coaching also examines how the team leader can develop his or her own capabilities and those of team members in the course of their project work. When multiple projects are running at the same time, team leaders themselves can share challenges and solutions, finding ways to support each other. The project rollout should include milestones, checkpoints, performance metrics, and midcourse process monitoring. In a perfect world, the project leaders' variable compensation would not only be tied to the project metrics, but also to their success in developing the skills of their team members.

Step 7: Applying project metrics

The project's success requires consistent involvement by the functional support groups. Is the learning project leader working only on the client side, or is he or she also focused on the development of the key behaviors in the team members? Are the milestones being reached, or are there obstacles that need to be overcome? Appropriate metrics naturally vary according to the type of project, but they should combine qualitative and quantitative elements. In our cross-sell example, the most obvious metric is increased revenue generated from new business opportunities with the target client. Standard measurements that may be appropriate in other situations include project completion on time and under budget or reduced costs. It is also useful to look at career advancement results for participating leaders and team members, pre- and post-project assessments of individual competencies, and measurements of team performance.

Step 8: Reviewing and scaling the project

Leader-led action learning benefits from a continuous feedback loop that extends beyond the boundaries of a common leadership program. The planning team, including the various functional support groups and the project sponsor, now needs to assess the effectiveness of the project and to more broadly socialize the learning outcomes across functional and business units. The team should, of course, evaluate metrics and share feedback from the team leader, participants, sponsors, coaches, and other stakeholders. The planning team can meet to discuss lessons learned and plan follow-up steps. Pilot projects that have borne fruit—say the trial of this cross-sell concept—may be scaled to larger numbers of teams in different regions and areas of the organization. Again, the structure of any next steps is best determined according to the demands of the business itself, not by a leadership program's schedules or deadlines.

Leader-led action learning of the kind outlined here provides significant advantages, especially during tough economic times, by bringing exactly the right people and the required level of resources together to advance global strategic objectives. By integrating high-profile projects with on-the-job learning opportunities, action-learning projects provide an intensive developmental experience for team leaders and participants with minimal added expense, and they are readily scalable across the organization to achieve major impacts. If truly optimized, such projects can become a normal part of a company's business cycle—a key component within an integrated and holistic system that employees value and to which they strive to contribute. This is a different and more complex venue than a formal program or training event, but it may be just what hard-pressed CEOs are seeking.

RETHINKING INTERNATIONAL ASSIGNMENTS

The leader-led action-learning framework offers a fresh way of viewing at least some international assignments, underlining the substantial investment they entail as well as their critical value for both accomplishing global business objectives and developing global leaders. Expatriates in executive roles, like the people we interviewed, have enormous leadership responsibilities that include developing future leaders across a country or region. Although some companies have sought to reduce costs by decreasing the number of expatriates around the world and outsourcing many of the touch points with assignees and their families to mobility service providers, there is a countertrend that views international assignments, either short-term or long-term (often defined as at least two or three years), in a more strategic light. Due to the transformational nature of the culture shock experience and the relentless resourcefulness required from the global leader at work outside his or her home country, expatriate assignments are increasingly being reevaluated as a consummate development opportunity. In some of the world's most advanced global enterprises, a work assignment in another region has long been considered to be a fast-track opportunity for leadership development and a prerequisite for attaining executive status—the trend in many other organizations as well is now to selectively invest in ensuring the rapid learning, adjustment, and success of key assignees. These assignees in turn are often charged with retaining and accelerating the cultivation of emerging market leadership talent, and play a crucial role in this high-stakes endeavor.

When properly supported and coached, expatriates can develop intercultural acuity, systems thinking, skill and comfort in working across functions, and a sound understanding of the firm's operational capabilities and opportunities on a worldwide basis. This experience results in a mindset of cross-border collaboration and coordinated activity that is often linked with organic growth and innovation. Expatriate assignments are indeed costly; however, the cost of the missed opportunity to leverage these work assignments as vehicles for global leadership development is even greater.

The project team for a leader-led international assignment project should be composed of representatives from all the groups connected with such assignments, and they must work together in a deliberate and strategic way like with other forms of leader-led learning. As Figure 11-4 outlines, the planning team members would work in alignment to address the business objectives and targeted performance goals for the assignment; in the selection, development, and compensation of the expatriate; and to achieve the organizational goals related to knowledge transfer and innovation. The figure also includes a snapshot of how these responsibilities could be designated. The global leadership behaviors described in earlier chapters can provide a template for the capabilities and mindset that the team cultivates.

Aligning the different functions that support expatriate assignments is just as essential as for other forms of action learning. Unfortunately, "ownership" of expatriate talent is like a hot potato in many firms: the tracking of career goals, accomplishments, next-in-line job opportunities, and succession plans are tossed between home and host locations, usually being dropped altogether at some point along the way. Handling at least the most critical international assignments in a form analogous to leader-led action-learning projects would help to bring structure and accountability to this vital form of talent development. The Organizational Development function, for instance, is usually absent from the expatriation cycle, leaving valuable learning up for grabs. The role of OD in the learning project is to repatriate the expatriate's learning, capturing and scaling such information to enrich the organization's global mindset and culture. Repatriation training is one way to help employees become more consciously competent with the skills they learned while on assignment, to better assimilate and retain them, and to foster knowledge transfer to other parts of the company. Some organizations have also initiated learning networks, facilitated

Human Resources	Assignee
■ Define nomination criteria ■ Determine the competencies for assignment ■ Help assess outcome ■ Introduce performance management tools ■ Identify and orient coaches for expatriates	■ Meet assignment goals ■ Balance global and local needs ■ Develop global competencies of self and local team ■ Seek feedback ■ Commit to continuous improvement
Global Talent Management	**Organizational Development**
■ Organize the review of high-potential talent capable of taking an expatriate assignment ■ Participate in assessment and election ■ Take part in succession planning	■ Align the contributing departments ■ Coordinate knowledge transfer and organizational learning ■ Scale the learning for broader application
Business Leaders/Sponsors	**Learning and Development**
■ Identify key business objectives to be achieved by the expatriate assignment ■ Determine assignment goals ■ Nominate key talent ■ Share ties to corporate network; preserve viable links to headquarters ■ Oversee ongoing performance management ■ Manage performance evaluation and recommendations ■ Identify a strategic role to leverage assignee's knowledge post-assignment	■ Develop program infrastructure ■ Create the leader-led learning "curriculum" for expatriates based on on-the-job opportunities to develop the competencies ■ Determine milestones and learning support tools
Relocation	**Compensation**
■ Administer benefits ■ Coordinate ancillary support such as home-finding and shipment of household goods ■ Oversee training providers, including language and intercultural training ■ Maintain link between home and host support functions	■ Coordinate cost of living differentials and payrolls ■ Manage variable reward programs based on assignment goals ■ Administer tax issues

FIGURE 11-4 Leader-Led Learning Roles and Responsibilities for International Assignments

by 2.0 websites and other self-serve options such as iMentor, a software program that connects would-be global leaders with those (such as expatriates) who are adept at the skill sets they are looking to develop. The real point, however, is less the specific tactics or technologies that are used than the alignment of the relevant functions to manage each stage of the global assignment cycle as a vital investment in future leaders. The assignment cycle must also be seen as part of a larger strategic and organizational context, as illustrated in Figure 11-5.

The global leaders we interviewed gave numerous examples of how their organizations could better utilize expatriate assignments as developmental initiatives. There is a sharp contrast between companies that have learned to leverage international assignments strategically and those that have not. The long-term, cumulative nature of this challenge is deeply systemic and goes beyond any particular assignment. As one interviewee remarked:

"We have a need for leaders who are really smart about portfolio management globally. We could be making decisions to go into a country on a six-month basis of information and making bad decisions. We need long-term thinking. Based on the perspective of people from a market where there isn't a lot of volatility, once they hit hard times, they walk away from opportunities because they just don't get it, and the opportunity is missed. This is true on other side, too, as they think volatility will last forever in other markets. We need to understand if we are catching a particular market on the upswing or downswing that this is not a long-term trend. Just because you don't understand, it doesn't mean it's not real or rational. The attitude is, 'If I don't

FIGURE 11-5 Global Assignment Cycle Stages

get it, it's screwed up' . . . rather than, 'I want to understand it, and need to talk to a person with experience.' We need a new model."

The more critical interviewee comments in Figure 11-6 are astonishing, considering the level at which all of these assignees were working and the scale of their employers' investments in them. On the other hand, these leaders do hold out hope and offer a number of good ideas about practices that have worked or that they would recommend.

Assignee Comments about Nonstrategic Approaches	■ "You have been out of sight, out of mind." ■ "You weren't there; you were on vacation as far as people at headquarters were concerned." ■ "No one really cares about where you've been." ■ "They are bored if you say too much about your experience." ■ "You have to scrounge for a job when you get back." ■ "From leadership down, the company does not put a value on international experience, doesn't reward it, doesn't identify it." ■ "There is no career planning for expatriates." ■ "My full potential and the competencies that I developed are not being used." ■ "Few in the company have been in real global leadership roles, so the company doesn't do a good job in capturing that experience." ■ "This is intelligence that the company has invested in; it is company priority property. But no one has come up with a way to get at it."
Assignee Recommendations for More Strategic Approaches	■ Share success stories. Talk about what happened and why it is beneficial. ■ Send high-potential employees on international assignments early in their careers so that they can start right away; recruit for this kind of experience. ■ Place assignees in stretch assignments on their return to utilize their greater breadth of vision and expertise. ■ Do not send someone abroad who displays a lack of curiosity or interest. ■ Appoint former assignees to top executive posts. ■ Use corporate publications to highlight global best practices. ■ Put senior people in the room and have assignees tell them about the market and business in that country; use them as experts. ■ Document the learning. Have assignees present case studies in different forums and workshops. ■ Develop a network of people on global assignments and knowledge sharing between them. In developing new business, their opinions and expertise are critical.

(continues)

FIGURE 11-6 International Assignments: Nonstrategic and Strategic Approaches

Assignee Recommendations for More Strategic Approaches (*continued*)	▪ Tap assignees as internal subject matter experts for relevant topics such as merger or acquisition activity in a particular geography.
	▪ Create links with new assignment candidates to ensure rapid learning and adjustment.
	▪ Hold guided discussion rounds with global teams to broaden the acceptance level of different behaviors and different needs.
	▪ Create links to business leaders doing business with a location for which the former assignee has expertise.
	▪ Apply global learning to improve leadership practices in a diverse domestic environment.

FIGURE 11-6 *Continued*

Leadership in a complex and connected world can only be developed with the mindful participation of all stakeholders. There are many ironies in the process of global leadership development, and many ingrained fallacies that companies must outgrow in order to become truly global in their thinking. Nonstrategic approaches to expatriate assignments, for example, only serve to insulate an organization and its leadership from the experiences of the very people who have firsthand knowledge of vital growth markets. As the neurological research discussed in Chapter 3 suggests, we literally don't see what we don't anticipate, even when it is in front of our eyes. Lack of interest reinforces lack of knowledge, which inhibits perception. Cracking the code for building a global mindset calls for reversing this pattern of self-reinforcing myopia in all corners of an organization.

Similarly, the assumption that international assignments are somehow a separate administrative realm that is not at the heart of global leadership development is patently absurd, and the proposition must again be reversed: How can the hard lessons and the everyday experiences of global assignees be transmitted most efficiently and effectively to everyone in the organization who touches global business or even domestic diversity in any form?

The advantage of leader-led action learning—whether it is applied to expatriate assignments or to other global leadership development opportunities—is that it not only helps to hasten the execution of business strategies, but also begins to alter the culture of an organization through careful cross-functional collaboration and transmission of new knowledge. The iconic companies of the future will achieve business results and build a true global leadership performance culture through the focused development of employees across boundaries of every kind.

Bibliography

BOOKS

Adler, Nancy, *International Dimensions of Organizational Behavior, Fourth Edition*. Cincinnati, OH: South-Western, 2002.

Bartlett, Christopher, and Sumantra Ghoshal, *Managing Across Borders: The Transnational Solution*. Boston: Harvard Business School Press, 1991.

Black, Stewart, Allen Morrison, and Hal Gregersen, *Global Explorers: The Next Generation of Leaders*. New York: Routledge, 1999.

Chandler, T., *Four Thousand Years of Urban Growth: An Historical Census*. Lewiston, NY: Edwin Mellen Press, 1987.

Charan, Ram, Stephen Drotter, and James Noel, *The Leadership Pipeline: How to Build the Leadership-Powered Company*. San Francisco: Jossey-Bass, 2001.

Christensen, Clayton, *The Innovator's Dilemma*. Boston: Harvard Business School Press, 1997.

Conger, Jay, *The Charismatic Leader: Behind the Myth of Exceptional Leadership*. San Francisco: Jossey-Bass, 1989.

Conger, Jay, and Ronald Riggio, *The Practice of Leadership: Developing the Next Generation of Leaders*. New York: John Wiley & Sons, 2007.

Connerly, Mary, and Paul Pedersen, *Leadership in a Diverse and Multicultural Environment: Developing Awareness, Knowledge, and Skills*. Thousand Oaks, CA: Sage Publications, 2005.

Cortez, Carlos, and Louise Wilkinson, "Developing and Implementing a Multicultural Vision." In *Contemporary Leadership and Intercultural Competence*. Thousand Oaks, CA: Sage Publications, 2009.

Covey, Stephen, *The Speed of Trust: The One Thing That Changes Everything*. New York: Simon & Schuster, 2006.

Friedman, Thomas, *Hot, Flat, and Crowded: Why We Need a Green Revolution—And How It Can Renew America*. New York: Farrar, Straus and Giroux, 2008.

Gardner, Howard, *Frames of Mind: The Theory of Multiple Intelligences*. New York: Basic Books, 1983.

Goldsmith, Marshall, Cathy Greenberg, Alastair Robertson, and Maya Hu-Chan, *Global Leadership: The Next Generation*. Upper Saddle River, NJ: FT Press, 2003.

Goleman, Daniel, *Emotional Intelligence: Why It Can Matter More Than IQ*. New York: Bantam, 1995.

Gundling, Ernest, *Working GlobeSmart: 12 People Skills for Doing Business across Borders*. Palo Alto, CA: Davies-Black, 2003.

Gundling, Ernest, and Anita Zanchettin, *Global Diversity: Winning Customers and Engaging Employees in Key World Markets*. Boston: Nicholas Brealey, 2006.

Gupta, Anil, Vijay Govindarajan, and Haiyan Wang, *The Quest for Global Dominance: Transforming Global Presence into Global Competitive Advantage*. San Francisco: Jossey-Bass, 2008.

Hofstede, Geert, *Culture's Consequences: Comparing Values, Behaviors, Institutions, and Organizations across Nations*. Thousand Oaks, CA: Sage, 2001.

———, *Culture and Organizations: Software of the Mind*. New York: McGraw-Hill, 1997.

Hogan, Terry, "Global Leadership and the Development of Intercultural Competency in Multinational Organizations," masters thesis for the University of the Pacific–Stockton, CA, and The Intercultural Communication Institute, 2008.

House, Robert, Paul Hanges, Mansour Javidan, Peter Dorfman, and Vipin Gupta, *Culture, Leadership, and Organizations: The GLOBE Study of 62 Societies*. Thousand Oaks, CA: Sage Publications, 2004.

Johansen, Robert, *Get There Early: Sensing the Future to Compete in the Present*. San Francisco: Berrett-Koehler, 2007.

Kelly, Eamonn, *Powerful Times: Rising to the Challenge of Our Uncertain World*. Upper Saddle River, NJ: Pearson Education, 2006.

Kotter, John, *What Leaders Really Do*. Boston: Harvard Business Review, 1999.

———, *Leading Change*. Boston: Harvard Business School Press, 1996.

Kouzes, James, and Barry Posner, *The Leadership Challenge: How to Keep Getting Extraordinary Things Done in Organizations*. San Francisco: Jossey-Bass, 1995.

Livermore, David, *Leading with Cultural Intelligence: The New Secret to Success*. New York: American Management Association, 2010.

McCall, Morgan, and George Hollenbeck, *Developing Global Executives*. Boston: Harvard Business School Press, 2002.

Mendenhall, Mark, Joyce Osland, Allan Bird, Gary Oddou, and Martha Maznevski, *Global Leadership: Research, Practice and Development*. New York: Routledge, 2008.

Mezirow, Jack, et al. *Learning as Transformation: Critical Perspectives on a Theory in Progress*. San Francisco: Jossey-Bass, 2000.

Naisbitt, John, *Megatrends Asia: Eight Asian Megatrends That Are Reshaping Our World*. New York: Simon & Schuster, 1996.

O'Hara-Devereaux, Mary, *Navigating the Badlands: Thriving in the Decade of Radical Transformation*. San Francisco: Jossey-Bass, 2004.

Pucik, Vladimir, Noel Tichy, and Carole Barnett, eds., *Globalizing Management: Creating and Leading the Competitive Organization*. New York: John Wiley & Sons, 1992.

Rock, David, *Your Brain at Work: Strategies for Overcoming Distraction, Regaining Focus, and Working Smarter All Day Long*. New York: HarperBusiness, 2009.

Rosen, Robert, Patricia Digh, Marshall Singer, and Carl Phillips. *Global Literacies: Lessons on Business Leadership and National Cultures*. New York: Simon & Schuster, 2001.

Schaetti, Barbara, Sheila Ramsey, and Gordon Watanabe, *Personal Leadership: A Methodology of Two Principles and Six Practices*. Seattle: FlyingKite Publications, 2008.

Schein, Edgar, *Organizational Culture and Leadership*. San Francisco: Jossey-Bass, 1991.

Schwartz, Peter, *The Art of the Long View: Planning for the Future in an Uncertain World*. New York: Doubleday, 1991.

Senge, Peter, *The Fifth Discipline: The Art and Practice of the Learning Organization*. New York: Currency Doubleday, 1990.

Solomon, Charlene, and Michael Schell, *Managing Across Cultures: The Seven Keys to Doing Business with a Global Mindset*. New York: McGraw-Hill, 2009.

Tapia, Adres, *The Inclusion Paradox: The Obama Era and the Transformation of Global Diversity*. Lincolnshire, IL: Hewitt Associates, 2009.

Tichy, Noel, *The Leadership Engine: How Winning Companies Build Leaders at Every Level*. New York: HarperBusiness, 1997.

Trompenaars, Fons, and Charles Hampden-Turner, *Riding the Waves of Culture: Understanding Diversity in Global Business*. New York: McGraw-Hill, 1998.

Weiner, Edie, and Arnold Brown, *FutureThink: How to Think Clearly in a Time of Change*. Upper Saddle River, NJ: Prentice Hall, 2006.

ARTICLES

Begley, Sharon, "West Brain, East Brain: What a Difference Culture Makes," *Newsweek*, February 18, 2010. *http://www.newsweek.com/2010/02/17/west-brain-east-brain.html*

Bennett, M. J. "Beyond Ethnorelativism: The Developmental Model of Intercultural Sensitivity." In Michael Paige, ed., *Education for the Intercultural Experience*. Yarmouth, ME: Intercultural Press, 1993.

Bernhardt, Stephen, "Technology for Global Teams: Using Technology to Support Global Drug-Development Teams: Basel, Switzerland: Franklin-Quest Consulting Group, 1997, p. 5.

Bhattacharya, Arindam K., and David Michael, "How Local Companies Keep Multinationals at Bay," *Harvard Business Review*, March 2008.

Bishop, Matthew, "Special Report on Globalization." The Economist, September 20, 2008.

"China's Dangdang Dabs $27M," *Red Herring: The Business of Technology*, July 5, 2006. *http://www.redherring.com/Home/17485*

De Rosa, Darleen, "Leadership in Action," *InterScience*, 28:6, January/February 2009.

Derven, Marjorie, "Managing the Matrix in the New Normal," *Training and Development Magazine*, July 2010.

Eldon, Eric, "The World's Most Lucrative Social Network? China's Tencent Beats $1 Billion Dollar Revenue Mark." March 19, 2009. *Social Beat, http://social.venturebeat.com/2009/03/19/the-worlds-most-lucrative-social-network-chinas-tencent-beats-1-billion-revenue-mark/*

Gladstone, Jack, "The Population Bomb: The Four Megatrends That Will Shape the World." *Foreign Affairs*, January/February 2010, p. 3; *http://www.foreignaffairs.com/articles/65735/jack-a-goldstone/the-new-population-bomb?page=3*

Gunther, M., "Warren Buffett Takes Charge," *Fortune*, April 13, 2009. *http://money.cnn.com/2009/04/13/technology/gunther_electric.fortune/*

Gurley, Bill, "How to Monetize a Social Network: MySpace and Facebook Should Follow Tencent," March 9, 2009. *http://abovethecrowd.com/2009/03/09/how-to-monetize-a-social-network-myspace-and-facebook-should-follow-tencent/*

Gutchess, A., R. Welsh, A. Boduroglu, "Cultural differences in neural function associated with object processing," *Cognitive, Affective, & Behavioral Neuroscience*, 2006, pp. 102–109.

Ho, Patricia, "China Passes U.S. as World's Top Car Market," *Wall Street Journal*, January 12, 2010. *http://online.wsj.com/article/SB1000142405274870365210457465183312 6548364.html*

Hole, David, Zhong Le, and Jeff Schwartz, "Talking about Whose Generation? Why Western Generational Models Can't Account for a Global Workforce," *Deloitte Review*; *www. deloitte.com/view/en_US/us/Insights/Browse-by-Content-Type/deloitte-review*

International Monetary Fund, "Global Demographic Trends. Finance & Development." 43 (3). September, 2006. *http://www.imf.org/external/pubs/ft/fandd/2006/09/picture.htm*

Jana, R., "P&G's Trickle-Up Success: Sweet as Honey." *Business Week Online*. March 31, 2009. *http://images.businessweek.com/ss/09/04/0401_pg_trickleup/5.htm*

Khanna, Tarun, and Krishna G. Palepu, "Emerging Giants: Building World-Class Companies in Developing Countries," *Harvard Business Review*, October 2006.

Leung, A., W. Maddux, A. Galinsky, C-y. Chiu, "Multicultural Experience Enhances Creativity: The When and How," *American Psychologist*, April 2008.

Population Reference Bureau; *http://www.prb.org/images07/62.3_12UrbanPop.gif*

Rock, David, and Jeffrey Schwartz, "Why Neuroscience Matters to Executives," *Strategy + Business*, April 10, 2007.

———, "The Neuroscience of Leadership," *Strategy + Business*, May 30, 2006.

Rowley, I., "China: Car Capital of the World?" *Business Week*, May 18, 2009. *http://www. businessweek.com/globalbiz/content/may2009/gb20090518_095449.htm*

Schein, V., "Would Women Lead Differently?" In J. T. Wren, ed., *The Leader's Companion: Insights on Leadership through the Ages* (pp. 161–67). New York: The Free Press, 1995.

Simons, Daniel J., "Selective Attention Test," Visual Cognition Lab: University of Illinois, 1999. *http://viscog.beckman.illinois.edu/grafs/demos/15.html*

Sull, Don, "Innovation Lessons from Emerging Markets: Live with your Customer," September 26, 2009. *http://blogs.ft.com/donsullblog/2009/09/26/innovation-lessons-from-emerging-markets-live-with-your-customer/*

Tibken, S., "Led by Asia, Global Chip Sales Rise 8%," *Wall Street Journal*, August 5, 2008, p. B5.

United Nations, Department of Public Information "World Urbanization Prospects," 1995.

Wikipedia, "TenCent QQ," *http://en.wikipedia.org/wiki/Tencent_QQ*

Yahoo! Tech News, "China Web Users Outnumber US Population," July 26, 2009. *http:// tech.yahoo.com/news/afp/20090726/tc_afp/chinatechnologyinternet*

Endnotes

CHAPTER 1

1. Examples of futurists and their work include Peter Schwartz, *The Art of the Long View: Planning for the Future in an Uncertain World* (New York: Doubleday, 1991); Robert Johansen, *Get There Early: Sensing the Future to Compete in the Present* (San Francisco: Berrett-Koehler, 2007); John Naisbitt, *Megatrends Asia: Eight Asian Megatrends That Are Reshaping Our World* (New York: Simon & Schuster, 1996); Mary O'Hara-Devereaux, *Navigating the Badlands: Thriving in the Decade of Radical Transformation* (San Francisco: Jossey-Bass, 2004); and Edie Weiner and Arnold Brown, *FutureThink: How to Think Clearly in a Time of Change* (New Jersey: Prentice Hall, 2006).

2. In addition to the sources listed in Footnote 1, the authors' thinking on megatrends has been particularly influenced by Eamonn Kelly's excellent book *Powerful Times: Rising to the Challenge of Our Uncertain World* (New Jersey: Wharton School Publishing, 2006), Chapter 8, as well as a presentation he delivered on this topic for the Human Resource Planning Society's annual conference in April 2008.

3. International Monetary Fund, "Global Demographic Trends," *Finance & Development* 43:3, September 2006. *www.imf.org/external/pubs/ft/fandd/2006/09/picture.htm*.

4. Jack Gladstone, "The New Population Bomb: The Four Megatrends That Will Change the World," *Foreign Affairs*, January/February 2010, p. 3. *www.foreignaffairs.com/articles/65735/jack-a-goldstone/the-new-population-bomb?page=3*.

5. Angus Maddison, "The World Economy: A Millenial Perspective," *OECD*, Paris 2001.

6. S. Tibken, "Led by Asia, Global Chip Sales Rise 8%," *Wall Street Journal*, August 5, 2008, p. B5.

7. Owen Fletcher, PCWorld Business Center, "China's Internet Users Outnumber U.S. Population," July 17, 2009. *http://www.pcworld.com/businesscenter/article/168596/chinas_internet_users_outnumber_us_population.html*.

8. Patricia Ho, "China Passes U.S. as World's Top Car Market," *Wall Street Journal*, January 12, 2010. *http://online.wsj.com/article/SB10001424052748703652104574651833126548364.html*. See also I. Rowley, "China: Car Capital of the World?" *Business Week*, May 18, 2009. *www.businessweek.com/globalbiz/content/may2009/gb20090518_095449.htm*.

9. Angus Maddison. The World Economy: A Millennial Perspective. (OECD, 2001), p. 28.

10. United Nations Population Fund, *State of World Population 2007*; and United Nations Population Division, *World Urbanization Prospects: The 2005 Revision* (2006). Population Reference Bureau: *http://www.prb.org/Articles/2007/UrbanPopToBecomeMajority.aspx*.

11. Tertius Chandler, *Four Thousand Years of Urban Growth: An Historical Census* (Lewiston, New York: Edwin Mellen Press, 1987).
12. United Nations, Department of Public Information, World Urbanization Prospects, 1995.
13. See, for example, Tarun Khanna and Krishna G. Palepu, "Emerging Giants: Building World-Class Companies in Developing Countries," *Harvard Business Review*, October 2006; and Arindam K. Bhattacharya and David Michael, "How Local Companies Keep Multinationals at Bay," *Harvard Business Review*, March 2008.
14. Clayton Christensen, *The Innovator's Dilemma* (Boston: Harvard Business School Press, 1997).
15. Reena Jana, "P&G's Trickle-Up Success: Sweet as Honey," *Business Week Online*, March 31, 2009. *www.businessweek.com/innovate/content/mar2009/id20090331_127029.htm*.
16. Marc Gunther, "Warren Buffett Takes Charge," *Fortune*, April 13, 2009. *http://money.cnn.com/2009/04/13/technology/gunther_electric.fortune/*.
17. Noel Tichy, *The Leadership Engine: How Winning Companies Build Leaders at Every Level* (New York: HarperBusiness Essentials, 1997), pp. 18–19 and 42–56.

CHAPTER 2

1. John P. Kotter, *John P. Kotter on What Leaders Really Do* (Boston: Harvard Business School Press, 1999), pp. 51–65.
2. Jay Conger, *The Charismatic Leader: Behind the Mystique of Exceptional Leadership* (San Francisco: Jossey-Bass, 1989), pp. 26–36.
3. See Ernest Gundling, *Working GlobeSmart: Twelve People Skills for Doing Business Across Borders* (Palo Alto: Davies-Black, 2003).
4. Tichy, *The Leadership Engine*, p. 11.
5. Ram Charan, Stephen Drotter, and James Noel, *The Leadership Pipeline: How to Build the Leadership-Powered Company* (San Francisco: Jossey-Bass, 2000), pp. 81–98.
6. Howard Gardner, *Frames of Mind: The Theory of Multiple Intelligences* (New York: Basic Books, 1993).
7. Daniel Goleman, *Emotional Intelligence: Why It Can Matter More Than IQ* (New York: Bantam, 1996).
8. Barbara Schaetti, Sheila Ramsey, and Gordon Watanabe, *Personal Leadership: A Methodology of Two Principles and Six Practices* (Seattle: FlyingKite Publications, 2008).
9. David Rock, *Your Brain at Work: Strategies for Overcoming Distraction, Regaining Focus, and Working Smarter All Day Long* (New York, HarperBusiness, 2009), pp. 195–97. See also David Rock, "SCARF: A brain based model for collaborating with and influencing others," *NeuroLeadership Journal*, Edition 1, 2008.
10. David Rock and Jeffrey Schwartz, "Why Neuroscience Matters to Executives," *Strategy + Business*, April 10, 2007; and "The Neuroscience of Leadership," *Strategy + Business*, May 30, 2006.
11. See, for example, Geert Hofstede, *Culture's Consequences: International Differences in Work-Related Values* (Thousand Oaks, CA: Sage Publications, 1997), and Fons Trompenaars and Charles Hampden-Turner, *Riding the Waves of Culture: Understanding Diversity in Global Business* (New York: McGraw-Hill, 1997).

12. The *GlobeSmart* web tool can be accessed at *www.globesmart.com*.
13. Sharon Begley, "West Brain, East Brain: What a Difference Culture Makes," *Newsweek*, February 18, 2010.
14. Robert House et al., *Culture, Leadership, and Organizations: The GLOBE Study of 62 Societies* (Thousand Oaks, CA: Sage Publications, 2004, pp. 669–719).
15. David Hole, Le Zhong, and Jeff Schwartz, "Talking About Whose Generation? Why Western Generational Models Can't Account for a Global Workforce," *Deloitte Review*. *www.deloitte.com/view/en_US/us/Insights/Browse-by-Content-Type/deloitte-review*.
16. Ibid.
17. Personal communication from Dr. Hammer, Intercultural Development Inventory certification program.
18. See Mitch Hammer's description of the IDI Inventory at *www.idiinventory.com/about .php*.
19. Joyce Osland, "An Overview of the Global Leadership Literature," in Mark Mendenhall, Joyce Osland, Allan Bird, Gary Oddou, and Martha Maznevski, *Global Leadership: Research, Practice and Development* (New York: Routledge, 2008), pp. 34–63.
20. Mendenhall et al., *Global Leadership Research*, pp. 62 and 79.
21. A similar point is made in Morgan McCall and George Hollenbeck, *Developing Global Executives* (Boston: Harvard Business School Press, 2002). McCall and Hollenbeck cite a Belgian expatriate who refers to the difference between the "what" and the "how," p. 36.
22. Allan Bird, "Assessing Global Leadership Competencies," in Mendenhall et al., *Global Leadership*, pp. 64–65. Bird further mentions "three standards that must be met to define an individual characteristic or capacity as a competency: (1) it must exist prior to performance; (2) it must be causally linked to performance; and (3) it must be possessed by superior, but not by average or subpar, performers."
23. Terry Hogan, "Global Leadership and the Development of Intercultural Competency in Multinational Organizations," master's thesis for the University of the Pacific–Stockton, California, and The Intercultural Communication Institute, 2008.

CHAPTER 3

1. The voices of global followers presented in this chapter and the five chapters to follow come from a variety of sources, including interviewees who described the perspectives of their global colleagues and other employees within the same organizations. In some cases we have combined the views of more than one individual who shared a common outlook.
2. See, for example, Ram Charan et al., *The Leadership Pipeline*, pp. 84–86.
3. *http://viscog.beckman.illinois.edu/grafs/demos/15.html*.
4. *www.redherring.com/Home/17485*.
5. *http://blogs.ft.com/donsullblog/2009/09/26/innovation-lessons-from-emerging-markets-live-with-your-customer/*.
6. *http://social.venturebeat.com/2009/03/19/the-worlds-most-lucrative-social-network-chinas-tencent-beats-1-billion-revenue-mark/*; *http://abovethecrowd.com/2009/03/09/how-to-monetize-a-social-network-myspace-and-facebook-should-follow-tencent/*; and *http:// en.wikipedia.org/wiki/Tencent_QQ*.

CHAPTER 4

1. For this example we have used a pseudonym and omitted the name of the interviewee's employer based upon her request. Comments in quotation marks in this section come from the interview but have been slightly altered to preserve anonymity.
2. Angela Gutchess, Robert Welsh, Aysecan Boduroglu, and Denise Park, "Cultural differences in neural function associated with object processing," *Cognitive, Affective, & Behavioral Neuroscience*, 2006, pp. 102–9.

CHAPTER 5

1. Christopher Bartlett and Sumantra Ghoshal provide a much more complete treatment of this topic of globalization stages in their well-known work *Managing Across Borders* and in subsequent scholarship. They use a more elaborate set of stages—domestic, international, multinational, global, and transnational—in which their version of the term "global" actually refers to an organization that is highly centralized for maximum efficiency. The "transnational" enterprise as they define it is a network of specialized, interdependent, and closely integrated national units that jointly develop and share knowledge worldwide. However, popular speech has outrun the distinctions made by Bartlett and Ghoshal, and has largely failed to adopt the term "transnational" in the sense that they intended it, so we have used the term "global" as in popular parlance to denote the integrated network model. See Christopher Bartlett and Sumantra Ghoshal, *Managing Across Borders: The Transnational Solution* (Boston: Harvard Business School Press, 1991), Chapter 4.
2. See, for example, ibid., pp. 96–97.
3. See Ernest Gundling and Anita Zanchettin, *Global Diversity: Winning Customers and Engaging Employees within Key World Markets* (Boston: Nicholas Brealey, 2007).
4. Sharon Begley, "West Brain, East Brain."

CHAPTER 7

1. Ram Charan et al., *The Leadership Pipeline*, pp. 27–29.
2. Angela Leung, William Maddux, Adam Galinsky, and Chi-yue Chiu, "Multicultural Experience Enhances Creativity: The When and How," *American Psychologist*, April 2008.
3. The idea for this model was inspired by a conversation with George Renwick. The authors are grateful to him for his support.
4. Portions of this last section are adapted from Ernest Gundling, *Working GlobeSmart: 12 People Skills for Doing Business Across Borders* (Boston: Nicholas Brealey, 2010), pp. 320–24.

CHAPTER 8

1. We have used a number of cases with success as examples of the need for frame-shifting on the strategic level. See, for example, José Sergio Gabrielli de Azevedo, "The Greening of Petrobras," *Harvard Business Review*, March 2009; Robert Burgelman, Andrew

Grove, and Debra Schifrin, "The Global Electric Car Industry in 2009: Developments in the U.S., China, and the Rest of the World," *Stanford Graduate School of Business*, 2009; and William Fischer et al., "Alcatel in China: Business as an Adventure," *International Institute for Management Development*, 2003.

2. We have withheld the individual's name at the company's request.

CHAPTER 9

1. There are many variations of the GROW model; its origins are attributed to Sir John Whitmore among others. See his *Coaching for Performance: GROWing Human Potential and Purpose—The Principles and Practice of Coaching and Leadership*, 4th Edition by Sir John Whitmore (London: Nicholas Brealey, 2009). The final "W," for example, has been referred to variously as signifying the Way Forward, Will, Wrap-up, What/Who/When, and so on.

2. The names of the coachees and other identifiers in this chapter have been changed to protect their anonymity at the company's request.

CHAPTER 10

1. This point was underlined for us recently in an interview with the senior vice president of executive development at a major global financial institution.

2. See, for example, Marjorie Derven, "Managing the Matrix in the New Normal" in *Training and Development Magazine*, July 2010. She quotes a manager at Verizon Communications to make the connection between matrix work environments and the need for shared vision: "Creating a shared vision is a key factor. One of the best ways to break down silos in large organizations is to have a clear vision that gives context to everyone's roles and responsibilities. Communicating frequently and consistently about goals and purpose is essential."

3. Darleen De Rosa, "Leadership in Action," *InterScience*, 28:6.

4. Peter M. Senge, *The Fifth Discipline: The Art and Practice of the Learning Organization* (New York: Currency/Doubleday, 1990), p. 9. See also, Carlos Cortes and Louise Wilkinson, "Developing and Implementing a Multicultural Vision," in *Contemporary Leadership and Intercultural Competence*, edited by Michael Moodian (Thousand Oaks, CA: Sage Publications, 2008), p. 28.

5. Stephen Bernhardt, *Using Technology to Support Global Drug-Development Teams* (Basel, Switzerland: Franklin-Quest Consulting Group, 1997). p. 5.

6. Marjorie Derven, "Managing the Matrix in the New Normal," *Training and Development Magazine*, July 2010.

7. Client interview, May 10, 2010.

CHAPTER 11

1. Jack Mezirow & Associates, *Learning as Transformation* (San Francisco: Jossey Bass, 2000).

2. From an interview in Terry Hogan's thesis, "Global Leadership and the Development of Intercultural Competency in Multinational Corporations."
3. This has been cited by many global leadership experts over the years, including J. S. Black, Terrance Brake, Hal Gregersen, Mansour Javidan, Tina Jokinen, Vijay Govindarajan, Anil Gupta, Mark Mendenhall, A. Morrison, and Stephen Rhinesmith.

About the Authors

Ernest Gundling, Ph.D.
Founder & Co-President
Aperian Global

Dr. Gundling has been involved with the organization Aperian Global since its inception in 1990. He is a Senior Asia Specialist and consults with clients on strategic approaches to global leadership development and relationships with key international business partners. He coaches executives with global responsibilities and works with multicultural management teams to help them formulate business plans based upon strong mutual understanding and a joint commitment to execution.

Dr. Gundling holds a Ph.D. and a Master of Arts from the University of Chicago, and a Bachelor of Arts from Stanford University. He also a Lecturer at the Haas School of Business at the University of California, Berkeley, where he teaches a course called Global Management Skills. He is the author of numerous publications, including several books: *The 3M Way to Innovation: Balancing People and Profits, Working GlobeSmart: 12 People Skills for Doing Business Across Borders*, and *Global Diversity: Winning Customers and Engaging Employees within World Markets.*

Terry Hogan—
Director, Citi Executive Development

Terry Hogan is Director of Executive Development at Citi where she is responsible for the design and delivery of global executive development, team training, and other organizational support interventions. In addition to her responsibilities for the company's Business Leadership Program, Chief Executive's Forum, and the Global Executive Leader Program, Ms. Hogan heads up the Citi Coach Center of Excellence. She joined Citi in 2009 from Aperian Global, where she managed the firm's Global Leadership Development Practice.

Previously, Ms. Hogan was a global General Manager for Cendant Corporation, where she led the development of new markets and products globally. Ms. Hogan has a Bachelor of Science degree from Oregon State University and holds a Master's Degree in Intercultural Relations and Global Leadership from the University of the Pacific and the Intercultural Communication Institute.

Karen Cvitkovich—
Managing Director, Global Talent Solutions,
Aperian Global

Karen Cvitkovich has worked in intercultural consulting, coaching and multinational team-building for over a decade. In her position as Managing Director of Aperian's Global Talent Solutions, she has designed and facilitated seminars for intact teams, team leaders and individual contributors on subjects including globalization, multinational teambuilding, global leadership and virtual communications.

Ms. Cvitkovich has a Bachelor's in Business and Human Resources from the University of Massachusetts Amherst and a Master's of Science in Training and Organizational Development from Lesley University. She is a frequent speaker at global conferences including SHRM, ASTD, and the Summer Institute for Intercultural Communication.

APERIAN GLOBAL

Aperian Global (*www.aperianglobal.com*) provides consulting, training and web tools for global talent development. Serving more than a quarter of *Fortune* 500 companies, Aperian Global is the largest privately held firm of its kind, widely recognized for its expertise in enabling companies to improve performance worldwide. The company has offices in Bangalore, Beijing, Boston, Dubai, Paris, Kolding (Denmark), San Francisco, Shanghai, Singapore, and Tokyo, and staff and associates on the ground in over eighty locations around the world. In addition to its Global Leadership practice, Aperian Global also addresses client needs related to Global Assignment Services, Global Teams, Global Diversity & Inclusion, and Global Business Skills.

Index

questions used to, 179–181
readiness to learn, 45–47
seeing what we don't expect to see, 47–49
tips from global leaders about, 51–52

J
Japan, 72, 91
Just-in-time approach, 207

K
Kelly, Eamonn, 7
Key markets, 7–8
Key stakeholders, 187–190
Knowledge sharing, 177, 189–190
Kwong, Abigail, 156–158, 163–164

L
Language skills, 49–51
Leader(s)
core values of, 106–107
definition of, 18
flexibility of, 85
future, developing of, 90, 92–93, 144–146
global. See Global leader; Global team leader
similarities among, 137–138
Leader-led action learning
advantages of, 213, 218
continuous feedback loop, 212
curriculum development, 207
definition of, 205–206
description of, 171
elements of, 206
limitations on, 206–207
potential of, 206
Leader-led action learning projects
aligning with other initiatives, 209–210
cycle of, 208
implementation of, 212
international assignments, 212–214
leaders of, 210–211, 214
metrics, 212
pilot projects, 210

reviewing of, 212–213
roles and responsibilities, 215
scaling of, 212–213
staff professional's role, 209
steps involved in, 209–213
team formation and orientation, 209, 211
Leadership
at all levels, 12, 16–19
common approaches to, 14–20
cultural variations in, 23
definitions of, 15–16
factors that affect, 22
intercultural perspectives on, 20–25
Kotter's definition of, 15
management versus, 15–16
multilevel approach to, 17
neuroscience views on, 19–20
succession of, 19
Tichy's concept of, 16–19
Leadership behaviors
adapt and add value, 99–102, 162–163
core values, 102–107, 160–161
cultural self-awareness. See Cultural self-awareness
expanding ownership. See Ownership, expanding of
frame-shifting. See Frame-shifting
for global teams, 173–190
growth of, 148
invite the unexpected. See Invite the unexpected
overview of, 119
results through relationships. See Results through relationships
shared vision, 172–173
stages of, 149
third-way solutions. See Third-way solutions
training of. See Training
Leadership conduct, 92
Leadership development. See also Global leadership development
description of, 90, 92–93
programs for, 129